Happy Birthd..

Enjoy your
We hope it fills you up
and emotionally!

Love, Tracy, Gregg,
Ann
Chris and Katie
2001

A Feast of Good Stories

For my mother
FROM WHOM I FIRST LEARNED
TO LOVE STORIES

A Feast of
Good Stories

A Special Collection
compiled by Pat Alexander

A LION BOOK

Selection, arrangement and introductory material
copyright © 1997 Pat Alexander
This edition copyright © 1997 Lion Publishing

Published by
Lion Publishing plc
Sandy Lane West, Oxford, England
ISBN 0 7459 3211 8
Lion Publishing
4050 Lee Vance View, Colorado Springs, CO 80918, USA
ISBN 0 7459 3853 1

First edition 1997
10 9 8 7 6 5 4 3 2 1 0

Acknowledgments
Text illustrations by Jonathan Williams

A catalogue record for this book is available
from the British Library

Typeset in 11/14 point Latin 725
Printed and bound in Spain

Contents

About This Book

Introductions are not for young readers. If a feast is on offer, they will want to get straight to the table. So this is a word for the grown-ups, who may be interested in the why and how of this book.

The title was there right from the start: *A Feast of Good Stories*. This had to be something special – festive fare, not simply bread and potatoes – a celebration of the great and the good in the world of story. There were many authors and stories I *had* to represent. And the word 'good' is important too: good stories, well-written, exciting, enjoyable – stories that express what is good at the same time as being fully aware of the badness and sadness in the world. The stories I have chosen express the deep-down goodness, the joy and the hope that is an essential part of my own Christian worldview, and that of many of the authors in these pages. All the stories breathe values that our world needs, not in a didactic way but simply in the way that stories do, by tugging at the heart-strings and reaching the parts that nothing else can touch in quite the same way.

Choosing has been very hard. In the end I decided to focus on relationships, since so many of the best stories are concerned in some way with understanding and getting on with one another. The sections then begin to form in sequence: from discovering what it is to 'be me', to family relationships and out in widening circles to explore the things that draw us together or keep us apart. Then there are the challenges which are part of the growing-up process, and the losses, since death is bound up with life as we know it. Yet here too there is hope and joy.

So here it is, my 'feast of good stories', set out for you to enjoy.

PAT ALEXANDER
Iffley, Oxford

1

Being Me

I am me and you are you – each of us different and special.
But what does it mean to 'be me'?
Finding the answer to that question can take a very long time.
We discover it bit by bit.
Sometimes we do it on our own – like David, the boy who has
escaped from prison camp in *I am David* and Jazz, in
A Half-Baked Bannock Cake. Half-Irish, half-Punjabi, Jazz is
'brown on the outside, white on the inside'.
But often it is other people who spot our hidden talents –
like Great Uncle Kaz in *The One and Only Delgado Cheese* and
old Mrs Walenski, who gives Malcolm the confidence to be
himself, in *Malcolm's Amazing Technicolor Waistcoat*. For, as Chad
discovers in *The Lark Who Had No Song*, we each have our own
special place in the scheme of things.

'The Journey'

CAROLINE SCOTT (AGED 9)

It's dark in here – it's warm and safe.
My very own space – for me to grow.
Inside this bubble, far away – yet very near.

I can hear the unceasing beat – beating for me –
A rhythm soft and sweet.
I cannot see, or smell or taste…
But I can touch within my place.

My place is changing…
I'm squeezed and pushed –
What's happening now?
Confusion… fear,
My place is left behind.

This is a dreadful thing,
I'm pushing downwards,
The rhythm has all gone.
Where am I now?

The pushing stops…
I'm somewhere else!
This somewhere does not push me now.
I'm feeling free – yet still afraid.
My eyes are opening,
I see, I feel, new things are here.
A soft sensation, like my special place.

A gentle touch, a murmur soft and sweet.
Loving hands – these are my friends.
I am born –
I am loved –
I am me.

The One and Only Delgado Cheese

BOB HARTMAN

Harvey Merritt was not the kind of boy people noticed.

Harvey was not bright enough for people to say, 'Oh, what a clever child!' Harvey was not good enough at football or baseball for people to say, 'Oh, what an athletic child!'

Harvey was not especially tall, nor extremely short. He wasn't ugly. He wasn't cute. He was just plain normal. And he didn't like it.

So when he moved from the Warren G. Harding School to Edward Everett Horton Elementary School, Harvey decided to do something about it.

One Monday morning when Harvey walked into his new school, he saw a sign hanging on the bulletin board.

'Talent Show:' the sign said, 'Sign up next Friday afternoon.'

Now, as you may have guessed, Harvey Merritt was not particularly talented either. But his desire to be noticed was so great, he was determined to find *something* he could do.

Harvey's first step was to talk with his Great Uncle Kaz.

Great Uncle Kaz was the reason Harvey's family had moved in the first place. He had to stay in a wheelchair and needed someone to look after him and his big house. Someone who could cook and clean. And someone who didn't mind the occasional bursts of what Uncle Kaz called his 'preachytelling' (and what his relatives called his 'funny ways').

13

Great Uncle Kaz stayed by himself most of the time in his faded, musty bedroom at the back of the house, thumbing through his Bible and preachytelling his stories to the wallpaper birds – or to Harvey, who often wandered in for a game of checkers and ended up listening to 'How the Lions Lost Their Lunch' or 'The Whale's Sour Snack.'

As far as Harvey was concerned, those old Bible stories of Daniel and Jonah had never been so interesting. He liked Great Uncle Kaz. In fact, of all the people Harvey knew, he felt most noticed by Great Uncle Kaz.

Uncle Kaz listened patiently to Harvey, nodding his bald, wrinkled head from time to time as Harvey talked about the school talent show poster.

'A talent show, eh? Well, what can you do, Harvey? Can you sing?'
Harvey shook his head, 'No.'
'Can you dance?'
'No.'
'Do you know any good jokes?'
Harvey didn't.
Great Uncle Kaz thought for a moment. Then he got a look in his eye like a preachytelling was coming on.

'Harvey,' he said, 'do you see that old trunk beside the bed? Take the blankets off the top, open it, and bring me the first thing you find inside.'

The first thing Harvey found was a paper tube with a rubber band around the middle. Uncle Kaz slid off the rubber band and unrolled the paper. It was a poster.

In the middle of the poster, which was now yellow, but was probably once white, big letters read:
'FROM THE STAGES OF ZANZIBAR, MADRID, AND GAY PAREE – DANCIN' DAN THE VAUDEVILLE MAN!'
'Who's that?' Harvey asked.
Uncle Kaz smiled a sly smile. 'That was me years ago.'
Harvey looked puzzled. 'But Mom said you were some kind of preacher.'
The old man chuckled. 'The Good Lord gave me a talent, Harvey – a gift for telling stories, for getting folks to sit up and pay attention.

But before the Lord grabbed hold of me to do that for him, I was
Dancin' Dan the Vaudeville Man.'

'What's Vaudeville?' asked Harvey.

'Oh, it's a bit like your talent show, really. A lot of people doing
a little bit of everything. Singing, dancing, juggling. Acrobatics,
comedy, magic acts. We weren't the best, but we enjoyed ourselves.
That was the most important thing – for me anyway.'

Uncle Kaz stopped. Like a light bulb had switched on in his head.

'Harvey,' he said, 'the Good Lord gave us all talents. Not all of us
the same ones. Not all of us the same number. But he didn't pass
anybody by. And the road to finding those talents starts with what
brings us joy. Harvey, what do you enjoy?'

Harvey's light bulb lit as well. Sure, there was something he
enjoyed doing. He liked to do...

'CARTWHEELS!'

Harvey almost shouted it, and Uncle Kaz jerked back his head in
surprise.

'Cartwheels?' he said.

'Last year, in second grade, we had to learn to do cartwheels.
I couldn't, at first, but I kept trying and trying. And one day I could.
I *like* to do cartwheels.'

'Then cartwheels it is!' announced Uncle Kaz. 'Or, at least, that
will be the main part of your act.'

'The main part?' asked Harvey, a little concerned.

'Sure. You can't just do cartwheels. You've got to build an act
around that. A little juggling. A little magic, maybe. But don't worry,
I can teach you how to do those things. OK?'

Harvey nodded his head a little hesitantly. He wasn't sure about
those other things, but he figured he could try. He'd managed
cartwheels, hadn't he? He smiled at Uncle Kaz and headed for the
door.

'One more thing,' Uncle Kaz called, waving the poster. 'You'd
better come up with a name. A stage name. Something people will
notice.'

It wasn't until two days later that a special name, a really *noticeable*
name actually hit Harvey. Mrs Finchley, his teacher, was talking
about geography. And, as usual, Harvey wasn't paying much
attention.

But somewhere between the cattle ranches on the Mexican border and the dairy farms in Wisconsin, he got an idea.

Harvey rushed home and started to draw furiously. Within an hour, he had made a poster. He rolled it up, wrapped a rubber band around it, and knocked on his uncle's door.

'What have you got there, behind your back?' asked Uncle Kaz.

'It's a poster,' said Harvey. 'A poster that people will notice. With a name they'll notice, too.' He unrolled it and held it in front of him.

The first thing Uncle Kaz did was to cock his head and squint really hard. And after he'd finished squinting, Uncle Kaz grinned. Slowly and proudly, he read:

'FROM THE STAGES OF ZANZIBAR, MADRID, AND GAY PAREE – THE ONE AND ONLY DELGADO CHEESE!'

'Delgado Cheese,' Uncle Kaz repeated. 'It's just the name I would have chosen.'

'Really?' said Harvey, lowering the poster so he could see over the top.

'Absolutely! It's... uhhmm... *exotic*, that's what it is.'

'Exotic?' asked Harvey, a little worried.

'Yes. Strange but wonderful. Like the cherubim and seraphim. Like manna in the wilderness. Like your Aunt Minnie's spoon collection. And now, Mr Delgado Cheese, what do you say we start teaching you a few magic tricks?'

Over the next few weeks, Harvey – or Delgado Cheese, as he now preferred to be called – stopped by his Uncle Kaz's room after school. For some reason, Uncle Kaz didn't seem to need as much rest as he used to. So Delgado saw him every day.

Using several items hidden away at the bottom of the trunk, Uncle Kaz showed Delgado Cheese a few tricks. He also taught Delgado how to juggle three small oranges.

Then they worked hard to combine the magic and the juggling with the cartwheels, so that Delgado had an 'act'. Delgado's mother joined in, too, and made him a silky red shirt with flowing sleeves and a pair of bright yellow trousers.

On the day of the talent show, it was plain to everyone in the house that Delgado Cheese was scared. So Uncle Kaz asked him into his room. He had a piece of notepaper and a small envelope lying on his lap desk.

'Who will be introducing the performers tonight?' he asked Delgado.

'My teacher, Mrs Finchley. Why?'

Uncle Kaz wrote something at the top of the notepaper, folded it, and slid it into the small envelope.

'Give this to Mrs Finchley tonight,' he instructed Delgado.

'All right,' said Delgado Cheese. 'What is it?'

'It's the *coup de grâce*,' smiled Uncle Kaz at a thoroughly puzzled Delgado. 'The rainbow after Noah's Flood. The walls of Jericho tumbling down. The final touch to what will be the perfect performance.'

Delgado looked solemnly at his feet. 'I don't think it's going to be very perfect. I'm really scared.'

Uncle Kaz reached over and put one large wrinkled hand on the boy's head. It looked like Delgado was wearing a five-fingered cap.

'Your performance will be wonderful. It will have to be. You're doing what you enjoy, right? You're using the talents God gave you, right? And besides, your mother's paid a buck and a half to see the show, and she deserves to get her money's worth.'

Delgado looked up. 'But what about you? You're coming tonight, aren't you?'

It was Uncle Kaz's turn to look at his feet. 'I haven't had any reason to go out of this house for years. And now that I do have a reason, I'm not sure I'm up to it. Maybe I'm like you, Delgado. Maybe I'm just a little scared.' He tapped on the note. 'You just remember to give this to Mrs Finchley, like I said.'

As he waited behind stage, Delgado Cheese folded and unfolded the small envelope Great Uncle Kaz had given him. He wanted to give it to Mrs Finchley, but she was busy giving last-minute directions and calming last-minute nerves.

Finally, gulping down his fear and shyness, Delgado pushed his way through the other performers and thrust the note into Mrs Finchley's hand.

'My uncle asked me to give this to you,' he said, as loudly as he dared. 'He says it's the *coup de grâce*.'

If it had been Harvey Merritt handing her the note, Mrs Finchley would probably have put it in her pocket without a word. But this little boy didn't exactly look like Harvey Merritt. This little boy didn't speak in that mumbling, unsure way that Harvey Merritt usually spoke. And that's because, as everyone who had a program knew, this little boy was not Harvey Merritt but Delgado Cheese.

Mrs Finchley opened the envelope and quickly read the note to herself.

She smiled.

'Thank you, Harvey. Excuse me... Thank you, Delgado Cheese,' she said.

Delgado Cheese smiled back.

As act followed act, Delgado's fear returned. What did he think he was doing here? What if he goofed? What if he embarrassed himself? He was almost ready to drop his trick cane and his sack of oranges and sneak out, when Mrs Finchley said, 'Delgado Cheese, you're next.'

It was too late to run. Too late to go back to being plain old Harvey Merritt.

Mrs Finchley put her hand on his shoulder. 'Just wait one minute,' she whispered.

Then she pulled out Great Uncle Kaz's note, stepped up to the microphone and read, in her best ringmaster's voice:

'FRESH FROM THE STAGES OF ZANZIBAR, MADRID AND GAY PAREE, EDWARD EVERETT HORTON ELEMENTARY SCHOOL IS PROUD TO PRESENT THAT JUGGLER, ACROBAT AND MAGICIAN EXTRAORDINAIRE – THE ONE, THE ONLY, DELGADO CHEESE!'

The audience applauded. Mrs Finchley grinned. And Delgado Cheese looked out at the crowd. The lights were so bright that all he could see clearly were the first few rows. But that was all he needed to see. For sitting in his wheelchair at the very front, with his top hat and cane, was Dancin' Dan the Vaudeville Man!

Delgado ran from Mrs Finchley's side and cartwheeled onto the stage. Once for Zanzibar. Twice for Madrid. Three times for Gay Paree. The audience applauded again.

Delgado Cheese picked up his oranges and started to toss them in the air. One for Zanzibar. Two for Madrid. Three for Gay Paree. He dropped Zanzibar halfway through, but the people clapped anyway.

Finally Delgado Cheese reached into the sack and pulled out his magic cane. *Voila!* The cane turned into a bunch of flowers. He called Mrs Finchley to his side and reached behind her ear. *Voila!* There was a fifty-cent piece. The audience applauded once more.

Delgado Cheese bowed to the audience and smiled. He was using the talents God had given him, and he was enjoying himself. At last he was more than just plain normal. He was being noticed.

But as he stood there amid all the applause, the thing Delgado Cheese noticed most of all was a wrinkled pair of clapping hands in the front row – from Zanzibar, Madrid and Gay Paree.

I am David

From *I am David*

ANNE HOLM

David lay quite still in the darkness, listening to the men's low muttering. But this evening he was aware of their voices only as a vague meaningless noise in the distance, and he paid no attention to what they were saying.

'You must get away tonight,' the man had told him. 'Stay awake so that you're ready just before the guard's changed. When you see me strike a match, the current will be cut off and you can climb over – you'll have a half a minute for it, no more.'

In his mind's eye David saw once again the grey bare room he knew so well. He saw the man and was conscious, somewhere in the pit of his stomach, of the hard knot of hate he felt whenever he saw him. The man's eyes were small, repulsive, light in colour, their expression never changing; his face was gross and fat. David had known him all his life, but he never spoke to him more than was barely necessary to answer his questions; and though he had known his name for as long as he could remember, he never said anything but 'the man' when he spoke about him or thought of him. Giving him a name would be like admitting that he knew him; it would place him on an equal footing with the others.

But that evening he had spoken to him. He had said, 'And if I don't escape?'

The man had shrugged his shoulders. 'That'll be none of my business. I have to leave here tomorrow, and whatever my successor may decide to do about you, I shan't be able to interfere. But you'll soon be a big lad, and there's need in a good many places for those strong enough to work.'

David knew only too well that those other places would not be any better than the camp where he now was. 'And if I get away without being caught, what then?' he had asked.

'Just by the big tree in the thicket that lies on the road out to the mines, you'll find a bottle of water and a compass. Follow the compass southwards till you get to Salonica, and then when no one's looking go on board a ship and hide. You'll have to stay hidden while the ship's at sea, and you'll need the water. Find a ship that's bound for Italy, and when you get there go north till you come to a country called Denmark – you'll be safe there.'

David stumbled, staggered, crawled: onwards in the darkness, uphill all the time, the going hard and stony: it must be a mountain slope... Then he came to a road and staggered across it without even remembering to see if there were people about... then farther uphill where something was growing in low straight lines... then over another stretch of mountainside with hard sharp-edged stones that hurt his feet. And then he could go no farther.

But there was no one to disturb his sleep that night, and when he woke he was no longer tired. He was not even cold – he was pleasantly warm, in fact. He lay awake for a while with his eyes shut, basking in the warmth of his own body while he listened as usual for sounds about him. But all was quiet. Then opening his eyes he sat up and looked.

David was familiar only with various tones of grey and brown, and of course the blue of the sky. Well, yes, he had once seen a little red flower that had strayed inside the camp wall. Apart from that, colour was something he had only heard of: he had seen only a pale and muddied reflection of it – in the ugliness of the camp and the equally ugly quarters of the guards.

He did not know how long he stayed there on the mountainside, sitting motionless, just gazing... only when everything grew strangely misty did he discover that he was crying.

Far below him lay the sea, a sea bluer than any sky he had ever seen. The land curved in and out along its edge: in and out, up and down, all green and golden, with here and there the red of flowers too far off to be clearly seen. Down by the sea a road ran along the foot of the mountain, and near it lay villages whose bright colours gleamed dazzlingly. There were trees with many changing tints of green, and over it all shone the warming sun – not white-hot and spiteful and scorching, as the sun had shone upon the camp in the summertime, but with a warm golden loveliness.

Beauty...

His tears continued to flow, faster and faster, and he brushed them angrily away so that the mist before his eyes should not veil that beauty from him.

Suddenly he knew that he did not want to die.

He did not want to be caught, he did not want to die... Now that he had learned about beauty he wanted to live...

For a long time David continued to sit and gaze upon the beautiful scenery that lay before him. He looked again and again upon the blueness of the sea, upon the coastline curving along its shore: he saw the colours of the landscape, its many kinds of green intermingled with gold and red, fade into one another towards the horizon until everything melted into the blue of sea and sky far away over the mountains.

David looked down at his own hand lying in the grass and knew at once what he was going to do first. The grass was green although summer was far advanced; there must be water not very far away.

He looked first at the sun, then at his compass, and then at the sun again: it was very early... he still had a good hour before he need find a hiding-place for the day. He took hold of his bundle and jumped up. And there was water: a lazy little brook glinting in the sunlight in the midst of a much wider river-bed which wound among trees and bushes where he could hide if anyone came along. David had his clothes off in no time: he had only a shirt and a pair of trousers kept up with string. He laid his trousers in the water and put a stone on top to prevent them from floating away. Then he soaked his shirt thoroughly and opened his bundle.

He stood there a moment, soap in hand. Sometimes when they first arrived in camp they were quite white and clean all over with no smell about them... He hardly dared try – then he made an attempt, beginning with his hands.

It worked... almost. David scrubbed away until he was in a sweat;

22

picked up his shirt to rub himself with and then he got on much better. He really thought dirt was much more difficult to get off... His head was a bit of a problem, but David would not give up: he was going to get all that dirt off, all that reminded him of the camp and smelt of it.

He lay right down, dipping his head in the water so that his hair was thoroughly wet, rubbed soap all over it until his arms grew tired, then ducked again and rubbed away with his shirt until his hair no longer felt sticky. He turned cold but he took no notice; his one thought was to be quite, quite clean. His shirt gradually took on a brighter colour, and then he set about his trousers as well. They, too, became brighter. Finally he sat down with his knife and whittled away at a twig until he had a sharp point of clean wood. He pricked himself a couple of times in the process, but in the end even his toenails were clean.

The sun glistened on a drop of water as it fell from his hand to his knee. David wiped it off but it left no tide-mark: there was no more dirt to rub away. He took a deep breath and shivered. He was David. Everything else was washed away, the camp, its smell, its touch – and now he was David, his own master, free – free as long as he could remain so.

Malcolm's Amazing Technicolor Waistcoat

From *Malcolm and the Amazing Technicolor Waistcoat*

HILARY BRAND

Malcolm had never stopped to think why he liked second-hand clothes. He just did. He'd never worn the same baggy jeans, lumberjack shirts, trainers or DMs as everyone else. When he was ten, he'd found a tailcoat for 20p in a jumble sale, and embarrassed Stacey rotten by wearing it home. He didn't wear it so much now, and he'd gone off his Prince-style frilly shirt – Stacey said he was a big girl's blouse – but he couldn't resist raking through the rails in the hope of finding something wild and wacky.

Nothing much today though. He found an old army coat, and tried it in the mirror. He sighed at the image that stared back. Why couldn't he be tall, dark, mysterious – not short, sandy-haired and skinny, in a coat six sizes too big?

He was about to give up, when the assistant, a round lady who wore a woolly hat even in summer, came out with an armful of men's clothes and hung them on the rails. *This is more like it,* thought Malcolm. These hadn't belonged to some old grandad. There were jeans with decent labels, silk shirts, baggy jackets and even a Leadbitter Riff T-shirt, but Malcolm had one of those. He looked at the prices and began to wish he hadn't bought the album, or at least the Big Mac. £2 for a shirt, £5 for the best of the jackets, £3.50 for the jeans.

He was about to turn sadly away when he noticed the waistcoat.

The back was black silk, but the front was a shimmering mass of colour. It was a rainbow, he realized, arcing across a background of deep blues and purples. Not a child's rainbow of bold brash stripes; this was much more like the real thing. Threads gleamed with gold and silver and blended so subtly that you couldn't quite tell where one colour ended and the next began. Malcolm looked at the price – only £1.25!

Glowing with the thrill of a bargain, he took it to the counter. He even knew when he could wear it. Next Saturday at the school disco. It might be just the thing to make Helena notice him at last...

Saturday was a Big Day... Malcolm leaped up early. Over two bowls of Weetabix and four slices of bread and jam, he thought about what to wear tonight.

Black jeans, he decided, black shirt and the waistcoat. He went up to his bedroom to try. He surveyed himself in the mirror. Not bad. He put on a cassette, tried gelling his hair back, and moved rhythmically to the music. Had to get it right – seductive with just a hint of menace. Yes, very cool. Oh, that zit on his chin – but then the lights would be low. They *would* be low, wouldn't they?

The waistcoat was a bit crumpled, he noticed. Perhaps he'd give it an iron. He transferred the cassette to his Walkman and went downstairs to put up the ironing board. He thrust his hips in time to the pulsating music. No one else was up. He swayed as he ironed.

'Love this bit.' He took off in a rave, iron in hand. He got tangled in the lead and put it down, dancing wildly, arms punching the air. He became a rock guitarist, bouncing sideways across an imaginary stage and finishing the last insistent chord with a huge flourish.

The music stopped and he noticed the smell. He went back and picked up the iron. A huge hole, the iron's neat imprint, lay smack in the middle of the waistcoat's silky back...

It was the end of a dream. Oh, well, Malcolm thought, he'd go round to his friend Marty's and watch some videos. But even that was not to be. His Mum caught him at the door. Malcolm had promised he'd go and tidy old Mrs Walenski's garden.

Gloomily Malcolm made his way to Mrs Walenski's. It was just around the corner, a tiny bungalow that he had never noticed before.

He saw now that honeysuckle almost obliterated the front door. Rose bushes sprawled fierce and rampant through the front garden. A blue-flowering plant crept and spread like a mat beneath.

What's she want a gardener for? Personally, Malcolm liked gardens like that. Much better than neat ones like their neighbours', the Sedges, with one marigold planted exactly every 15 centimetres along the path. He'd even seen Percy Sedge take out a ruler to get it right.

On Mrs Walenski's front door was a faded note in spidery writing. 'Please come round side. Knock and wait.'

He ducked his way under a rickety trellis to the side door. He knocked. Nothing...

Then he heard it. Deep inside the bungalow a strange shuffling noise. Shuffle, clunk, shuffle, clunk. He began to see movement through the cobbled glass – a bent figure creeping nearer.

Eventually the door opened and he looked down into Mrs Walenski's face. It was a shrivelled prune of a face, framed in wispy white hair. She looked at him suspiciously. There were a few wispy whiskers on her chin.

'Gardening – I've come to do the gardening.'

She waved a misshapen hand towards him. 'You come,' she said. 'Garden, time chop back... boy... Come in.'

Can't even talk proper, thought Malcolm as he followed her slowly shuffle-clunking her walking frame up the dingy corridor. *S'pose she's foreign.*

He followed her into the sitting room, adjusting his eyes to the gloom... Drapes hung everywhere. A filmy fabric dotted with sequins covered the lamp shade. The patterned velvet curtains were looped back with huge, gold-tasselled cords. A shawl with long silver fringes was thrown across a sofa.

Spooky, thought Malcolm. *Perhaps she's a fortune teller – or a witch!*

Where there weren't drapes there were photos – some brown and faded, some black and white, some with scrawling signatures across the corner. The people who smiled from them clearly thought they were something. Women in beaded frocks with feathers in their hair. Men with white scarves and top hats at a jaunty angle. Women with flowing skirts, tiny waists and absurd little saucer hats. Portraits of people by now long gone, or else as faded and shrivelled as their owner.

'You like?'

'Er, yes.' Malcolm realized he was staring.

'My cly... My cly... I dress... clothes...'

Great, thought Malcolm. *She's not just foreign, she's batty as well. Let's just do the gardening and get out of here.*

'About your garden, Mrs Walenski,' he said loudly and slowly in the sort of voice people reserve for foreigners, idiots or the deaf. Mrs Walenski appeared to be all three.

She wasn't listening to him now, but leafing through a big red desk diary. She passed it to him, open at the front.

'I have had a stroke,' it said in spidery scrawl. 'I cannot speak very well. I also have arthritis.'...

'Look, Mrs Walenski, about this gardening...'

It could have been worse. She took him outside and showed him a battered electric lawnmower in a dank coal house. Mowing was OK... It didn't take long... Malcolm put the mower away... He shut the coal house door, then jumped. Mrs Walenski and her frame were right behind him. 'Cuppa tea.'

'Thanks but really I must get...'

Oh no! It really wasn't a question. The tea was already in the pot, knitted teacosy on top. There was milk in a jug and sugar lumps with tongs. She peered hopefully at him with sad watery eyes. Malcolm noticed a plateful of Jaffa cakes behind her. *Oh well... and he had to admit he was thirsty...*

Malcolm ate and gulped the hot tea in an effort to be gone. He peered at the nearest photo, a lady in a jewelled gown. It was signed, Malcolm noticed, 'To darling Eva'.

'My fa...' said Mrs Walenski.

Oh no, not again.

'My fa... fa... fa...'

'Family?' tried Malcolm helpfully.

Mrs Walenski shook her head emphatically. 'Fa... Fa...'

'Father?' tried Malcolm.

'No, no,' said Mrs Walenski helplessly. 'Fa...'

'Famous!' said Malcolm. 'They're famous people.'

'Ah ye-e-s,' said Mrs Walenski doubtfully, then, 'No-o-o, my fa... fa...'

She picked up her pincers and drew towards her a dog-eared photo album. 'Fa...' she said triumphantly and thrust it towards him.

The first page had black and white photos cut out of a magazine. The caption read:

Society dressmaker Eva Walenski showed her first collection this month after leaving Hartnell's illustrious salon. Her exquisite use of fabrics and attention to detail meant the clothes were snapped up quickly by the fashionable set of Kensington and Chelsea.

'Fashion!' said Malcolm.

'Ah, fashion!' repeated Mrs Walenski, a broad beam spreading over her wrinkled features.

Malcolm turned the page. A photo showed a tiny lady with swept-back, black hair, pinning the sleeve of a tall, willowy model. 'Is that you,' asked Malcolm, 'the little one?'

'Me,' agreed Mrs Walenski.

'You used to make clothes?'

'Make clothes,' repeated Mrs Walenski. 'Look.'

Malcolm looked. The album was filled with glossy photos of models. Long satin ballgowns encrusted with jewels. A bridal gown frilled with lace. A slim, tailored suit in black and white, curling feathers embroidered down the front.

'Very nice,' said Malcolm, flipping the pages and thinking how sad it was that someone from this glamorous world had shrunk to a batty old prune in Broad Heath.

He turned over to where a woman in black floaty chiffon held the arm of a man in a bow tie and satin waistcoat. That reminded him.

'I've got a waistcoat,' he said, to fill the silence, 'but I've just ruined it.'

Mrs Walenski looked up enquiringly.

'Put the iron through the back of it. Made a dirty great hole.'

Mrs Walenski chuckled. 'Dirty great hole,' she repeated.

'Ruined it,' said Malcolm, wistfully.

'No, no, you mend,' said Mrs Walenski.

'Nah, not me. Wouldn't know how.'

'I help,' insisted Mrs Walenski. 'You mend,' she said. 'I show how.'

Malcolm headed home. No one in... He picked up the waistcoat and went out.

'Once she sees it, she'll know it's hopeless,' thought Malcolm as he knocked on the honeysuckle-covered door.

Mrs Walenski looked at the waistcoat. 'Easy done,' she chuckled and ushered him in. She rifled through her boxes of fabrics and came up with a black silk dotted with tiny diamonds. 'OK?' she asked.

'Yes, OK,' said Malcolm, 'but...'

'You lift.' She pointed to the sewing machine.

'Now thread.' She gestured to a tin marked Peek Frean's Biscuits. It was full of cotton reels.

She expects me to thread a sewing machine? thought Malcolm.

She did, but pointing to each bit in turn made it far easier than he'd expected. Then she handed him a tiny forked metal prong. 'Unpick,' she said.

Malcolm thought about how frustrated she must feel as he clumsily unpicked the waistcoat's seams. He looked at her hands, lumpen and twisted, and tried to imagine them smooth and straight, whizzing fabric through the machine. He glanced at her cloudy eyes and wondered when they last saw well enough to push a needle into an intricate design. He wondered what it was like, the day she finally decided it was over. She met his gaze.

'Come, come, don't stop,' she chided. 'We finish today.'

And they did. Malcolm became Mrs Walenski's hands, and she became his brain as they cut, pinned, tacked and machined together. 'You good,' she told him as he cut out. 'Very good,' she said as he sewed. 'This boy, a natural,' she proclaimed as he pressed seams.

There was only one point when Malcolm began to think Mrs Walenski really was batty after all. She had made him turn the waistcoat inside out and stitch until it seemed impossible that it could ever turn the right way out again. *Very useful*, thought Malcolm. *She's mended it, but it's permanently inside out.*

And then suddenly, the sewing was finished. All except one tiny gap. 'Push through,' she insisted, and he did, miraculously pulling all the waistcoat right way out through the tiny gap. It looked as good as new.

'That's brilliant,' said Malcolm.

'Ah,' said Mrs Walenski and sat back beaming with pride. 'You like needlework?' she asked hopefully.

'Yes,' said Malcolm, to his surprise...

He put the waistcoat on and admired himself in Mrs Walenski's gold-curlicued mirror.

'You come,' said Mrs Walenski. 'You come again. I make you great couturier.'

A great what? thought Malcolm. 'Dunno about that, but OK, I'll come again.'

Mrs Walenski's beam lit up her face. 'Really?'

'Yeah, honest. I promise.'

'Name? Phone?'

Malcolm wrote his name and address on the scrap of paper she handed him. She added it to a pile of similar scraps on her table.

The cherub clock chimed 7.30. Twenty minutes to go home and shower, and ten minutes to school. Just in time for the disco – amazing. Malcolm smiled to himself in the mirror. He was going to the disco and he was looking good.

A Half-Baked Bannock Cake

From *Princess Jazz and the Angels*

RACHEL ANDERSON

Born in Glasgow, with an Irish mother (Bridie) and a Punjabi father (Rajinder), Jazz is still working out who she is. Torn between west and east, she describes herself as 'brown on the outside, white on the inside, like a half-baked bannock cake'.

'Mrs Bridie O'Hare Singh?' asked the postman, looking doubtfully at Jazz in her Mickey Mouse pyjamas.

'Aye. That's me,' said Jazz, reaching out for the packet.

'It's a special delivery, hen. To be signed for.'

'Surely,' said Jazz, taking the form and writing Bridie's signature in a near-perfect forgery which even Bridie herself might be tricked by. Long ago, Jazz had discovered how useful it was to be able to sign her mother's signature when writing a sick-line for school.

'If anyone else calls, I'm not opening up,' said Jazz to the postman as she slammed the door of the flat after him and chucked the special-delivery packet on top of the pile of coats, magazines, and the old baby buggy, missing one wheel, which had been lying there since way before Billy Connolly was born.

A long while back, Bridie used to say the three-wheeled buggy was for the next wean, but after her dad Rajinder died, Jazz's hope of a wee sister went out of the window, though the broken buggy stayed.

She listened to the postie's feet trip-trapping away down the four flights of stone steps of the tenement close. She heard him reach the bottom and close the main door. She nodded with satisfaction and went back to her bed, taking Bridie's pink blanket as well as her own blue one.

After a while it stopped being so grand to be on her own.

Jazz was hungry.

She found a brown carrot, two potatoes, already sprouting eyes, and one tin of broth which she opened and drank, cold, straight from the tin. She was still hungry.

Or perhaps she was bored. Or lonely. Or annoyed with Bridie to be away without so much as a word about where, or how long. Sometimes a person had so many different feelings that they were all in a carfuffle so you could not tell which one it was.

At school, they would soon be sitting down in the bustling hall to a steaming plate of tatties and neeps, boiled mutton and pearl barley, followed by a bowl of pink rhubarb and yellow custard.

Jazz pulled her mother's blanket over her Mickey Mouse pyjamas, went down to the telephone kiosk on the corner and dialled 999. That would soon stir things up.

'Which service do you require?' said the voice.

'All of them,' said Jazz. 'And meals on wheels while you're about it.'

'Which service do you require?' said the voice again.

That was so like a grown-up, not to listen properly the first time.

'I already told you,' said Jazz.

'You have dialled the emergency number. If this is not an emergency, please replace the receiver so that others may use this service.'

'Ach, this *is* an emergency,' said Jazz. 'If you can no do something about it, I shall ring the evening paper and tell the people there instead.'

The voice went back into its parrot-speak. 'Which service do you require?'

Jazz took a breath and yelled into the telephone receiver.

'I require a rescue! Here is my description. I'm female. Ten years old. I'm wearing my Mickey Mouse pyjamas. I have curly brown hair, even longer than my friend Susheela's.'

This was a lie. Susheela had the longest hair in class. She could sit on hers even when it was braided.

'I have greenish almond-shaped eyes. And if you're still listening, I'm standing in a phone box on the Great Western Road just beyond the bridge. And I'll tell you for nothing, my feet are that cold for the person who shall be nameless, and who should be looking after me, will no buy me slippers. The clarty rat. Says I may wear my old trainers but I've left my trainers upstairs. I've been abandoned by her. My feet are that freezing. It is my guess, she has done a flit. For she is a lazy useless besom who cares more for herself and her own black moods and miseries than she does for me.'

Jazz wondered if Bridie had gone back to her folks in Galway like she sometimes threatened she would if Jazz misbehaved one more time. But sure, she would not have left without Jazz?

If she has, Jazz thought, then I'll be really extra dead annoyed.

'Abandoned?' said the emergency services voice, abruptly changing from its parrot-tone.

'This is so. On my honour. And it is the second parent to do so. Now I have none left.'

'How long back, pet?'

It came to Jazz that perhaps Bridie hadn't done a flit at all, but had nipped down to fetch milk for their tea, and instead of going to Ahmed's All-Day Store just over the road, she'd gone on a whim all the way to the big supermarket. Once there, she'd noticed the cut-price things on the bargain shelf.

She'd done that once before...

'I said, how long ago, dear?'

'How long, who?'

'When did you last see your mother?'

'Centuries back. So long I can no more remember. And I'm near dying of hunger. Which is why I'm calling for your help.'

The emergency-services' voice became soft and sleekit like those teachers at school when they wanted something from you.

'So what would you like to eat, pet, if you could have anything you wanted?'

Jazz guessed that the voice had no more interest in her favourite food than Bridie had, but was gaining time. Then the call would be traced.

Jazz liked the thought of three squad cars being despatched and coming screaming down the high road towards the bridge, blue lights flickering and sirens screaming, to rescue her. But she didn't want to give the fire, police and ambulance services the satisfaction of finding her too easily by standing here. They should put some elbow into it.

They should also walk up the seventy-two steps, just like *she* had to every day of her life.

She gave her address to the voice, then quickly replaced the receiver and returned to the flat to wait. She knew she wouldn't have to wait long. Weans were not supposed to be left unattended for weeks and weeks, as Jazz felt she had been, though she knew it was probably not such an offence to fail to buy slippers with fluffy puppy faces on them.

For the benefit of the emergency services, she left the door to the flat on the sneck for she reckoned on Bridie being none too pleased, when and if she ever returned, to find her front door hacked to splinters by a frantic fireman's axe.

While she waited for her rescuers, Jazz turned down the sound on the telly in the kitchen...

Jazz moved the dirty dishes, climbed into the sink the better to look from the window. Peering eastwards, she could see towards Gallowgate in the centre of the city. Craning her neck the other way, to the west, she could see the distant hills of Kilpatrick. That's where Bridie must be, running about the open hills pretending she was back in Ireland.

She had done that one time before. It'd been Lammas so there'd been no school and Bridie had taken it in her head to go brambling. But she didn't just bramble. She ran around blethering about the brambles in Galway. It was so embarrassing. Jazz wanted to fall into a burn and drown herself. Jennie Stewart was there too. She just picked and picked and took no notice.

Bridie still said they must *always* look westwards from the kitchen window, towards those hills, because west was the direction of Ireland.

'Sure, Kilpatrick's not a patch on Galway. But it's the same kind of thing, all soft and green. And I'm telling you, Jazz, that's the selfsame reason why they call that colour in the paint pots Galway green, because that's the living likeness of Galway in summertime. Sure, you remember the time we were there?'

Jazz remembered. It was like a video of summer in her head. But that was years back, even before Rajinder died. And maybe it had been changing in her memory, going mouldy just like bramble jelly forgotten at the back of the cupboard?

'And with wee Patrick? And our Moira and Tomas. Do you remember Tomas? Oh, what a high old time we had. And my Aunty Caitleen. Don't you just wish we could be there again?'

Jazz didn't listen once Bridie began her blethering.

'And another thing, Jazz, that I may tell you, there's no health in you looking always towards the east. For it's all hunger and dirty foreigners that way.'

How could Bridie be so sure if she'd never been there?

Jazz had once asked if Rajinder had been dirty, since he'd come from there.

'Dirty? He was so clean he near washed himself away. It was unhealthy, washing all the time, wasting all that water. Once a week, Friday nights, I said to him. That's what I did in my childhood. And that's what we do in this country. Not every day like you. Spendthrift, that man.'

So spendthrift had he been that he'd even wasted his own life by getting himself killed, and not yet seen the back of twenty-five years.

'So you'll not go keeking towards the east with those big eyes, do you understand?'

'Why must you run my life for me? So you're even telling me today which way I'm to look from the window? If that's the way you'll be, I shall no look from the windows at all! Ever again. I shall run away to America and I shall get myself adopted by a lady who is rich enough to care. You'll see and you'll be that sorry you ever crossed me.'

Jazz had slammed the window down with a shudder and marched away to take shelter under her blue blanket.

Now, free of that eejit Bridie, she craned her neck still further out to look towards the east. Through the drizzling grey she thought she could just about make out the shape of the cathedral. Or maybe it was only an office block.

Her father had been a foreigner from the east. Bridie came from Ireland. But Jazz herself belonged right here. She was born, like half the kids in class, at the Queen Mother's Hospital which sat resplendent on its mound, lighted up by night and day as bright as a magic palace, getting new people into the world.

Her father was supposed to marry the bride his parents had

chosen for him. But he'd gone away after a job and met Bridie instead. She'd come over from Ireland, looking for a job or trouble, whichever came first.

Jazz wondered what would have happened to her if he and Bridie hadn't each set out that Friday night and so had never met. Would she have been born as Bridie's girl, Irish through and through, or as Rajinder's all-Punjabi daughter, instead of as she was now, brown on the outside and white on the inside, like a half-baked bannock cake?

Or perhaps she would never have been born at all?

Jazz wished that people could send letters from heaven, or the Land o'the Leal or wherever it was they went. She wished that the little parcel could have come from Rajinder himself. She needed to get to know about him before it was too late. She could still remember him, but only just, and the certainty of the image was fading all the time.

At St Mungo's Road Primary School, they did not perform nativity plays at Christmas time as Bridie would have wished, on account of there being so many people whose parents might have been offended. It was, Jazz noticed, only the adults who liked to take offence about these things, never the children themselves. However, last Christmas, or perhaps it was the one before that, but certainly it was at least two winters after Rajinder had died, the teacher, Mrs Macpherson, had read the Christmas story straight out of the Bible. And when she'd got to the bit about the wise men from the east, Jazz had felt all strange and excited, as though the world had stopped still.

She shot her hand up. 'Please, Mrs Macpherson, will you do that last bit again?' she said. 'Jamie's been nudging so I could no hear properly.'

'Behold, there came wise men from the east,' Mrs Macpherson read and again the world round Jazz was hushed. Jazz loved those words. She repeated them to herself. Wise men from the east. Men from the east. From the east.

That's where he was from. If only he had lived, he might have been one of the men in the story.

When Bridie, soon after, was in one of her rare chuckling moods, Jazz asked, 'Was he a wise man?'

'Who's that then, flower? Santa Claus?'

'No, Rajinder.'

36

'Was he wise? Don't make me die laughing. Course he was never wise. Would a wise man go against his parents' wishes and stick with me? Would a wise man go getting himself killed, would he now?'

So Jazz had not talked about it any more. But she had seen the pictures in the books at school of three wise men wearing brocade robes and richly coloured cloth around their heads.

Rajinder had worn a turban too.

Jazz remembered the long, long hair, smooth and shiny as black satin ribbons when he combed it out, but all day knotted up and secretly hidden beneath the turban.

Rajinder had been a Sikh and Sikhs must never cut their hair.

And now, there was no Rajinder and no Bridie either.

Jazz's rescuers were no carload of police officers, nor a fire engine full of firemen, nor an ambulance-load of paramedics, but two social workers. The dour-faced one waited at the bottom of the close in case Jazz did a plunk, and the other, grateful for the open door, crept stealthily across the sticky kitchen lino and grabbed Jazz down from the draining board, then held her fast so she couldn't get away. She feared that Jazz, in distress at her abandonment, might throw herself from the window down to the mucky middens four floors below.

Jazz had no intention of doing such a thing, not now when her life of freedom was just beginning.

And besides, she was that hungry.

The Lark Who Had No Song

CAROLYN NYSTROM

Chad's world began in a hollow tree.

He could not see the sun, but he felt its golden warmth spread down through his mother's body into his ivory shell.

He could not see the clouds sailing in the breeze, but he felt the brittle limbs of the ageing tree groan and ache in the wind. And he felt his mother tuck her wings further down to keep him safe.

One day Chad shivered inside his shell.

He heard lightning crackle and hiss above him.

He heard the wind and the tree shriek in chorus.

He heard a roar of thunder echo a splintered roar from within the tree. Chad felt himself sail high, high through the air: soaring, sinking, wings tucked tight inside his shell.

A soft plop ended his fall.

Chad felt cold, cold – colder than he had ever felt – and very, very sleepy.

Slower and slower beat his heart.

But God, who made wind and rain and thunder and lightning, loved the little bird still hidden inside his shell.

Hours went by.

Then through foggy brain, Chad felt himself move again: the

gentle cupping of a small hand, a settling down into a soft tidy nest, a rustle of departing feet.

Moments later, Chad felt a warm feathered body shut out the cold and light.

And from the distance he could hear the silver music of a lark.

Chad slept a long time.

Inside the egg, his body grew and grew.

Chad moved his beak from side to side, trying to find a more comfortable spot.

His wings pressed against the sides of the shell.

His head pushed harder and harder against the top.

His feet tried to stretch, but the shell held them close to his tummy.

Was his egg home getting smaller?

No, Chad was getting bigger. And bigger!

One day when Chad tried to straighten his neck, his beak scratched the inside of the shell.

He tried again.

A tiny hole opened all the way to the outside.

He wiggled a wing.

Crack! A piece of the shell fell off.

He stretched a foot hard against the bottom of the shell.

Crunch! Crumble! Craaaaaack!

Surprised, Chad sat back on a tiny bit of shell and stretched his neck.

Soon Chad's mouth joined four other tiny mouths reaching skyward.

Mother Bird scurried back and forth bringing seeds and bugs and spiders and even juicy caterpillars.

Chad's brothers and sisters liked the seeds best. But Chad liked bugs.

He didn't like seeds at all.

Chad and his family grew healthy and strong.

'Peep, peep, peep,' said the other little birds as they reached for the seeds.

But Chad's voice didn't say 'Peep, peep.' Chad squawked a noisy 'Chu-urp, chu-urp, chu-urp' as he reached for a fuzzy caterpillar.

Before long the five little birds had grown enough to leave the nest for a short time.

Chad watched the others walk in measured steps through the grass under the fence as they looked for seeds. But try as he might, Chad's feet always moved in hops.

Chad felt proud of the way his family looked.

He liked their soft brown feathers, the gold on their chests, the black stripes at their throats.

He especially liked the way they could crouch in the weeds, so low that their little bodies looked like dried tufts of grass.

But Chad lost every game of hide-and-seek. He wondered why.

One day the parent birds lined their family up for flying lessons. 'God made the earth where we walk and the sky where we fly, and God made us,' Father Bird said. 'We meadowlarks praise God as we sing and sail through the sky.'

And he lifted from the fence post, fluttered a moment or two in the soft air, and floated high, high, high towards a white cloud.

A moment later he landed back on the post.

'Your turn,' he whistled to the others. After a few tries, all the birds but Chad began to sail. How beautiful they looked!

Chad wondered if they could feel the wind as it slid through their feathers.

They flew a perfect circle, then landed back on the fence rail with a bristle of white tails and a chorus of proud peeps.

'Next,' said Father Bird, and he looked at Chad, still glued to the fence.

Every inch of Chad wanted to cut the air with his beak, to hear the wind swoosh past his face, to feel the sky lift his wings.

But when he stepped off the rail, he forgot to flap his wings at all.

Thud! Chad came up from the weeds below with a mouthful of seeds and a frightened squawk.

Chad tried again.

This time he remembered to beat the air with his wings.

They jerked him right and left, up and down. They carried him a short distance into the breeze. But they would not sail.

Singing lessons were just as bad.

The young larks already whistled three-note trills, but Chad's best efforts brought only a raspy *kar-rump*. And the *kar-rump* was getting louder every day.

From earliest memory, Chad had seen one or the other of his parents glide to a fence post, open a beak and sing as if a whole choir of birds hid inside the tiny throat.

How Chad wanted to say thank you to God with a song like that!

How did they do it?

Was it the way they planted their feet on the post?

No, he tried that and it didn't work.

Was it the way they stuck out their yellow chests?

No, he tried that too.

Was it the way they tilted their heads high with beaks raised towards heaven?

Chad tilted his head the same way. He felt his throat open wide. Surely this was the secret!

He opened his beak and pushed with all his might, ready to hear his own beautiful song.

'Kar-rump! *Kar-rump!* KAR-RUMP!'

Chad was so embarrassed by the last loud *Kar-rump* that he fluttered to a nearby tree to hide.

Suddenly, Chad's beak began to itch.

He tried to rub it against his wing feathers, but it still itched.

He tried to scrape it against his foot, but it itched even more.

Then Chad spotted the rough bark of the tree trunk behind him. He leaped over to the trunk and stood sideways on the tree. It was funny how well his feet gripped the tree trunk. Much better than a fence rail.

Chad closed his itchy beak tight and plunged it into the tree bark.

Rat-tat, his strong beak squeaked as it scraped through the wood.

Chad pulled his beak out and discovered a juicy grub hiding just under the bark. He gulped it down and tried another spot.

Rat-tat, thunked his beak against the wood. *Rat-tat, rat-tat.*

Chad's beak didn't itch any more, but he kept finding more grubs.

Rat-tat,

Rat-tat,

Rat-tat-tat-tat,

Tat-tat-tatty-tatty-rat.

From far away, the trilling song of the meadowlark family trickled back to Chad. Its notes soared as high as their wings sailing through the clouds.

Chad stopped his drilling for a moment and opened his beak to try once more to join their song.

Then he stopped, listened to the high clear notes, each tumbling over the other.

For the first time Chad knew that something was missing in the lark's song. What the song needed was an added sound,

a different sound –

low notes, rhythm –

his own music.

Chad listened again, caught the flow of the song, closed his sturdy beak tight, and turned back to the tree.

Ratty-tat-tat. Ratty-tat-tat, sang Chad's beak against the wood.

Ratty-ratty-ratty-tat.

Chad's music lifted all the way up to the larks, joined their song and made it whole.

And God, who loved all the birds he had made, smiled.

'Just a Thought'

ANITA SEEHRA (AGED 17)

I, myself. Myself, I.
I, myself can only see another.
I, myself cannot see me as myself.
I can see myself as a reflection, although I cannot see
myself like I see you.

You, yourself. Yourself you.
You yourself can only see another.
You yourself cannot see yourself.
You can see yourself as a reflection, although,
you cannot see yourself like you see me.

2
Family Matters

The stories in this section are all about home and family –
but most of all about love. We may be born into our family
or chosen, like Winston in the first story. But having a place
where we belong and are safe and accepted is the next most
important thing to 'being me'.

But sometimes things go wrong, even in the best of families.
In these stories, Ramona thinks that no one likes her and
packs her case to run away. Davie is worried sick about his
rabbit. Frank's Dad has hit the headlines by painting the Bank
bright green. And Appleby is too ashamed about what she's
done to face her family. But all kinds of problems can be
sorted out, when love and understanding find a way.

'My Home'

ZOE WHITTINGTON (AGED 13)

Home, the place
   of all comforts,
The foundation
   of all ideas,
The birth
   of all opinions.

Home, the start
   of all arguments,
The end
   of all angry words,
The forming
   of all warmth.

Home, the beginning
   of a future,
The decision
   of a life,
Where the problems
   of growing up
    are told.

Winston's Important Weekend

From *The Day the Fair Came*

RACHEL ANDERSON

Two people looked after Winston. Aunty Pat was there all week, then Aunty Carol came on Saturdays and Sundays.

'I think I like you best, Aunty Pat,' said Winston. 'Aunty Carol looks cross.'

Sometimes Winston wished he had Aunty Pat all to himself, and didn't have to share her with the others.

One weekend, Aunty Pat didn't come. A new Aunty came instead. Winston crawled under the table and stayed there.

'Well, I don't care about Aunties either,' said Carmen. 'I've got a real mum and dad now. They're all my own. I'm going to live with them for ever and ever, till I'm grown up.'

Aunty Carol packed Carmen's clothes and her doll and Carmen went away with the mum and dad she said were all her own now. She looked pleased with herself.

Winston wished he could get a mum and dad too. He asked Aunty Carol. She said, 'We'll have to ask your social worker next time she comes.'

Winston's social worker brought a photograph of a man and a woman. They didn't look as nice as Carmen's new mum and dad. The mum was holding a baby in her arms.

'They would very much like to be your parents,' said the social worker.

Aunty Carol pinned the photograph up in the dayroom and

everybody looked at it. The mum and dad came to visit Winston. He ran and hid behind the dryer in the laundry. The mum found him.

'We've been looking for a lovely big boy just like you.'

'You don't want me!' shouted Winston. 'You've got a baby in your car already.'

'But we need you too, to be big brother for the baby,' said the mum.

Winston didn't want to leave, but Aunty Carol said, 'You'll come back and see us very soon.'

Winston sat in the back of the car with the baby. She held his finger and gurgled. They drove for a long time.

The mum and dad's house was much smaller than the children's home. But it had some nice toys in a cupboard. There was a photograph of Winston already in the kitchen.

'I like that,' said Winston.

'We've been waiting for you for a long time,' said the dad.

Winston didn't like the supper.

'Aunty Carol knows I don't like carrots!' he said, and threw his plate on the floor, and then crawled under the table. He wondered if the mum would send him away.

The mum cuddled him and read him a story. The dad went out to dig the garden. Winston went to help. That was fun.

Upstairs, there was a little shelf by Winston's new bed.

'To put your things on,' said the new mum.

'I haven't got any things,' said Winston.

'Then we'll find you some.'

They went round the house together and the mum found a fir-cone, three picture books, a postcard of a train and some marigolds in a mug. They arranged them on the shelf.

'Can I keep them?'

'Of course.'

Winston was in the room all by himself. It was very lonely.

'I'll leave the door open so you can see the light on the landing,' said the mum.

In the morning, Winston looked at the baby asleep in her room, and he looked at the mum and dad asleep together in the same bed. The dad opened his eyes.

'Would you like to come in and have another cuddle?' he said.

So they were all in bed together, and the baby had her bottle.

'I think I might stay always,' said Winston.

Winston, and his new mum and dad, and his new sister drove to the children's home to fetch Winston's anorak and his boots.

'Mum Dad and Me'

JAMES BERRY

My parents grew among palmtrees,
in sunshine strong and clear.
I grow in weather that's pale,
misty, watery or plain cold,
around back streets of London.

Dad swam in warm sea, at my age.
I swim in a roofed pool.
Mum – she still doesn't swim.

Mum went to an open village market
at my age. I go to a covered
arcade one with her now.
Dad works most Saturdays.

At my age Dad played
cricket with friends.
Mum helped her mum, or talked
shouting halfway up a hill.
Now I read or talk on the phone.

With her friends Mum's mum washed
clothes on a river-stone. Now
washing-machine washes our clothes.
We save time to eat to TV,
never speaking.

My dad longed for a freedom in Jamaica.
I want a greater freedom.
Mum prays for us, always.

Mum goes to church
some evenings and Sundays.
I go to the library.
Dad goes for his darts at the local.

Mum walked everywhere, at my age.
Dad rode a donkey.
Now I take a bus
or catch the underground train.

Mama, Do You Love Me?

BARBARA M. JOOSSE

*This is a story from the people often called Eskimos, though they
call themselves Inuit. They live in the lands around the
North Pole where it is freezing cold and dark in winter,
and in summer the sun never sets.*

'Mama, do you love me?'

'Yes, I do, Dear One.'

'How much?'

'I love you more than the raven loves his treasure,
more than the dog loves his tail,
more than the whale loves his spout.'

'How long?'

'I'll love you until the umiak* flies into the darkness,
till the stars turn to fish in the sky,
and the puffin howls at the moon.'

'Mama, what if I carried our eggs – our ptarmigan eggs! –
and I tried to be careful,
and I tried to walk slowly,
but I fell
and the eggs broke?'

'Then I would be sorry.
But still, I would love you.'

51

'What if I put salmon in your parka,
ermine in your mittens,
and lemmings* in your mukluks*?'

'Then I would be angry.'

'What if I threw water at our lamp?'

'Then, Dear One, I would be very angry.
But still, I would love you.'

'What if I ran away?'

'Then I would be worried.'

'What if I stayed away and sang with the wolves
and slept in a cave?'

'Then, Dear One, I would be very sad.
But still, I would love you.'

'What if I turned into a musk-ox?'

'Then I would be surprised.'

'What if I turned into a walrus?'

'Then I would be surprised and a bit scared.'

'What if I turned into a polar bear
and I was the fiercest bear you ever saw
and I had sharp, shiny teeth,
and I chased you into your tent
and you cried?'

'Then I would be very surprised
and very scared.
But still, inside the bear, you would be you,
and I would love you.

'I will love you, forever and for always,
because you are my Dear One.'

* An *umiak* is a big kayak canoe; *lemmings* are little creatures like mice, and *mukluks* are the Inuits' fur-lined boots.

'Tact'

LUCY UPWARD (AGED 14)

Oh, you're such a wonderful mum,
Mum, do you know that I really love you,
You're just the best mum in the world,
What do I want?
Nothing, why do you ask?
I'm just saying that I like you,
Because you're much better than other mums.
Yes, I know I've never said it before,
Yes, and that I always say you're awful,
The worst mum in the world, yes,
But I was just thinking how nice you are,
OK, wonderful,
Yes, even fantastic,
Yes, yes, the best mum ever.
What do you mean?
No, I'm not in trouble,
Thank you, well actually,
No I have no bad news,
Well, not really anyway,
It's just that, well,
OK, don't rush me,
It's just that um,
I've just lost something,
It's just my little sister's watch,
Well, and her shoes and socks,
and her clothes and hair clips,
Yes, very careless and stupid,
And also mum,
I seem to have lost my sister.

Davie's Rabbit

From *Shadrach*

MEINDERT DEJONG

There was this boy, Davie, and he was going to have a rabbit. His grandfather had promised it. A real, live rabbit! A little black rabbit, if possible. In a week, if possible...

The week passed, the rabbit arrived, and Davie was overjoyed. He called his rabbit 'Shadrach'...

It was almost unbelievable, and it was still a miracle. Every morning you woke up it was a miracle all over again, that there in a barn across the village sat a little rabbit, and he was yours. Something breathing, nibbling, hopping, and it was yours! In all the world it was yours. It was alive, and it was yours!

Oh, but it had been nice the way they all had come to look at Shadrach that first great day. It was even nicer because they had come one by one. First there had been Mother, of course, because she'd helped him carry Shadrach from Maartens' wagon to the barn. But Mother had gone to get Grandpa. And Grandpa had come with a plate, and on it was a fried herring. Grandpa had put two potato crates right in front of Shadrach's hutch, and Grandpa had sat there with him.

'Now while you look your fill, you go and eat your fill of that delicious herring,' Grandpa had said. 'Grandma kept it warm for you.'

It had been wonderful sitting there close, talking and talking about the little rabbit. All about Shadrach, the way he hopped, the way he nibbled and wriggled his little nose, about how black he was – black as sin – about his ears, his little bit of a tail – that's what Grandpa had called it – and everything and everything all over from the beginning again about Shadrach. Grandpa had kept reminding him to eat, and he'd kept forgetting because there'd always been something else again to point out to Grandpa about Shadrach. Shadrach, Shadrach, little black rabbit...

Then Grandma had come, and Grandma had sat in the exact spot where Grandpa had sat. She had sat there just like Grandpa, leaning forward, peering into the hutch with her old eyes. She had even cleaned her glasses with the inside bottom edge of her apron. That had been nice, too – Grandma there – because he had been able to tell Grandma not only everything about Shadrach, but also everything that Grandpa had said about Shadrach. And Grandma had just sat there saying: 'My, oh my, oh my, Davie.' Finally he'd just had to put down his plate with the herring and lay his head on Grandma's knee and say: 'Oh, Grandma!' He had loved her so.

Then Mother had been back again, with dry clothes. There in the barn she'd made him undress down to his skin, right before Grandma! But she'd first put a potato sack down on the earthen floor for him to stand on. Mother had said: 'I just thought I'd better bring these here, because I know you won't stir from this barn the rest of this day.'

She'd rubbed him so hard with a dry towel to get the chills and dampness all out of him that he'd had to put his hands on Grandma's shoulders – otherwise Mother would have rubbed him right down to the floor. And Grandma had said: 'My, oh my, oh my, Davie, to think that your grandfather thought of giving you a little rabbit! I don't think he could have thought of anything better in all the world.'

Grandpa couldn't have!

Then Dad had come! There all of a sudden Dad's voice had come through the open doorway: 'Is this where that eighth wonder of the world is kept? Is it in this barn? Can anybody tell me?'

He'd dragged his father over to the hutch, but Dad had been in too big a hurry to sit down on the potato crate. He'd just stood stooped over the hutch, slowly wiping the rain spots from his glasses.

It had made him so impatient, he'd just yelled at Dad: 'Look at him, Dad!'

Dad had said: 'I'm looking and looking with my whole pair of eyes, and even an extra pair of glasses thrown over them.' Dad always had such funny sayings!

But then he'd said: 'Is that the little beastie, Davie? Isn't he black! I don't think I could have made a better black rabbit myself out of a piece of black ebony.'

He'd told Dad: 'Your old wooden rabbit you would make would just sit!'

'So.' Dad had said. 'SO! I'm good enough to make your rabbit hutches, but not your rabbits.' Dad had tried to look terribly hurt but he hadn't managed at all. Oh, he loved his dad!...

But Davie's rabbit didn't do well. He got thinner and thinner, and Davie got more and more worried about him...

'Mother, may I just run to the barn quick a minute and see if Shadrach is all right?'

'It's Sunday, Davie. And with your good clothes in that barn... There isn't time. You're going to church with Dad this morning, just you and Dad out to the church in Nes. I thought that would be a big surprise treat for you, walking way out to the village of Nes with Dad. He wants to hear the new preacher there.'

'Oh, good!' It was a fine surprise, but he didn't let himself forget Shadrach. 'Mum, I'll just look, I won't touch a thing, and I'll come running right back.'

'Well,' Mother said doubtfully. 'All right, then. Otherwise I'm sure you'll just sit worrying about Shadrach all morning in church, and it doesn't seem quite right to sit worrying about a rabbit in church. But be right back!'

In the kitchen there was a bun with spice cheese on his plate on the table. He snatched it and ran hard across the village to the barn.

Shadrach was gone! The hutch was empty! Shadrach wasn't in his hutch. He stood there in his horrible scare, the forgotten bun squeezing to pieces in his hand. He stared at dim corners of the dark cluttered barn. There was nothing. Nothing moved. The whole barn felt empty. It was frighteningly quiet. He peered at the hutch in the dimness, poked at it, his face close. There was nothing. The cover of the hutch wasn't open – the brick was still on it. There wasn't any hole, not a single one of the slats was loose, nothing was disturbed, but Shadrach was gone.

He crouched at the hutch, frightened and forlorn. In the total Sunday silence of the barn and the village it seemed as if he could hear his own heart thump. He stared at the cluttered dim corners again, but there were so many nooks and holes, he didn't know where to look. He felt utterly helpless, and inside he began crying, but he did not cry out loud. The quiet was too awful to cry in. Now across the village the bell on the church tower started its solemn deep Sunday tones. Faintly far away the bell of the village of Nes began answering it. The two bells talked solemnly back and forth. It was church time.

The two bells went on ringing, there wasn't another sound. There hadn't been any sound in the barn, not a sound, but all of a sudden – there was Shadrach! There he came slowly hopping across the empty middle of the barn. Straight towards the hutch. Davie did not dare move for fear of scaring Shadrach. He crouched there, squeezing the bun. Shadrach came right to him, he even stood up against his knee like a squirrel. Why, Shadrach wanted to sniff the bun! Then he had the little rabbit, he pulled him up in his arms, he hugged him. 'Oh, Shadrach, you came. You came. You came,' he said brokenly. 'Aw, did you want the bun?' He held the bun to Shadrach's mouth, and Shadrach started nibbling it. Shadrach liked buns!

There were quick hard footsteps in the barn. It was Father. 'What's this?' his father demanded sternly. 'Didn't you promise you'd come right back?'

'Dad,' he said, 'Shadrach was out. Shadrach was gone and I couldn't find him anywhere. And I don't know how he got out. He just came back, just now.'

'Nonsense!' his father said, not believing it for a moment. 'You're just making up that story because you started playing with your rabbit and forgot to come back. Now put him in the hutch. We're late, because I was sitting at home waiting for you.'

Silently he dropped Shadrach in the hutch. He hurriedly glanced up, and when he saw his father wasn't looking, he dropped his bun in the hutch with Shadrach.

Straight from the barn they set out for the church in the village of

Nes. He was glad they hadn't gone home first. His clean starched blouse was all smudged, there was even a black cobweb on the sleeve. He couldn't brush it off, because Dad had him by the hand. Dad didn't notice the blouse. Dad didn't notice anything, he just walked fast, staring straight ahead, not saying a word. His father walked so fast it had him running at a dog trot to keep up, but Dad still kept tugging him along.

He looked up at his staring father. Dad was still angry. He trotted on the best he could so his father wouldn't notice him. It wasn't a nice surprise trip at all. It was a headlong run without a word between him and his dad. His father seemed to be thinking hard. Well, he was thinking hard too – about Shadrach's getting out – even though it was hard to run and think at the same time. It was a mystery how Shadrach could have got out, but not a nice mystery like the ones you made up in your mind. Suppose Shadrach got out again and got lost, what then?

Words formed on the end of his tongue, but he swallowed them. Dad hadn't believed Shadrach had been out. His father thought he had fibbed. It gave him a lost, unwanted feeling. He didn't remember his father ever being really angry with him before. Oh now and then short stern words, but not really angry, not a long going-on anger like this.

All of a sudden his side started to ache and stab. It felt like a thick pincushion full of stabbing sharp pins. It felt so thick, he couldn't breathe. He still tried to trot along.

'Dad,' he had to whisper at last. 'Dad!' He tried to loosen his hand from his father's grasp. His father didn't even notice. 'Dad! I can't any more!' He wept aloud, angrily and ashamed.

His father stopped, startled. 'My side,' he explained to his father between gasps. 'I can't catch my breath.'

'Oh Davie, why didn't you yell? Son, I forgot all about you.' His father sounded sorry, his father wasn't angry!

'Here, sit down quick in the grass. Stitch, hunh? Why didn't you yell, Son?'

'I thought you were angry with me.' It was hard to talk between gasps, but he had to get it out now, all of it. 'Dad, I wasn't fibbing – honest! Shadrach was out! I didn't let him out. And Dad, nothing was open or broken, but he was out.'

He still couldn't talk right because his side was still stabbing, but he wanted to talk and talk. It was so enormously wonderful – his dad wasn't angry with him!

His father sat down in the grass beside him. 'Just take deep breaths and don't try to talk. No, Davie, I wasn't angry with you. In fact, I'd forgotten all about it. Why boy, I'd even forgotten you were with me, or I never would have walked so fast. But I was thinking hard about that big farmhouse I'm building. I was worrying out some of the problems in my mind.'

'I was too, Dad,' he said eagerly. 'I was worrying out problems about Shadrach. I was worrying it out in my mind how Shadrach could have got out.' He laughed a little chummy laugh and shifted closer to his father. To think they'd both been worrying out problems!

'Tell me about it, Davie.'

Now the ache was all gone. It was wonderful sitting there in the deep grass with just his father on this quiet Sunday morning. There was peace in the fields, and the whole road stretched peaceful and empty... But they'd be late for church!

He forgot about church the next moment, for now he was telling his father everything, everything. About Shadrach's skinniness and about what Rem* had said. Though he'd never picked up Shadrach by the ears or given him even one single stalk of tall red clover, still Shadrach stayed skinny. And now he had got so skinny, he could even get out between those narrow up-and-down slats – because that's how he must have got out. He must have squeezed out between the slats, there was no other way. He even told his father his real deep worry – something he hadn't yet dared admit to himself. There were rats in the barn – big rats, big rat holes. If Shadrach got out again, could the rats take him down one of those holes and eat him?

Off and on he almost cried a little as he talked, but that wasn't because of his worries. That was because Dad listened so seriously. Then he was finished with all he had to say, but his father didn't have a quick grown-up's answer ready for him the moment he was finished. He didn't make a joke. He sat and thought! He thought about it!

'Well, Davie,' Father said at last, 'I've got to admit I don't know much about rabbits. I don't know why little rabbits get skinnier and skinnier. All I know is that your mother and grandmother tell me that you take the most wonderful care of your Shadrach. Why don't you ask Grandpa – he might know... So I can't do much about your rabbit, but maybe I can do something about that coop so he can't get out. However, even though he's as skinny as you say he is, I still can't see how a rabbit could squeeze through the narrow spaces between those slats... Are you sure there wasn't a loose slat, or maybe Shadrach gnawed a hole in the bottom under the straw where you didn't see it – rabbits can gnaw through wood, you know.'

'I looked the hutch all over, Dad, but there were no holes, and there was nothing broken except the crib that Rem broke, but that's because you've never fixed it.'

His father smiled a little at that, then he thought about the hutch again. 'You're worried sick about all this, aren't you, Son?' he said. He pulled out his watch, looked at it and made a surprised sound, then pushed his watch back in his pocket. 'Davie, it's much too late to go on to church now. And I've a notion that even if you and I went on to church, that preacher could preach and preach, but I'd be in that farmhouse I'm building, and you'd be in your rabbit hutch with your little rabbit. So, what do you say if we go back and look at that hutch of yours?'

Oh, that was clever – the preacher could preach and preach. Why, that could be an inside song:

> The preacher could preach and preach,
> But you'd be in that rabbit hutch
> With your little rabbit.

He loved it. He tucked it away for an inside song to remember and jumped up, eagerly ready to go back to the barn.

'We'll go back and see what we can find wrong,' Dad said as they walked along. 'We'll just be a little wicked today, you and I. But don't you tell anybody, not even that Grandpa of yours!'

Now it was different. Now that they were going back, he was walking eagerly ahead, almost tugging his father along. And his side didn't ache one bit. Oh, he had a wonderful father.

* Davie's big brother, who teased and worried him.

Ramona's Suitcase

From *Ramona and her Mother*
BEVERLY CLEARY

Ramona Quimby, aged seven, is afraid that her big sister Beezus
(Beatrice) is the favourite; that her mother can get along without
her. In this story all her worries come to a head and she
decides to run away.

'Nobody likes me. Nobody in the whole world,' said Ramona,
warming to her subject as the cat walked disdainfully through the
room on his way to peace on Beezus's bed. 'Not even my own mother
and father. Not even the cat. Beezus gets all the attention around
here. Even Picky-picky likes Beezus more than he likes me!' She was
pleased that her father stayed in the living room and she didn't lose
any of her audience. 'You'll be sorry someday when I'm rich and
famous.'

'I didn't know you were planning to be rich and famous,' said
Mr Quimby.

Neither had Ramona until that moment.

'What do you mean, I get all the attention around here?'
demanded Beezus. 'Nobody tapes my schoolwork to the refrigerator
door. We can hardly find the refrigerator, it is so buried under all
your drawings and junk!'

Both parents looked at Beezus in surprise. 'Why, Beezus,' said
Mrs Quimby, 'I had no idea you minded.'

'Well, I do,' said Beezus crossly. 'And Ramona always gets out of things like washing dishes because she is too little. She'll probably still be too little when she's eighty.'

'See?' said Ramona. 'Beezus doesn't like me because my artwork is stuck to the refrigerator.' Her parents weren't supposed to feel sorry for Beezus. They were supposed to feel sorry for Ramona.

'I'm always in the way,' said Ramona. 'You have to park me with Howie's grandmother so you can go to work, and Howie's grandmother doesn't like me. She thinks I'm so terrible she probably won't want me around anymore, and then there won't be anybody to look after me and you can't go to work. So there!' Ramona flopped down on the couch, waiting for someone to tell her she was wrong.

Ramona's mother and father said nothing.

'Everybody picks on me all the time,' said Ramona. Maybe she really would be so bad Howie's grandmother would say, I simply cannot put up with Ramona another day.

Silence.

Ramona made up her mind to shock her parents, really shock them. 'I am going to run away,' she announced.

'I'm sorry to hear that,' said Mr Quimby as if running away were a perfectly natural thing to do.

'When are you leaving?' inquired Ramona's mother politely. The question was almost more than Ramona could bear. Her mother was supposed to say, Oh, Ramona, please, please don't leave me!

'Today,' Ramona managed to say with quivering lips. 'This morning.'

'She just wants you to feel sorry for her,' said heartless Beezus. 'She wants you to stop her.'

Ramona waited for her mother or father to say something, but neither spoke. Finally there was nothing for Ramona to do but get up from the couch. 'I guess I'll go pack,' she said, and started slowly towards her room.

No one tried to prevent her. When she reached her room, tears began to fall. She got out her Q-tip box with all her money, forty-three cents, in it. Still no one came to beg her not to leave. She looked around for something in which to pack, but all she could find was an old doll's nursing kit. Ramona unzipped it and placed her Q-tip box inside. She added her best box of crayons and a pair of clean socks. Outside she heard the cheerful *ching-chong, ching-chong* of roller skates on cement. Some children were happy.

If nobody stopped her, where would she run to? Not Howie's house, even though Howie was no longer mad at her. His grandmother was not paid to look after her on Saturday. She could take the bus to Aunt Beatrice's apartment house, but Aunt Beatrice would bring her back home. Maybe she could live in the park and sleep under the bushes in the cold. Poor little Ramona, all alone in the park, shivering in the dark. Well, at least it was not raining. That was something. And there were no big wild animals, just chipmunks.

She heard her mother coming down the hall. Tears stopped. Ramona was about to be rescued. Now her mother would say, Please don't run away. We love you and want you to stay.

Instead Mrs Quimby walked into the bedroom with a suitcase in one hand and two bananas in the other. 'You will need something to pack in,' she told Ramona. 'Let me help.' She opened the suitcase on the unmade bed and placed the bananas inside. 'In case you get hungry,' she explained.

Ramona was too shocked to say anything. Mothers weren't supposed to help their children run away. 'You'll need your roller skates in case you want to travel fast,' said Mrs Quimby. 'Where are they?'

As if she were walking in her sleep, Ramona pulled her roller skates from a jumble of toys in the bottom of her closet and handed them to her mother, who placed them at the bottom of the suitcase. How could her mother not love a little girl like Ramona?

'Always pack heavy things at the bottom,' advised Mrs Quimby. 'Now where are your boots in case it rains?' She looked around the room. 'And don't forget your Betsy book. And your little box of baby teeth. You wouldn't want to leave your teeth behind.'

Ramona felt she could run away without her old baby teeth, and she was hurt that her mother did not want to keep them to remember her by. She stood watching while her mother packed briskly and efficiently...

When Ramona said her mother did not love her, she had no idea her mother would do a terrible thing like this. And her father. Didn't he care either? Apparently not. He was too busy scrubbing the bathroom to care that Ramona was in despair. And what about Beezus? She was probably secretly glad Ramona was going to run away because she could have her parents all to herself. Even Picky-picky would be glad to see the last of her.

As Ramona watched her mother fold underwear for her to take away, she began to understand that deep down inside the place where her secret thoughts were hidden, she had never really doubted her mother's love for her. Not until now... She thought of all the things her mother had done for her, the way she had sat up most of the night when Ramona had an earache, the birthday cake she had made in the shape of a cowboy boot all frosted with chocolate with lines of white icing that looked like stitching. That was the year she was four and had wanted cowboy boots more than anything, and her parents had given her real ones as well. She thought of the way her mother reminded her to brush her teeth. Her mother would not do that unless she cared about her teeth, would she? She thought of the time her mother let her get her hair cut at the beauty school, even though they had to scrimp and pinch. She thought of the gentle books about bears and bunnies her mother had read at bedtime when she was little.

'There.' Mrs Quimby closed the suitcase, snapped the latches, and set it on the floor. 'Now you are all packed.' She sat down on the bed.

Ramona pulled her car coat out of the closet and slowly put it on, one arm and then the other. She looked at her mother with sad eyes as she grasped the handle of her suitcase and lifted. The suitcase would not budge. Ramona grasped it with both hands. Still she could not lift it.

Hope flowed into Ramona's heart. Had her mother made the suitcase too heavy on purpose? She looked closely at her mother, who was watching her. She saw – didn't she? – a tiny smile in her mother's eyes.

'You tricked me!' cried Ramona. 'You made the suitcase too heavy on purpose. You don't want me to run away!'

'I couldn't get along without my Ramona,' said Ramona's mother. She held out her arms. Ramona ran into them. Her mother had said the words she had longed to hear. Her mother could not get along without her. She felt warm and safe and comforted.

'Reasonable Parents'

CORAL RUMBLE

Some nights I hear my parents come into my room,
And I poke my book under the pillow,
And I pretend to be asleep.
And that's when it happens...
They forgive me everything.

Mum says, 'He didn't mean to be so rude,
He just forgot himself;
And I think he's tried to tidy his room –
Well, at least his large bookshelf.
And it is quite hard to remember to say
"Thank you" all of the time,
In fact, I think he does very well,
We forget he's only nine!'

Then Dad says, 'I know he should have asked before
He took my tools from the shed,
But kids forget things like that
When they've got an idea in their head.
And it must be hard to go to bed
When you don't feel tired at all;
I remember reading under the covers –
A monkey I was, I recall!'

And when I hear my parents go out of my room
I slide my book out from under the pillow,
Snuggle down, all safe,
And thank God for giving me such reasonable parents!

Calum's Swan

ELAINE BROWN

It was hard for Calum, living alone with his mam. She was often cross and tired because she worked for long hours growing tatties and turnips on their lonely croft. She had to look after the cow, and a few sheep and hens too. Once Calum had seen tears streaking down his mam's pale thin cheeks.

'What's wrong, Mam?' he'd asked gently.

'Nothing!' she'd snapped, and jerked away. He guessed his mam felt sad because his dad had gone away. Calum could hardly remember his dad, he'd left so long ago. But he was angry with his mam. He sat on top of an old mossy wall and hammered his heels against its damp grey stones. Then he jumped down.

'I'll go and see Sandy!' he decided. Sandy worked as a woodcutter. His home was a wooden wagon which had stood under a clump of pine trees for so long that its heavy iron wheels had sunk deep into the brown leafy carpet. Sandy was Calum's friend.

'A bit like my Dad, maybe!' Calum thought. Sandy was tall and strong. His round face was as brown and creased as the tatties Calum's mam used for soup. It was a happy face, not tired or cross.

'Why do you smile so much?' Calum had asked Sandy once.

'Why there's so much to smile about, lad!' he'd answered. 'It's all around! Trees n' birds n' flowers. And animals n' insects n' fish. Things God's thought up and made… Aye, they matter very much to him, too!'

At that Calum's face had screwed up into a frown. 'Those things dinna make *me* smile,' he'd snorted. 'Nor my Mam.'

66

Calum ran along the path through the wood. Autumn mist had begun to creep in from the river. He shivered. Sandy would have a log fire burning outside his wagon – 'And there'll be tatties baking in the ashes!' Calum guessed. So he ran even faster.

Just then a patch of white beside the river bank caught his eye. He stopped and peered through the mist. What could it be? An old shirt? A lost ball? Maybe someone lying there, hurt? Or even drowned?…

Calum's heart began to thump in fear. He held his breath and eased the reeds apart. Suddenly two huge wings began to stretch, a tall thin neck uncurled, and a pair of dull eyes gazed at Calum. It was a wild swan – a whooper swan – pure white, except for a bright yellow patch which reached almost to the end of its black bill.

Calum was still very afraid, but he didn't run away. Instead he crouched as near to the swan as he dared, because the swan seemed to need him. It stayed quite still, watching Calum with sad eyes.

Then, all at once, the swan's neck drooped, its head fell back against its body, and the two huge wings crumpled. Calum gasped. What had happened? Was the swan ill? Or hurt?

Calum's heart thumped harder still.

'I *must* help her!' he cried. But when he reached out to the swan his feet began to slip down the muddy bank. Calum shrieked. He knew the river was deep and dangerous.

'Hey, why the noise?' a deep voice boomed. It was Sandy.

'See – the swan!' Calum cried. 'I must help her. She's very ill!'

Sandy lifted the swan out of the cold dark water. She was too weak to struggle. He settled her on a soft pile of leaves, felt her chest and sighed.

'Aye, she *is* very ill,' he told Calum. 'Looks like lead poisoning.'

'How did she get *that*?' Calum asked, eyes wide with concern.

'Shotgun pellets in the grit she's eaten,' Sandy said grimly. 'Grit's good for her, mind, but lead? Deadly. The poison's spread right through her, that's why she's so weak. Feel here…'

Sandy took Calum's hand and put it against the swan's chest. 'That's her crop, full of food,' he went on, 'but the swan's thin, 'cause her poisoned body can't digest food any more. Before long she'll starve to death.'

'No! No! She mustn't!' Calum blurted. 'We've got to help her!' Hot tears rushed to his eyes. He began to feel desperate.

'Does the swan matter to God?' Calum whispered.

Sandy nodded. 'Aye, she matters very much.'

'Then he'll show us how to help her, won't he?' Calum insisted.

'Well, maybe he will!' Sandy replied. He was thinking hard. 'The swan needs a warm place to rest. My wagon's too cold. Would your mam let her stay in the log cupboard by the stove?'

Calum frowned. 'She might.'

'Let's try,' Sandy suggested. He lifted the swan and they walked out of the wood together.

When they reached the gate, Calum took the swan in his arms. She felt heavy, cold too, so he rubbed his cheek against her feathers to comfort her.

'Mam must let me take you indoors!' he murmured. 'She *must!*'

Calum tapped the back door with his foot. It opened a crack and a streak of pale lamplight fell across his face.

'Whatever ha'e you there, lad?' his mam demanded.

'A wild swan, Mam. I found her. She's dying. I must keep her warm...'

'Nae in my kitchen!' Calum's mam snapped. 'You can take that swan right back to the river. Then come straight home!'

'But, Mam, she'll die!' Calum pleaded.

'Do as I've telt ye!' his mam ordered, and slammed the door.

Calum stood on the step trembling with cold and fury. He looked down the lane, but Sandy had gone, so he struggled back to the wood alone.

Calum laid the swan in a bracken hollow by the mossy wall. She was far too ill to lift her head or even stir. He knelt and stroked the swan's long limp neck, and his heart ached with love and fear for her. Then, full of dread, he crept home.

That night Calum hardly slept. Over and over he whispered to God: 'Please make the swan better... and please help Mam to stop raging me.'

At dawn he crept out of the cottage and raced to the swan. She was still alive! But only just. Her eyes stayed closed and she felt cold when Calum put his arm right round her. If only he could have taken her indoors for the night...

As soon as he'd gulped down his breakfast porridge, Calum rushed to tell Sandy about the swan and how his mam had raged him.

'Come and see the swan – *now*!' he begged, tugging at Sandy's sleeve.

'She matters very much to you, doesn't she lad?' Sandy said as they strode back along the path.

'Course!' Calum snapped, ''cause she needs me!'

'Seems like you n' God feel the same way about the swan,' Sandy went on. 'God feels like that about people too, mind. All kinds. Even ones that rage.'

Calum jerked to a stop.

'Even my Mam? Does *she* matter to God?' he demanded, eyes wide with surprise.

'Aye, lad, even your Mam. And he'd like you to help her, ''cause she needs you. You're all she has now your Dad's gone.'

Calum didn't answer. He just strode on.

It was very frosty that evening, but the swan was still alive… just.

'What's on your mind, lad?' Calum's mam asked at suppertime.

'Nothing,' he grunted. His mam frowned.

'Maybe…,' she began. 'Maybe the swan could sleep in the log cupboard for just *one* night!'

'Could she? Now? I'll go and fetch her!…' Calum rushed to the door.

'No! Come back at once!' his mam ordered. 'Tomorrow will do.'

'But Mam, she'll die before then!' Calum pleaded. His mam didn't listen. She just marched him up to bed.

But Calum's mam didn't forget about the swan. Next day she helped him to settle her in a straw nest among the logs.

'Just for *one* night, mind!' Calum's mam warned.

Calum stroked the swan's soft breast and felt a first faint warmth in her feathers. She stirred and opened one brown beady eye. Calum winked back and laughed.

'That's right! That's right!'

Then his smile faded.

'But you'll never be better, *all* better, by tomorrow,' he sighed.

Before dawn the first angry storm of winter began to howl around the cottage. All day long it rattled the windows and thumped the back door. Thick snow burst in over the hills and settled in deep drifts. As dusk fell, Calum grew very afraid. The swan was still so ill.

She would die if his mam made him take her out into the storm.

'Och the swan will have to stay another night,' Calum's mam muttered as she turned bannocks on the thick iron griddle.

Calum jumped for joy! He ran to hug his mam's thin waist, but not too hard because she didn't really like being hugged. Then he dashed to the log cupboard and whispered the news to the swan. She stirred, and while Calum helped, tried to sip water from the tin dish, then her head flopped down onto her back again.

Calum's mam began to pile bannocks onto a warm plate. She always made bannocks when the snow came. Calum loved them.

'Shall I put the bannocks on the table?' he offered shyly. 'And shall I fetch the butter?' His mam nodded. She watched him reach up to a high shelf and lift down the butter plate. A faint smile crossed her pale thin face. Calum saw it. He paused. His mam was *always* tired and cross. Or silent. She never smiled. Never. Why had she changed, just for those few moments? Was it because he'd helped her? Calum set the plate carefully down on the table. Sandy's words flashed back through his mind. 'God would like you to help her, mind, 'cause she needs you.'

A few days passed. The angry wind blew on, leaving the snow to lie, glistening white, beneath a cold, sunlit sky. Now the storm was over, Calum was certain his mam would make him take the swan back to the bracken hollow. He waited, quiet and fearful, but she said nothing.

More storms came. More snow. The swan liked the warm cupboard. She tried to lift her head and stretch her wide webbed feet. One day she nuzzled up to Calum, tapping him with her bill.

'Look Mam! Look!' Calum cried out in joy, as he put his arm round the swan's thin neck. 'You will get better!' he told her. 'You *will*!'

Calum helped his mam by feeding the animals and sweeping snow from the back step. Sometimes he fetched logs or peeled tatties for the soup. Once or twice the same faint smile crossed his mam's face. Calum loved to see her smile. He wanted to hug his mam again, but felt too shy, so tried to help her more instead.

At last spring came. The snow dripped away. New grass shoots poked up, tight snowdrop buds opened, and one morning the first black and white oyster-catchers flew in from the sea, shrieking with delight.

The swan heard their calls. She stirred and lifted her head, then began to nibble the sliced tatties and turnip Sandy had brought for her.

Later Calum joined Sandy on the pine-log step of his wagon.

'The swan *is* going to get better now, isn't she?' he insisted.

'Aye, I think so,' Sandy answered, and his deep blue eyes beamed.

'That means God *did* show us how to help her!' Calum pointed out, then added shyly, 'I think he's showing me how to help my Mam too.'

'Aye, I've noticed,' Sandy said. 'And has she raged you lately, lad?'

'No, she hasn't. I'm not so angry with my Mam now, mind,' he told Sandy.

Sandy squeezed Calum's hand, then he went into the wagon and fetched a strip of bright yellow cloth.

'What's that for?' Calum asked.

'To tie round the swan's leg,' Sandy explained. 'Then, when she comes back we'll know she's ours.'

'But... but she isn't going awa' is she?' Calum demanded. A sudden sharp pain stabbed his chest, the same pain he'd felt long ago when his father had left home. Sandy sat down and put his arm round Calum. 'Spring's here, lad, and the swan will want to feed in the river again,' he began. 'Then, once she's strong enough it'll be time for her to set off with other wild swans for Iceland.'

Next day, when Sandy visited the cottage, he lifted the swan out of the cupboard. She struggled hard.

'That's a good sign!' Sandy said. 'Shows she's much stronger. And look how her eyes shine in fun when she tries to peck me!' Calum laughed.

He and his mam tied the yellow band to the swan's black leg while Sandy held her still. Then he tucked her under his arm and the three of them walked to the river. Sandy set the swan down on the bank. At first she wobbled and flopped, then she stood and tried to wag her thick tail. Calum grinned.

Suddenly the swan stood straight up and stretched her huge wings. Calum gasped. They were massive! She beat them back and forth twice, then folded them down against her body again. Calum jumped up and down and cheered. His mam laughed too. Then, 'Come awa' hame, lad!' she said. 'We must let the swan live her ain life now.'

☆

Calum went to the river every day. He loved to watch the swan. One morning, he heard wild swans calling – whooping – overhead. His heart sank. Had his swan joined them? Had she gone? He dashed to the river bank, but she was still there.

'Please don't go!' Calum pleaded.

Sandy came striding down the path.

'Did you hear the wild swans?' he asked. 'Maybe our swan will join them. Swans always fly together. It's safer.'

Calum stiffened. If only the swan didn't have to go!

Suddenly a dozen whooper swans flew in low over the river. What a flypast! Then, as Calum held his breath, his own swan gave an answering cry and stretched her massive wings. Her webbed feet paddled fast across the shining water, then, all at once, she soared into the clear morning air. Calum cried out to her and she called back, then flew higher still. Above the old wall, above the tall trees, above the small cottage. At last she reached the other swans. She was one of them now. Her long journey had begun.

Calum gazed after the swan until her beating wings faded far into the distance. Then he leapt down from the wall.

'I must tell Mam!' Calum called back to Sandy as he raced home.

'Whatever's happened?' Calum's mam cried when he burst in.

'It's the swan! She's flown off with the others. To Iceland. But she *will* come back. In October, Sandy says…' Calum's words tumbled out, excited and sad all at once.

Without thinking he ran and flung his arms round his mam's thin waist.

'Sandy says God will take care o' the swan,' Calum cried into his mam's warm apron, ''cause she matters to him…' Sobs choked his voice. 'And Sandy says people matter to God, too. All kinds, even ones that rage…'

Calum stopped, horrified.

What had he said. What was he doing, hugging his mam like this? She'd be angry. She'd push him away. She'd rage. He waited, tense with fear. But this time his mam didn't rage. She didn't push him away. This time, she bent down and gave him a very quick kiss.

Frank's Dad and the Green Paint

From *Our Kid*

ANN PILLING

*Frank lives with his Dad and his nineteen-year-old brother
Malcolm, whom Frank has privately christened 'Slob'. Frank's
Dad has lost his job and wants to set up his own electrical
business at home. But that depends on money from the Friendly
Northern Bank, and as he waits for a reply, he gets gloomier
and gloomier. At last the letter comes. It's a turn-down,
and Frank's Dad flips...*

It was still dark when Frank reached Shorrock Street, but there was
a street lamp opposite the squat concrete and timber hut that housed
Dad's branch of the Friendly Northern. He propped his bike against it
and stared across the road, a sour sick feeling in his stomach, dragging
unwilling eyes upward till they were level with the building opposite.
Please don't let it be true.

But it was. Dad was very nifty with his paint brushes and rollers.
All the people he'd done jobs for had commented on how neat he
was, how thorough, yet how quick. Well, he must have been quick,
to have painted all this overnight. It was only small but it still
represented several hours work for one man, and he'd done a good
job too.

Frank had crossed the road and was examining his father's
handiwork with hideous fascination; no runs, no drips, no brush-
marks, no bits left out. The whole of the Friendly Northern Bank,

Shorrock Street Branch, Darnley-in-Makerfield, was a glossy bright Buckingham green, including its flat roof, its door handles, and all its windows. Someone had made a feeble attempt to scrape some of the paint off, to see out, but it was obviously a job for the experts. According to the report, high pressure hoses were going to be necessary to restore the place to its former glory.

You could always tell if a bank belonged to the Friendly Northern because they were all painted yellow and black, with the eagle logo on the windows and doors. This shiny green hut resembled something from Legoland.

Dad must have chosen 'Buckingham' because green made you think of Ireland, land of the Shamrock, the Emerald Isle. The report in the *Examiner* said he'd done it as 'a protest', because he wanted to speak out for all the hundreds of people like him who'd gone to their banks in good faith and been turned away, *'An official at the Friendly Northern'*, it had stated, *'denied that Mr Feargus Tanner's application had been turned down because he had an Irish name. "Frankly, we are bewildered," local manager, Mr Brian Brocklehurst (37) said last night. "He even painted my car tyres with green paint and I am having considerable difficulty getting it off. He should have made his complaint to us in person, instead of resorting to these childish tactics." Mr Tanner, aged 45 and a widower, lives at 14 Bailey Street, Darnley with his two sons. A former electrician with Morland's Electrical, he has been unemployed for some time and said he had also recently suffered a disappointment in his private life. "I'm afraid everything just got on top of me," he told our reporter on the telephone last night. "It was a very silly thing to do and I apologize to all concerned." The Friendly Northern has yet to decide what action to take against Mr Tanner.'* Frank had read the report so many times, he'd more or less got it off by heart.

As he climbed back on to his bike he stared across at the silly-looking green hut. True, his father had behaved like a lunatic, creeping out at dead of night to slap gloss paint all over it, and he would probably end up in debt now, for years and years. He might even go to prison for committing criminal damage. Yet deep down, Frank felt he understood.

He could see exactly how things had 'got on top' of Dad: Rita Stone taking him for a ride then ditching him; the jobs he went after that never came to anything; the bills he couldn't pay – and underneath all this, the running sore of the bank loan. He must really have believed that they'd lend him the money in the end, even though they'd said his front-room conversion scheme wasn't 'practical'.

That final refusal from Brian Brocklehurst had arrived the same day Rita had chucked him, and it had all been too much. Some people would have banged their heads against the wall and screamed; some would have gone out and got drunk. Others might have found out where the bank manager lived and punched him in the face. But Dad, silently brooding about everything for weeks and weeks, till he couldn't stand the tension any more, had crept out with all his painting tackle in the middle of the night and given vent to his disgust at life in general by painting the offending bank green.

If it had been anybody else's father Frank would probably have laughed, like the people at school. But it was his own, and he wanted to cry.

On his way back to Bailey Street he stopped at Midwood's, bought a tube of Polos and took a free *Spotlight* from the pile on the counter. Their headline was even worse than the *Examiner's* – BANK MAN SAYS IT WITH PAINT.

He ran his eyes over the report underneath. It wasn't much different from the other one, except that they said the Tanners lived at 4 Bailey Street, not 14, and that Dad was an unemployed plumber.

Well, there was no way he was going to do his paper round this morning...

Sister Maggie was the only person he could talk to about all this. He'd go and see her today...

Instead of knocking at the front he went through the side gate and peered in at the kitchen window. Sister Geraldine stood at the sink, her arms up to their elbows in soapy water. Everybody did menial tasks here, Maggie had told him, nobody was considered 'too grand' for cleaning the brasses, emptying the dustbins or washing old men's feet. It was part of what they believed, part of the 'Love of God', like it said on the gate.

Frank steeled himself, ducked out of sight and tapped on the back door. He'd have to go through with this now...

She opened the door at once, still drying her hands on a tea-towel. 'I'd like to speak to Sister Maggie,' he blurted out in a rush, but taking immediate refuge in a close inspection of his own feet. Those keen blue eyes of hers always unnerved him, the way they seemed to see through everything.

'She's not available just now,' he heard, a calm unruffled voice from the other side of a solid purple bust. 'Perhaps I could help?'

'But can't I speak to her? Just for a minute? It's urgent like.' Frank's voice was wavering now, in spite of his efforts. Why couldn't she just go and fetch Maggie? Surely she could see what a state he was in?

There was a pause, then the door was pulled open. 'Come in then, Frank. Take a seat, I'll just go and see what's happening.'

He pulled a stool out and sat waiting at the kitchen table. Some meat was simmering in a pan on the old Aga cooker. Above it, where other people would have fixed a clock, a wooden Jesus hung on a wooden cross. He'd often looked at that when he'd had cups of tea in this kitchen, with Maggie and Sister Ursula of the Teeth. That cross, she'd told him once, stood for everything the nuns believed, all the love in the world. Frank didn't really understand how someone jolly like Maggie could be associated with all that gloom and suffering. All the nuns were cheerful though, humming as they went about their menial tasks in the echoey rooms and corridors of 105. Even Sister Geraldine cracked the odd joke.

Through the kitchen door he could hear them singing a hymn. Usually, he quite liked the sound but today, with all that he'd got on his mind, solemn music like that upset him. They were obviously in the middle of singing practice for their 'chapel', a dark narrow room at the back of the house. Maggie wouldn't be allowed to come and see him.

Gloomily, he began to fold up the two newspaper reports about Dad which he'd spread out on the table for her to read. Then he felt a hand on his shoulder and he heard the door being shut behind him. It was Maggie.

'Hi, Frank,' she said, 'how are you doing?' and she sat down at the other end of the long table.

Four feet of scrubbed pine stretched between them now, acres of wood separated them, sharpening up the panic and loneliness he felt inside. There she sat, all fresh and country-looking with her face raised to his, her neat head on one side as usual, wondering why he'd come.

But how could he tell her he'd come for comfort, that he wanted her to come to his end of the table, and put her arms round him so he could cry about Dad? That he wanted her to be the sister he'd always wanted, the mother he'd never known, not a young nun whose life was already dedicated to that mysterious thing, 'the love of God'? At that moment, he needed her more than God did. Silently, he pushed his two cuttings down to her end of the table... Then he sat firmly on his hands, because they were shaking so much.

All the time she was reading the articles he watched her carefully. At first he thought she was going to laugh because her mouth twitched very slightly, now and again. Then he saw her hands go up to her face. When she dropped them she looked much more serious but he detected she was having to make an almighty effort to keep her face straight.

At last she said, 'I'm really very sorry, Frank,' and she pushed the two cuttings back along the table.

'What am I going to *do*, Maggie?'

She shrugged and gave a little smile. 'Well, what can you do? It's not your problem, is it? Have you talked to your father?'

'No. We've been avoiding each other, but knowing him, he won't want to discuss it when I do try. I knew something must be up on Sunday, when the police came round. All he said was that it'd probably blow over and that we'd not hear any more about it. But I never realized he'd done something as daft as this. I thought he'd just nicked a telly I found in the cellar. I mean, honestly, fancy painting a *bank*. He's off his chump.'

Maggie did laugh then. 'What do you mean, Frank?' she said. 'I've never heard that expression before.'

'Well, off his rocker, like, y'know, crazy.'

'But I like crazy people! Not many people would have thought of painting the bank, as a protest, now would they? I do like it, Frank. I could just see it on television, couldn't you? It's wonderful.' She was laughing so much now that for one terrible moment Frank wanted to hit her. It wasn't 'wonderful', it was dreadful, and it might land his father in debt for years and years, if not actually in prison. She must be overtired or something because of all that cleaning and scrubbing they did in this place. She just wasn't thinking straight.

He didn't hit her, but he suddenly shouted very loudly, 'Don't laugh, Maggie, please. They were all laughing at school. They'll all have gone to look at it, knowing that lot. I can't stand it. Please don't laugh like that.'

'I'm sorry Frank,' she said at once. 'Listen, I'm sure it'll just blow over, honestly. And as for these silly newspaper stories, well, you know what reporters are like. It'll be something different tomorrow. Everybody will have forgotten the whole thing by next week, you'll see.'

'But Maggie, it's my *Dad*! They've made him sound such a *fool*!' And he brought his fist crashing down on the table, making everything in the kitchen rattle.

This time she did walk round to his end. He felt her hands come down on his shaking shoulders, giving them a little squeeze. 'I do understand, Frank,' she said.

'No, you don't,' he muttered. 'How would you like it, if it was your dad? Everyone poking fun at him and that?'

There was a long pause, then she said, 'Frank dear, my old dad was a bit of a problem too, you know. He wasn't, well, original like yours but – '

'So you think it's "original", do you?' he interrupted sourly, 'painting a bank in the middle of the night, just because it won't give him a loan for a silly scheme, making everyone laugh at our family?'

'My dad,' she pressed on firmly, 'was a bit of a drinker. My brother and I were always sent to fetch him home from the bar. If my mother went they usually ended up having a fight. And we were only young, Frank, much younger than you and your Malcolm.'

'But you still don't *understand*,' he said, rubbing viciously at his raw red cheeks down which, in spite of all his efforts, the tears had started falling.

'OK, Frank. You win. Nobody understands.' Abruptly, she took her hands away from his shoulders and resumed her seat at the other end of the table.

But the tone of her voice worried him now and he got to his feet. She'd always been so kind to him before, so willing to see his side of things. Now it sounded as if he'd really hurt her feelings by losing his temper and wallowing in self-pity. Perhaps she'd ask him to leave in a minute and never come back. He couldn't bear that, not at the moment when he needed someone to stick up for him.

'I'm very sorry,' he grunted, then he rushed straight on before she could say anything else. 'But why are you so sure it'll "blow over"? It says in the *Spotlight* that the bank might sue for damages.'

But Maggie shook her head. 'I'm sure they won't, Frank.'

He stared at her. How *could* she be 'sure'? Religion wasn't supposed to be about foretelling the future, you were supposed to trust in God for that. And while they were on the subject, where was God, when Dad painted the bank? Asleep? But he'd better not say that or she'd be really offended. In confusion he sank back on to his stool and put his face in his hands. 'You just can't be sure, Maggie,' he said through his fingers. 'They might send him to prison, and he's all I've got. I love my Dad.'

'Sorry'

CORAL RUMBLE

Why is the word 'sorry'
So very hard to say?
Your mouth goes dry,
Your arms go stiff,
Your knees start to give way.
And even when that little word
Is ready to pop out,
It rolls around
Upon your tongue
Until you have to shout,
'I'M SORRY!', just to get it past
Your gums, your teeth, your lips;
And then your mum says,
'Well, my girl,
It doesn't sound like it!'

The Showdown and After

From *The Mennyms*

SYLVIA WAUGH

The Mennyms are a family of life-size rag dolls: living, walking, talking, breathing – but made of cloth and kapok. Teenage Appleby has been found out after hoaxing the whole family with a series of letters from Australia, from someone called Albert Pond. Rather than face a showdown with her Granpa, Sir Magnus, she runs away. Vinetta, her mother, is frantic with worry as Soobie (Appleby's brother, the twin of newly discovered Pilbeam) goes out into the storm to search for her.

Vinetta did not move. She listened to the rain on the windows and she grew more and more intensely miserable. The agony of wondering where her daughter could be on a night like this felt like a fist in the stomach taking her breath away.

'Oh, Appleby,' she groaned, 'where, oh where, are you?'

But it was Soobie who answered her. He was there at the lounge door, dressed in the hooded coat again and the blue wellington boots. In his hand was the golf umbrella.

'I'll find her, Mother. I will find her. She's wilful but she is strong and resourceful. I think I know where to look.'

This time when he went out into the stormy night he did not turn towards the town and the well-lit shops. He turned left, past the first church which was closed up and in complete darkness, on to the second church which was dimly lit but still closed. He walked right

81

up to the arched doorway of this second church and looked carefully in the corners of the porch. A little boy of about nine or ten was sitting in a huddle with his knees up to his chin. But there was no sign of Appleby.

The third church had two entrances. A large double door in the centre of the front facade was firmly shut. Soobie even tried the metal ring that formed the handle. It looked promising. There were lights in the stained glass windows. There was a definite air of a building that was not closed and shuttered. Soobie looked along to the right and his eye fell on the second door. It was smaller, no bigger than an ordinary house door, and narrow and, what was more to the point, a little bit ajar.

Cautiously, Soobie went in. He found himself in an inner porch where there were noticeboards on the walls, and two coat stands. Looking through the glass partition into the nave, he saw that there were three or four individuals sitting, or kneeling in silent prayer, well-separated from one another, very private people in a very private place.

He watched for a while before slipping quietly into the far end of the back pew. He knelt before the statue of a lady with a child in her arms. Appleby was not there, but the prayerful mood of the place gave him another straw to clutch at.

In deep shadow he pushed his hood back just far enough to make it clear that he knew to bare his head in church. Being Soobie, always honest to himself, he was prepared to be no less than honest to God.

'I do not know who made the part of me that thinks. I do not know who I really am or what I really am. I am never satisfied to pretend. I cannot pretend that you are listening to me. I can only give you the benefit of the doubt. And it is a massive doubt, I can tell you. I do not know whether I believe in you, and, what is worse, you might not believe in me. But I need help and there is nowhere else to turn. The flesh-and-blood people who come here have something they call faith. Please, if you are listening to a rag doll with a blue face, let the faith of those others be enough for you to help me. I must find my sister, or my mother will be the first of us to die. Dear God, I don't even know what that means!'

It was all he could say. After he had said it, two things came to his mind. First, he knew now just why he had come to find Appleby.

Secondly, he had the feeling, and it was no more than a feeling, that someone somewhere had heard his prayer.

He went out into the wet autumn evening and wandered in the direction of the park. The gates were closed, but times being what they were, the railings by the gate had been vandalised and there was a gap of ample size for even Soobie to pass through.

He wandered down the broad path till he came to a junction. To the left a narrower path led upwards among some tall leafless trees. To the right the broad path continued downwards past a grassy playground to the lake. Weak, old-fashioned lamps lit both paths and were reflected in the rainwater. The rain was still falling, thin but steady. Soobie's coat was soaked. It was fortunate that the blue wellingtons were more waterproof than the old golf umbrella.

He stood at the junction for a few seconds. Then he decided to follow the more sheltered, narrow path up among the trees. After a few yards, he passed a park-bench and then another one. They were arranged at intervals all along the path facing, through the trees, the green, the playground and the more distant lake.

Soobie walked slowly and bleakly on. At the top of a walk that came up from the lake and split the green into two large areas there was a wooden building, all shuttered, with what looked like the face of a clock just perceptible through the darkness in a little lantern tower. Soobie kept on walking towards it.

Just before he reached the building, on the last seat, he saw what looked like a very large bundle of dirty rags. Soobie knew at once that it was Appleby, for no other reason than that for the past ten minutes or more he had expected to find her there. Some instinct had told him that she would be lying just as she was, scruffy and desperate, not knowing where to turn.

Soobie was pleased to find her. He was overjoyed to find her. But he didn't show it.

He went up to the seat and grabbed her wet arm.

'Come on,' he said. 'You're coming home. Your mother's worried sick.'

Appleby looked up at him wildly. Still defiant, she made herself say, 'So what?'

Soobie bit his blue lip and was about to say something salutary when Appleby's defiance suddenly crumbled and she slumped back on the seat and sobbed.

There was nothing more to say. Soobie took her by the arm and, without a word, supported her wet weight along the path, through the gap in the railings, and out into the dark street.

By the time they had struggled home, Appleby was in a dreadful state. None of the Mennyms had ever had a bath before, but that was what she needed. And afterwards a long dry-out in the airing cupboard. But still Appleby refused to meet the family. She shut herself into her room and would not come out. Then Sir Magnus decided to write her a letter and push it under the door...

Appleby, lying on her bed and getting more and more bored by the minute, saw the envelope edge its way through the door. She waited at least half an hour before going to pick it up. She wouldn't give them the satisfaction of hearing her move, if that was what they were waiting for. She did not trust any of them.

'My dearest Grand-daughter,' she read, when at last she decided to retrieve it and open it, 'We have had enough of this stuff and nonsense. It is making your mother very upset. Pull yourself together, girl, and come and join the family. There'll be no reference to things past, no recriminations. No one will ever mention the name of Albert Pond.
    Your loving Granpa,
    Magnus Mennym.'

'Some hopes!' exclaimed Appleby. 'The minute I'm out of that door it'll be "Why ever did you do it?" "Where did you go?", "How did you get so dirty?" and those twins might even ask if it was fun.'
    Taking the airmail stationery, of which she still had a fairly large supply, she tore off a flimsy blue sheet and wrote in large letters the words:

'GET STUFFED'

Then she put it in an airmail envelope and addressed it in her best handwriting to 'Sir Magnus Mennym'.
    It was Vinetta who picked up the envelope as she was on her way to Granpa's room in the early evening, just after the family hour.
    Sir Magnus took his silver paperknife and opened it with a flourish. When he read the contents he nearly bounced out of his bed with rage.

84

'There'll have to be a conference,' he shouted. 'Tell everybody to come here now, this minute.'...

Vinetta glimpsed the words on the paper as it fluttered to the floor. Then she steeled herself to say what she had to say.

'There will be no conferences. There have been too many already. Leave it be. I'll write to her. She's obviously willing to read letters and to answer them, however objectionable the answers may be.'

Sir Magnus still looked furious. 'A conference...' he spluttered, black beady eyes popping.

'Stop that,' said Vinetta sharply. 'If you don't you might just be the first rag doll ever to die of a stroke. Leave it to me. I know what I am doing.'

The next letter Appleby received was from her mother.

'Dear Appleby,' she read. 'I won't dwell on anything wrong you may have done. I can't be your judge. I can't even be so condescending as to forgive you. How do I know what there is to forgive?

All I can offer you is my unconditional love. And if you come out, there will be nothing said to you about the past, not by me, not by anyone. No doubt Granpa made you a similar promise. There is a difference. I will make sure, absolutely sure, that the promise is kept. I have never realised till now just how much power I have in this family. I can restrain them and I will.

If some day you wanted to talk to me about what happened, I would be happy to listen. But you would have to speak first. I will never broach the subject with you again. The truth is a gift in your possession. You can decide to keep it, or to bestow it on whomever you choose. No one will ever ask you any questions. We can pretend it never happened, if that is what you want.

Please join us. We love you. Do not make yourself a stranger.
Mother.'

Appelby sobbed when she read the letter. She read it two or three times and then put it away safely in a drawer.

Taking paper again, she wrote on it just two words:

'I CAN'T'

Pilbeam it was who found the airmail envelope addressed to Vinetta. She dashed down with it to the kitchen where Vinetta was busy ironing.

'She still won't come out,' sighed Vinetta.

Pilbeam, looking over her mother's shoulder, corrected her.

'She doesn't say "won't". She says "can't".'

'It amounts to the same thing.'

'No it doesn't. She says "can't" and I think she really means it. I almost understand her. She is my sister, after all, and nearer my age than any of yours.'

'You don't even know her,' said Vinetta bitterly.

'Yes, I do,' declared Pilbeam with sudden clarity of vision. 'I was born knowing her.'

At those words, with that thought, the next move became obvious.

'I am going up to see her,' she said.

'Don't,' said Vinetta anxiously, but Pilbeam was already out of the kitchen door and half way up the first flight of stairs. Vinetta hurried after her. They paused outside Appleby's door. Pilbeam knocked once, quite firmly. There was no reply. So she pushed open the door.

'Who are you?' screamed Appleby. 'Get out of here. This is my room.'

'I'm Pilbeam,' answered Pilbeam sharply. 'I'm your sister and Soobie's twin. You know perfectly well who I am. So stop being stupid.'

Pilbeam went into the room. Vinetta, standing in the hall, had the good sense not to follow. She closed the door and, a little reluctantly, left them to sort it out between themselves.

The next day, Appleby rejoined the family. She became her old, perky, abrasive self again. There were no apologies, not even an explanation. Nobody mentioned Albert Pond. For good or ill, that was what Vinetta decreed and everyone was made to agree to it. It was her side of the bargain. Like the old lease on the house, it was very much in favour of the owner. In this case, the owner was Appleby; the property, her mother's unconditional love.

'The Final Straw'

STEVE TURNER

I hit my sister.
My dad got mad.

Dad said, 'Get right in your bed. Now.'
So I did. I got right in.
I slit open the mattress
With a sharpened blade
and I slid right in.
It was a tight fit
between those springs.

So Dad said, 'That's destructive.
Stay in your room. And don't you dare come out.'
So I did.
Monday, Tuesday, Wednesday,
Thursday, Friday.
I stayed in my room.
I got lonely. And hungry.

So Dad said, 'Come down here
and eat some food.
Now you eat everything. You hear?'
So I did.
I ate the egg, the chips and the beans.
The plate, the knife, the fork.
The table.

So Dad said, 'You've gone too far.
You make me sick to death.'
So I picked up the 'phone.
I called an ambulance.
'Come quickly. My dad's sick...
How sick? Sick to death.'
The sound of sirens
soon filled the street.

They carried Dad off on a stretcher.
They had to strap him down
to stop him struggling.

So Dad said, 'That's the final straw!'
(But it wasn't.
There was a spare one
stuck onto a carton of fruit juice
in the fridge.)

3

Not Like Me?

'I wonder what it's like to be you?'
That's a good question to ask, especially when it helps us to
see and feel things the way someone else sees and feels them
– especially someone who is different from us. That's what
the poems and stories in this section are all about.
In *The Choosing*, white girl Mary Jemison learns about the
American Indians by living with them. Billie's arrival in his
foster home is a disaster until Robert unlocks the love
beneath all the anger and hurt. And *I See Music* takes us
into the silent world of Alex, who is deaf.

'Look'

EMILY DOUGLAS (AGED 11)

I
    wonder
            what
                it's
                    like
                        to
                            be
                                you
                                    and
                                look
                                at
                            me
                        from
                your
            point
        of
view!

The Choosing

From *Indian Captive*

LOIS LENSKI

Mary Jemison (Molly in this story) is only twelve years old when a band of Indians carries her off from her family's farm in Pennsylvania. For a long time she is very unhappy and she finds her new life hard. But the Indians are kind and teach her many things. They give her an Indian name – 'Corn Tassel'. Now, at last, she is given the chance to return to the world of the white men...

'Don't leave us! Don't leave us! Don't leave us!' The children's cries kept ringing in Molly's ears as she left them beside the door and entered the council house. She took one fleeting glance round the room. The Chief was there, the sachems and warriors, but not only these – the women were there, too – Panther Woman, Red Bird, Earth Woman, and all the others. The council house was filled with faces and all of them were staring at her.

Then she saw the white man, dressed in red – a red so red it almost hurt her eyes. She saw gold lace and shining buttons of brass, and then above, his smiling face.

'Captain Morgan has come to us from Sir William Johnson.' Molly turned her eyes away from the shining red to hear what the Chief was saying. 'He brings a message of thanks for our offer to join forces with the English.'

Chief Burning Sky paused, then went on: 'It has not been our policy, heretofore, to sell or exchange captives, as you know, for we

consider our adopted captives our own flesh and blood. But now
that we fight with the English, our policy has altered. Sir William
Johnson says that as soon as the French are subdued, all white
captives in the hands of the Iroquois will be given up by treaty
agreement. Since this is undoubtedly true, it would seem the better
part of wisdom to listen to Captain Morgan's offer. Because the treaty
has not yet been drawn, Captain Morgan has generously offered to
ransom you himself.

'The Sachems and I have decided in council to give you your
freedom, if you desire it. If you do not desire it, you may stay quietly
and undisturbed with us for the rest of your life. You are not to be
sold without your own consent.'

Sold! The word hit Molly like the sharp sting of an arrow from
a tightened bow. Looking up, she saw Gray Wolf's face against the
bark wall, leering down at her. When had he come? Was he waiting
to get the money? Was he already holding out his greedy hand to
the Englishman?

Sold! A white girl sold – to buy Gray Wolf a white man's suit
at Fort Niagara, to buy Gray Wolf fire-water to turn him into a
worse beast than he was! Molly's breast heaved up and down with
righteous anger. Her eyes flashed as she stared at the man's wicked
face against the bark wall.

But the Chief was speaking again. She turned to him and looked
up into his face. There she saw real sorrow, which moved her deeply,
as she drank in his words:

'My daughter, these are men of the same colour as yourself, who
speak the language you spoke in childhood. Soon a treaty will be
signed which says you must go free. But you need not wait for that.
Captain Morgan offers you a home and every comfort of the pale-
faces, if you wish to go.

'My daughter, for many moons you have lived with us. I call upon
you to say if Red Bird has not been a mother to you; if she has not
treated you as a mother would a daughter of her own? I call on you
to say if Shining Star and Squirrel Woman have not treated you as
sisters?'

'Red Bird has been a mother to me,' said Molly, in a low voice.
'Shining Star and Squirrel Woman have been like my own sisters.'

A murmuring sound ran through the crowd of waiting Indians
like the hum of a rising storm, then died away, as the Chief spoke:

'My heart rejoices to hear you say so, daughter. The women have taught you many things. They have taught you to grow corn, to prepare food, to care for the younger children, to tan skins and make clothing. Earth Woman, who has no daughter, has taught you an old, old art – how to make fine pots of grace and beauty. You mean as much to Earth Woman as if you were her daughter. She is growing old – you will be a support to her in her old age. She will lean on you as upon a staff. If you are going to leave us, we have no right to say a word, but we are broken-hearted. I speak for the women. I speak for the children. I speak for the men and boys, and for myself.'

A vision of Earth Woman's kind face rose up before Molly's eyes. She remembered the look of pain upon it when Running Deer went away, never to return. Could she, who loved her so much, bring her still more sorrow?

'With us for many moons you have made your home,' continued the Chief. 'With us you have eaten bread and meat. When we have had plenty, you have shared in it. When we have had nothing, you, too, have known the pinch of hunger. You have learned what giving is, without thought of return. You have learned what truth and courage are. By the hardships which you have suffered with us, you have learned bravely to live and, because of that, when your time comes, you will the more bravely die.

'If, my daughter, you choose to take the hand of this man of your own colour and follow the path where he leads, I have no right to say a word. But if you choose to stay with the Senecas, then the pale-faces have no right to speak. Whatever you choose, no pale-face, no Seneca, shall change your decision. Now reflect upon it and take your choice and tell us. It shall be as you decide. I have spoken.'

The room was very still. It was still with all the silence of complete emptiness, as if no man breathed or moved or stirred. It was still with the silence of mingled hope and fear, for hope and fear, with desperate strength, struggled against each other in the breasts of the waiting Indians.

Molly thought of everything, and yet it seemed as if the turmoil in her mind was so great, she could not think at all. She thought of the children she had just left crying at the door. She thought of her special friends – Turkey Feather, Beaver Girl, Shining Star and Earth Woman. She thought of her home and family, her parents, brothers and sisters – all gone, never to be recovered. She thought of the

Englishman in red and his smiling face. She looked at him and he was speaking – speaking to her only, in English, so that the Indians might not understand.

'My child, you were torn away from home and family by the ruthless Indians,' he said, speaking fast.

'Don't let their fine words blind you to the crime which they committed against you, in destroying your family, in stealing you away from your home, from white people. Don't fool yourself, or let them fool you into thinking that you can forgive them. You may at the moment, but later you will come to hatred. You will never stop hating till you have had your revenge.

'These Indians, who profess to be so friendly, have caused you to suffer every hardship – hunger, sickness, pain and distress. They are a cruel, relentless, wicked and savage people. They are revengeful and cannot be trusted. They are letting you grow up, an untamed savage, like a wild animal in the forest. They will marry you to an Indian whom you cannot love; your children will be Indian children, who will be hated by the white people.

'From this, my child, I will take you away. I shall give you a good home, send you to a school to acquire education and a polish of good manners. I shall give you all the benefits of civilized life. I shall make a lady out of you. Surely you would prefer to be a cultivated lady rather than a savage! Surely there is only one choice you can make!'

His words brought back to Molly a picture of the woman in shining silk at Fort Duquesne. What if she had stayed there as she had so much wanted to do? She wondered what life with the white people would be like – rich people, who wore not homespun, but silk in glistening, bright colours.

Then she remembered the Englishman's words. He was right. It was true. She was an untamed savage, growing up like a wild beast in the forest. She looked for a moment at the open palm of her hand and saw how hard and calloused it was – from work. It would never lie soft and idle on shining silk. She was not meant to grace a rich man's home – to be an elegant lady. An inner conviction told her so.

At that moment she saw Old Shagbark looking at her, his brown eyes overflowing with kindness and understanding. He knew how hard it was for her to decide. She did not need to say a word – he knew what was going on in her mind. She saw the Englishman, too. His lips were smiling, but his eyes of cold gray were hard. Even if she were able to put all her thoughts into words, she knew he would never, never understand. Better to live with those who understood her because they loved her so much, than with one who could never think with her, in sympathy, about anything. Better to stay where she belonged, with the Indians who loved and understood her, and whom she could always love and understand in return. Squirrel Woman's scowling face and even Gray Wolf's wicked one no longer held any terrors, because she understood them.

Perhaps the Englishman was right – she ought to hate the Indians for the crime which they had committed against her – but in her heart there was no feeling of revenge, no hate. It was only war that she hated – war which set nation against nation; the French against the English, and the poor Indians between them both. It was war which had deprived her of her family. As she had suffered once in losing her family, so did the Indians suffer like losses, over and over. Her loss was no greater than theirs.

No, by coming to the Indians, she was the richer. She had learned much that she might not otherwise have learned. No matter what lay in store for her, she was willing now to go out to meet it. All that she had suffered in coming to the Indians would make the rest of her life easy by comparison. No pain, no sorrow which the future held, would be too great to bear. She was sister to the animals, to all growing things; she was sister to the Indians, because she had suffered pain with them. Because her pain had been so great, she would be sister to the suffering as long as she lived. Washed clean by pain, she faced the future unafraid.

Molly turned and faced the assembled people. She held out her arms.

'I cannot go!' she said, in a clear, steady voice. 'I wish to stay. The Senecas are my people. I will live and die with the Senecas.'

There was no hesitation. The words came with deliberate calm. Her decision was made. It was a decision born of a long ripening and so there was no faltering, no regret.

A hubbub of excitement filled the council house. Cries and exclamations were heard on all sides. The Englishman stalked out without ceremony, followed by his men and Gray Wolf.

Shining Star whispered in Molly's ear: 'Gray Wolf did not earn his gold pieces, after all. But he goes to Fort Niagara with Captain Morgan just the same. The Englishman has promised him a white man's suit and all the fire-water he can drink. We are well rid of them both.' Outside, Molly heard little Blue Trout cry out. 'Corn Tassel is going to stay!' The other children took up the chorus: 'Corn Tassel is going to stay – Corn Tassel is going to stay with us!'

As Chief Burning Sky raised his hand, the people quieted down. 'Your name, Corn Tassel,' said he, 'was given to you by the women on the day when your two sisters brought you to us, because your hair is the colour of the tassel on the corn. But now you have earned your real name.

'By the sympathy, perseverance and courage which you have shown since you came among us, by your willingness to give up the life of a white woman cheerfully to become an Indian Woman, you have earned the name, *Little-Woman-of-Great-Courage*. Cherish this name and do not tarnish it. Like this piece of silver, cut in delicate design, which I bestow upon you, keep it shining bright.'

He placed a delicately wrought silver bracelet upon her slender wrist. 'You are now a woman, and the women of our tribe will welcome you as one of themselves. Welcome to the Senecas, Little-Woman-of-Great-Courage.'

Again Molly heard her mother's voice speaking and the words sounded like an echo of Chief Burning Sky's: 'It don't matter what happens, if you're only strong and have great courage.'

Molly went out of the council house, surrounded by her happy, smiling friends. The children came running joyously to meet her. Swiftly she caught up little Blue Trout and held him to her breast.

Inside, her heart was singing: 'Oh, Ma! You are pleased, too, I know – with your Little-Woman-of-Great-Courage!'

'Third Time Lucky'

PAVANDEEP LOCHAB (AGED 13)

I am now adopted for the third time;
Third time lucky they always say.
Maybe this adoption will bring me luck –
For my first adoptive parents I was too lazy.
For my second adoptive parents I was too fat.
For my third parents I might be just right.

I stand alone in my room staring at the ceiling.
I look around, everything seems just right.
The room looks expensive
The parents can't really be rich
If they were I definitely wouldn't be here.

My so-called parents keep staring at me:
Maybe they're wondering
'What have we adopted?'
My new mother says
'Don't touch the iron, it's hot.'
I know, I am fourteen, I say to myself.

My new father says
'Don't talk to strangers.'
I say to myself
I am already talking to strangers.

Billie

ANN PILLING

Dad said, 'Oh, and he's called Billie by the way,' very casually, just like that, as if your name was the last thing that mattered. Robert knew that his father wasn't feeling casual, just the opposite in fact. He was as tense as a drum skin; so was Mum. 'Billie,' Robert repeated softly, 'the three Billy Goats gruff,' and he laughed.

His parents flicked uneasy looks at each other, then his mother inspected her hands, waiting for his father to speak. She had wanted to foster a child for so long but Dad hadn't been quite sure and the family discussions had been endless. Now 'Billie' was coming and the tension in the house was thickening by the minute.

Robert's little joke obviously hadn't helped. 'Now *listen*,' his father flashed, 'we don't want any funny business about this boy.'

'Sorry.'

'I should think so,' and he bent down to remove a bit of fluff from the carpet.

Mum gave Robert an anxious smile. She knew he was nervous about the foster child. He'd said he didn't mind at all if they looked after someone for a bit, it might even be good fun, but why for heaven's sake had they made such elaborate preparations? It wasn't just the spare room that had been redecorated, it was a proper 'little boy's' room now with Superman wallpaper, but they'd done the bathrooms and the kitchen, this room too, with its expensive new carpet. Billie surely wasn't likely to stay very long.

Liz his older sister, who was away at music college, wasn't so sure.

She'd left home, he was nearly fourteen and the third child their parents had wanted had never happened. Then this 'Billie' had come up for fostering and the Harbournes had been deemed 'suitable'. They'd hoped – Robert had too – that he might be older, someone who could become a friend. But he was only eight and according to Dad was bringing a few problems with him. They'd been prepared to tell Robert the whole story but he'd said no, not yet. From the bits Liz had let out it all sounded too heartbreaking and he didn't think he could bear it. Let the child come first, and settle in.

The minute he saw him Robert knew Billie spelt trouble. Everything about him felt alien and there was a kind of deep hostility pulsing through him in great waves. Physically he couldn't be more different from the two Harbourne children who were long and gangling with light blond hair and blue eyes; Billie was four-square and thick-set, very swarthy with a mass of tight black curls, his enormous dark eyes two great glossy pools. He had the sort of film-star good looks that turned heads in the street. Next to him the Harbourne children looked wishy-washy, almost two-dimensional.

His first act was to ruin the new living-room carpet. At tea, the day he came, Mum, unusually bright and breezy and obviously trying hard to hide her nerves, dropped a bag of sugar which split, scattering its contents all over the kitchen tiles. 'Sugar's the very worst thing, Billie,' she said, down on her hands and knees with a dustpan and brush. 'It gets everywhere, like sand at the seaside, you know.' From behind a chair (he always tried to put some solid object between himself and other people, Robert had noticed) the boy watched carefully as she swept up the grey gritty grains. 'Wine's the worst,' he said belligerently, 'my mam said.'

Mrs Harbourne didn't react but Robert saw her looking at his father. According to Liz one of Billie's 'problems' had been parents who drank, not just one parent, but *both*. So what on earth must have happened to him when they were both drunk at the same time? What else must have gone on in his eight years of life and why, when there was no furniture to hide behind, did his hands always fly up to his face?

In the living room that first night Billie stayed awake for hours, curled up on Mum's knee like a cat, watching television through his fingers. The Harbourne parents had always had strict rules about going to bed, they liked order, routine, cleanliness. But every time Dad tried to prise Billie from Mum's arms he went rigid, doubled himself up on her lap and let out a spine-chilling high-pitched squealing noise, like tom-cats having a fight. In the end Mr Harbourne gave up and carried on with his Saturday night ritual, bringing in the usual tray with its two glasses and its half-bottle of red wine. They always had a drink at the weekend though Robert was a bit surprised when the wine appeared, in view of what he knew about Billie's parents. The boy asked for a drink too so Dad went back to the kitchen and returned with mugs of hot chocolate. 'Here you are, you two,' he said. 'Put your own sugar in. Let's all drink to Billie,' and he gave a rather unconvincing smile.

It seemed to be the signal for Billie to spring out of Mum's lap, very suddenly and silently, like a coiled spring released, to grab the sugar bowl and to scatter its contents over the new carpet, then to water it in with the bottle of wine. *'Billie!'* cried Mrs Harbourne. 'What on earth are you – ' But Dad raised the flat of his hand. 'It's OK, it's *OK*. No damage done,' he said in a whisper as the dark red seeped into the thick pile of the immaculate beige carpet. From behind the television the child peeped out, his fingers laced across his eyes which were now fixed greedily, with a kind of joy, upon the spreading stain. The mess he'd made seemed to have calmed him down and he went off to bed without a word.

While Dad was upstairs with him Robert helped his mother to attack the carpet. She put salt on it, then soapy water, but the harder she rubbed the worse the great dark patch seemed to become. She was crying as she bent over it, but whether it was for the carpet or for Billie Robert couldn't quite decide.

Every night he threw a tantrum at bedtime, spent hours kicking at his wall then wandered round the house when they were all asleep, banging doors to wake everybody up. Mornings were even worse because they meant going to school and he hated that. Every day at breakfast, for nearly a week, he waited until Mum's back was turned then spat into Robert's bowl of cornflakes. 'Don't react,' Dad begged, when he heard about it. Robert didn't. He simply threw the cornflakes away, made himself toast and ate it walking round the room. But something made him persist with his cornflakes routine. He was a Harbourne and he liked his usual breakfast.

On the Friday Billie ruined the cornflakes for the last time.

Gathering together all the spit that he could muster Robert bent over his bowl and gave him the same treatment. The child's mouth dropped open, he slid off his stool, gave Robert a little kick, and waited. 'Don't *do* that, Billie, and don't keep spitting into my breakfast. If you kick me again I'll kick you back, *hard*.'

There was a long silence in which they stared at one another, Robert's pale blue eyes searching the deep brown pools of Billie's. 'OK,' he said at last, and he squatted down on the floor and started playing with some toy cars. When it was time for school he went off with Robert quite happily, actually holding his hand as they walked down the street.

'I think you're winning,' Mum said, when she heard about it. 'He really likes you.'

But Robert was still cautious. He'd seen the joy in Billie's face as the wine had spread over the new carpet and he borrowed Dad's tools, bought a padlock and fitted it on to his bedroom door. After a whole year of saving his paper-round money he'd recently bought himself a hi-fi system. He could just see Billie creeping in, twisting off the delicate pick-up arm, gouging great scratch marks across all his records, pulling the tapes from the cassettes. Every day now, before going to school, he carefully locked up his room. He was frightened of the wild hard energy in Billie, of that awful anger deep inside the small tense body which suddenly broke out for no apparent reason and sent him screeching round the house, flinging himself against the furniture and pulling endlessly at Mum and Dad so he could get up on to their laps, or into their arms.

'He's just a little attention seeker,' Robert said one night when Billie, having worn himself out by screaming, had collapsed in bed and actually fallen asleep. This 'experiment' of his parents was beginning to get on his nerves. There was no peace any more, no order, no family time.

Mum said sadly, 'I know, but he's had no love, Robert. All he's ever known is violence and unhappiness. That's all we're trying to do, trying to give him a bit of love. But it's obviously going to take time. Oh, I *do* wish you'd not put that lock on your bedroom door...' Regularly, like a record stuck in a groove, she returned to the subject of the padlock. Dad always supported her.

Only when Liz came home for a weekend did they see Robert's side of it. She was studying the violin and on the Saturday night

101

Mrs Cousins, her old piano teacher, came round so that they could play together. At first Billie sat on Mum's knee and listened. Robert watched him very carefully, thinking the sad, sweet music might calm him down. Dad had explained once that there was a thing called 'music therapy', which sometimes helped people to relax and to sort out all their tangled hurt feelings. But Billie was obviously bored. Liz and Mrs Cousins had only played a few bars when he asked to have the television on. When Mum whispered 'no' he slid off her lap and crawled under the table where he started banging at the legs with one of his toy trucks.

Mrs Cousins was very interested in Liz's new bow, an eighteenth birthday present from Grandpa Harbourne, who had once played the violin himself in an important orchestra. 'It's a *very* good one, Elizabeth,' she said, examining it carefully. 'I shouldn't think there was much change out of a thousand pounds, was there?'

Liz shrugged. 'I don't really know. Grandpa gave it to me. It does play beautifully, doesn't it?'

'I'd no idea a violin bow could be worth so much,' Mum said, as they went to the front door with Mrs Cousins. 'We must get it insured. John, you'll have to ring your father.'

While everyone was in the hall saying goodbye there was a snapping sound in the living-room. Billie, standing on the new carpet, just in front of his wine stain, had broken the bow into two pieces and was waving it slowly round his head, wide-eyed and at peace now, a satisfied little smile on his face. Liz gave a little scream then burst into tears.

For once, Dad wasn't gentle. Without a word he grabbed Billie, took him up to his room and shut the door on them both. It was nearly midnight before he came down again and Billie was still screaming, and kicking at the wall. Nobody got any sleep that night. At breakfast next day everyone was pink-eyed and irritable. Only Billie had slept, blissful in his new Superman bedroom.

They talked for hours that Sunday about whether Billie ought to go back. Liz was still smarting about her ruined bow and rather in favour of getting rid of him. She brought his cheap cardboard suitcase down from the loft and dumped it in the hall. Robert said nothing. It seemed to him that Billie always wrecked the things that people particularly cared about, the things that gave them joy, Mum's carpet for example, the new rose bushes that Dad had just planted out in the front, which Billie had torn up and trampled on, Liz's precious bow. It must be that he himself had never been allowed to love anything, or at least, not love it for very long. Liz had whispered that his mother used to shut him in a cupboard if he misbehaved and that she never played with him or allowed him to have any toys. So he was jealous of the things that other people had which took them into their own private world, away from his incessant demands; he had to put an end to them.

Billie stayed.

Sometimes, late at night, when his parents were dropping with tiredness and Billie was still kicking at his bedroom wall, Robert would creep in and read to him. He liked stories and he would snuggle under the duvet, stick his thumb in his mouth and listen. When at last his eyes started to close Robert would stroke at his cheek and at his thick dark hair. Always, in response, Billie would make gentle purring noises like a satisfied cat. All the anger and rage packed up tightly inside his squat little frame was like a great black tangle of endless string. If only someone could find the end, tease it out gently and give him release. Dad had hoped the clue to him might be music but the bow episode had knocked that theory on the head.

Robert decided that Billie needed a pet. He was always mesmerised by animal programmes on television and he seemed to understand animals better than people. He even purred or grunted when he was happy, and scratched and spat and bit when something upset him. A pet would be something he could relate to when human beings got too complicated and demanding, something he could give all his love to. For Robert had decided that there *was* a kind of love in Billie.

On the way to school they often passed Boris the chip-shop cat, sitting on its favourite bit of wall. Billie always stopped and fussed the old ginger tom, tickled its flea-bitten ears and kneaded its neck, drawing great rapturous purrings from it. And after the bit of fuss he positively skipped the rest of the way to school. On the days when there was no Boris to love Robert usually got a kick or a punch.

The Harbournes had never allowed their children to have pets They associated cats with hairs, dogs with noise and smells, and long walks at anti-social hours. But Robert pleaded so hard that they caved in and spent a large sum of money on a tank of tropical fish.

It was installed in Billie's bedroom on gleaming white shelves and they showed him how much food to scatter in each time, how to check the water temperature and clear out the algae with a special net. There were bright green plastic plants in the tank and a hoop-shaped rock through which the fish could swim endlessly in and out.

Billie was interested for about twenty-four hours, then he got bored. He took to banging on the glass with his fists to liven things up, overfed the fish because he liked to watch them swim greedily up to the surface of the water and flop their mouths open. One day Robert went into the room and found that they were all dead. Billie had put sugar and salt in the water 'to see what would happen'. Dad emptied the tank, took it downstairs and put houseplants in it. There was no more talk of 'pets'.

And Billie got steadily worse. Three times his little suitcase was packed and put in the hall and they got as far as dialling the social worker, to ask her to remove him. Always, though, they hung up before anyone answered.

That phone call meant that he would be automatically returned to the children's home and they couldn't do it to him. 'It's got to get better,' Mum said tearfully. Robert wasn't so sure.

One day, when they'd had Billie for about six weeks, Robert met mad Mrs McCann from Dogs Rescue. She lived in a sprawling run-down bungalow near the canal and took in not only lost dogs and cats but had rabbits and hamsters too. People said the place was overrun with wild life. Sometimes she knocked on the Harbourne's door and held out a rusty tin, for her 'work'. She smelt strongly of cats and sweat and her clothes were so filthy and so full of holes they'd have been rejected for a jumble sale. Mum always gave her something, just to get rid of her. Afterwards she sprayed all round with air freshener.

Mrs McCann had a dog on a bit of rope. It was an extraordinary-looking creature, a bit labrador, a bit collie, a bit poodle. It had outsized ears and a lavatory-brush tail, a silky gold coat, a huge shaggy head and melting brown eyes. She'd found it abandoned by the gates of the old slipper factory. 'I'll have to find a home for this one,' she told Robert, 'he's a terrible eater. Cruel what some people do to animals. Not looking for a dog, are you? Your mother always supports my work.'

'As a matter of fact we are,' said Robert.

'Well, what about this one then? He's not much more than a puppy and he's going to be a real beauty.' Mrs McCann's faded blue eyes grew round with love as she tickled the curious creature's ears while the lavatory brush tail whirred like a propeller. 'I've called him Prince,' she said, 'but of course you can choose your own name.'

'Prince is fine,' Robert told her, amazed at his own daring as he took the rope lead and fished in his pocket. 'Er, I've only got 50p, Mrs McCann. I don't get my paper-round money till Saturday.'

'You keep it, sonny,' Mrs McCann said magnaminously. 'Buy him a tin of food with it.'

By the end of the day Prince was installed in a big shed on the edge of some abandoned allotments, about a mile from home. It was a place Robert remembered from his early childhood, when Dad, who was a keen gardener, had been mad on growing prize vegetables.

Nobody went there any more and the nearest houses were far enough away not to be bothered by Prince's barking. Not that he made much noise, he was a placid sort of creature. For all his ugliness you looked into his great brown eyes and loved him on the spot.

For a few days Robert experimented, taking him for walks after his morning and evening paper rounds and slipping out of school at lunch-time to give him a quick run on the allotments. Then, one Friday afternoon, he brought Billie. He'd never deceived his parents before and this thing with Prince was big, *big*. But the minute he saw them together he knew that his instinct had been right. Billie immediately knelt down, flung his arms round the dog and buried his face in the soft neck. Prince sniffed him all over then licked his face. The little boy laughed, tickled his stomach then they were rolling over and over together, on the floor of the shed. Robert felt superfluous and, somehow, moved. He'd never seen Billie look happy before. His sharp little face had miraculously softened now and all the grown-up fear and suspicion had drained away.

It wasn't difficult to explain that for the time being Prince was a big secret and had to live in the shed. Billie was sharp as a needle and old for his years, he understood about Mum's pride in her house, that was why he'd ruined the carpet. He understood, too, about the need to deceive grown-ups. With his own parents he must have been constantly on his guard, Dad had said, keeping out of their way at the worst moments, ducking flying objects and dodging blows. The

Prince secret was nothing compared with that. 'Yeah, yeah, I get it,' he said impatiently when Robert said they had to keep quiet. 'But when can he come and live with us? I want him in my bedroom.'

Robert began to make promises, hopeless he felt, at first, but as the days wore on and Billie's behaviour at home and school improved dramatically, he began to think he really might be able to persuade his parents to have the dog at home. Since Prince had come into his life Billie had started to act like an ordinary eight-year-old boy. Just as long as he knew he could see the dog every day, play with him and take him for runs, he was happy. On the day Robert had to stay in bed with a stomach bug and nobody could go to the shed Billie went mad with frustration, pulled the cloth from under the dinner table and smashed all the crockery. But he never said a word about Prince. He trusted Robert now and he knew that the Harbournes mustn't be told yet.

The day after his bug Robert did tell them. He could see that the secret couldn't last for ever and he'd proved that Prince was a big part of the answer to Billie's problems. But, anxious as they were to help, they wouldn't hear of having Prince. A big dog like that, they argued, was expensive to keep and a terrible tie, besides, they all led such busy lives. If Billie wasn't satisfied with something easy like fish, they told him gently, perhaps they'd buy him a rabbit. You could certainly stroke and cuddle those, they were like dogs, really. Dad could make a special hutch for it, out in the garden.

That afternoon, when Robert went to the primary school to collect Billie, he wasn't there. He wasn't at the house either. He'd obviously slipped away just before home time, so nobody knew. He was missing for three days and nights during which Robert's parents were wracked by anguish and guilt. If only he'd come back, they said, he could have his precious dog. For all his problems they were growing to love him. The old shed was the first place they checked on but its door was open and Prince had gone. Billie's cardboard suitcase and the pathetic cache of 'treasures' he had brought with him had gone too, from his room.

There were many 'sightings' of Billie and Prince – down in the town, wandering along the bypass, in an amusement arcade in Bradford. Someone even said they thought they'd spotted a little boy with a dog climbing into a lorry in an M1 service area near Northampton. It was terrible at home. Mr Harbourne spent his evenings constructing an elaborate dog kennel. Mrs Harbourne obsessively polished all the floors then started spring-cleaning her immaculate kitchen cupboards. Nobody spoke much but whenever the phone rang they all hurtled towards it. Sometimes it was the social services, sometimes the police. But nobody ever rang with news of Billie.

On the fourth day Mrs McCann knocked on the door with her rusty money tin. Dad was down at the police station, begging them to hot up their search, Mum was asleep upstairs. She'd not been to bed for three nights. 'I'm sorry, Mrs McCann,' Robert said, feeling in his pockets. 'I've not got anything for you today.'

'That little boy of yours,' she said, thrusting her big crumpled face right up to him and letting out a blast of foul breath, 'he's been by the canal, I saw him this morning. Shouldn't be wandering round on his own like that, you know. It's dangerous that canal, the dog might pull him in. Our Cissie's kiddie...' But Robert didn't wait to listen to any more. He pushed past her, pulled his bike out of the garage and pedalled off towards the allotments. It was getting dark and he'd not stopped to put the lights on. In the town centre a policeman hollered at him to stop, but he took no notice.

Billie was in the shed with Prince and they were both fast asleep. The child lay curled round inside the curve of the pale gold belly of the dog, his head pillowed against its softness, one hand round the neck. Prince was making little snoring noises and a large paw was stretched across Billie's body as if to say, 'Don't touch, this is my friend.' At Billie's feet was the little cardboard case. On top, neatly arranged, were all the precious animal postcards that Robert had given him. As he looked at Billie and Prince his eyes filled with sudden tears. He'd once read about a famous explorer going to sleep in the presence of a lion. The lion had also slept, a sleep, he had written, that must surely be the ultimate act of trust.

They kept Prince and they kept Billie. The funny-looking dog filled out and eventually grew into its ears and into its extraordinary tail. It loved living with the Harbournes and as the months passed it became big and brave and lovely. Billie did too.

I See Music

LINETTE MARTIN

Alex is deaf. His world is full of pictures and shapes,
but no sounds.

The car went by in a hurry. It made Alex jump because he didn't
see it coming. It went through a big puddle by the side of the road.
Water leapt out sideways and up on to the pavement, then the drops
fell down and the puddle rocked and settled to the shape it had had
before. The car went on down the High Street in the dusk till it
vanished over the curve of the hill. It was a tiny car now, lifting
and dwindling, going out of sight like a candle flame.

Alex touched his Dad's arm, and his Dad turned from looking at
the bus timetable.

'It's a big puddle,' said Alex. He said it mostly with his hands,
but he used his mouth too, the way he had learnt at school. 'Big.
Big. Big. Pud-dle.'

Alex's Dad looked at the puddle, then he looked at Alex, 'I hope
the bus can swim!'

Alex was glad his Mum and Dad were not like the lady in the
flat downstairs. She didn't look at him the right way so he couldn't
understand what she said. Once the lady had jerked a question to his
sister Margaret and screwed her greasy finger to the side of her grey
head. Margaret had stormed and raged and gone red in the face. She
had hugged Alex and shouted 'No!' Alex could see the round mouth
she made and knew she was shouting because he could feel the

power of it coming through her old blue jumper when she hugged him.

Their bus came towards them now like a bright smile, red and lighted, sliding through the wet evening. Alex said, 'Busss' to himself over and over again as they went inside and sat down. He could feel his mouth pushing out the word when his lips opened. The conductor smiled. Two ladies sitting in front of them turned round.

Dad touched his arm, looked at him and said, 'Well done, Alex. Good. But now wait till we are home.'

So Alex sat with his mouth shut and looked at the line of street lights sliding close and sliding away. When the bus got past one lot of shops, the places between the lights were dark. When they passed each lamppost, light slanted through the bus windows and leapt over the backs of the seats. It was a pattern he could look forward to; dark, light, slant and leap, like a dance, again and again.

It was going to be a wet Easter, but that didn't matter. Dad had the paper bag with the secret Easter presents for Mum and Margaret. He was going to hide them somewhere in the flat, and they would be on the breakfast table on Easter morning. That was tomorrow.

Alex put his hand on the paper bag and smiled at Dad. 'Time to get off the bus now,' said Dad.

As they waited to cross the road, Alex watched the bus go round the corner by the betting shop; red against grey and black, a warm colour against cold colours. A lot of the grey things around him were sparkled with shiny surfaces; lampposts, the tops of cars, and the silvery-grey bicycle chained to the railing by the bakery. There were points of light on the buttons of a man's coat, and the handles of a pram, and there was a tiny red jumping patch on the collar of a lady's poodle.

The traffic stopped and Dad took his hand and went over the road, but they weren't going home yet. Something was happening on the other side. Some people in blue uniforms were standing on the pavement. One held a trumpet in both hands and stared at a piece of paper slotted through a wire stand. The wind pushed the corner of the paper and the man edged his head sideways to read it while he blew into the silver trumpet and twiddled his fingers. A lady had a round thing that she held up and shook and hit. Alex remembered they had a tambourine like that at school. He knew the name of another thing and said it: 'Drum.'

They both stopped to watch and Dad tapped his foot in time to the movements of the man with the drum. Dad put ten pence into Alex's hand and showed him the lady with the collecting box. Alex put the money in and stared at the lady's uniform.

Dad told him, 'They are playing music.'

Alex frowned at him. If music was blowing and twiddling and shaking things, it was silly. The people were silly. So was Dad. He swung back his foot and kicked at the wire stand. The trumpet man grabbed at it as though he had had a lot of practice. He grinned at Alex, shook his head warningly and blew into the trumpet again. But Dad looked Alex straight in the face and told him off, right in front of everyone. Alex slid his eyes round to the side and saw the people laughing.

He pointed at the drum and enjoyed the feel of the word on his lips and inside his mouth. 'Drum. Drum. Drummm.' The feel of it was like the look of it; round and solid. The man with the drum smiled at Alex and beckoned to him and Alex put his hand on the beautiful drum and felt the thump as the man began to play again. He laughed and the lady with the collecting box laughed. His Dad laughed and so did the other people who were watching the music.

That was something special to happen on their way home. Alex hoped he could tell Mum about it in a way she could understand. Maybe he could draw her a picture to help him when the words weren't enough.

When they got home, Margaret was there. She and Mum were talking the way everyone else did, not having to look at faces or hands or anything, but just talking and being understood by someone on the other side of the room.

Alex went up to Mum and told her as well as he could about the smiling bus and the street lights and the drum, while Dad went and hid the Easter eggs. Alex and Margaret laid the table for their tea, then Alex pulled Margaret into the hall. He put on the light and told her with his hands about Mum's shiny Easter egg with the plastic daffodils up the side.

Margaret asked, 'What did you get for me?'

Alex laughed, butted her with his head and ran back to the kitchen. Margaret's present was a bottle of pink bath salts. But that was part of the Easter morning surprise.

As they ate their tea, Alex thought about tomorrow and how nice it was going to be. He was so old now he could remember Easter last year. He had been given a set of Magic Markers and he had drawn a picture of each of the family; Dad in his overalls with his blue lunch tin, Mum in her Thursday apron for when she cleaned Mrs Buchanon's house, and Margaret dancing near the radio with her hair flying out. He had drawn squiggly lines round the radio to show it was on, and that was why Margaret was dancing.

He touched Mum's arm and she put down the teapot and looked at him. 'Mum, will we go to church?'

She looked puzzled and had to ask again.

'Go where?'

He thought he had got the word right, so he tried with his hands. It wasn't a word he used much and he couldn't draw a picture of it, not the brightness and beauty of candles and coloured glass and all. It would take more than all the Magic Markers in the world.

He couldn't draw it and he couldn't say it. He made an angry feeling in his throat and kicked the table leg, feeling the wood jarring hard against his shoe. The tea in Dad's cup jiggled like a puddle and Mum touched his arm and said, 'Stop it, Alex!'

Then Margaret said something and Mum understood, 'Oh, church! With the flowers? And the red and blue windows?'

Alex nodded hard and looked at Dad.

'Yes, we will go tomorrow,' said Dad.

Margaret reached her toe under the table. Alex looked at her and she said, 'Do you remember Christmas in church? Christmas?'

Alex nodded again, and while they talked to each other in their own way, he sat enjoying the pictures in his head. The church had trembled inside like the balloon at school when the teacher put her mouth against it. It felt like the excitement of Christmas. He had felt the quiver all along the place where they were sitting, and on the wooden floor boards, but not on the stone slabs down the middle of the church. Dad had told him then, that the feeling was music.

He touched Mum's arm and asked, 'What is music?' And after tea they all tried to explain it to him again. Mum made the radio go and had Alex put his hands on it. Dad pursed his lips and made Alex feel the cold thin air that came from them. Then Margaret took Alex into her room and put on one of her pop records and jumped about. Alex jumped about with her and bounced on and off the edge of the bed.

Mum ran in and said, 'The lady downstairs! The lady downstairs!'

But it was too late. The lady came up and stood in the flat doorway and shouted at Mum and Dad. She pointed at Alex and made a face at them all.

Margaret hugged Alex. They all stood and shouted at her. Alex shouted too. Without words. Then they put on the telly and tried to forget her. But Dad was worried and wouldn't tell Alex what the cowboys were saying when Alex asked him.

Alex didn't dare ask about music any more but he still wondered about it. When he cleaned his teeth that night, he stood on the laundry basket and looked at his face in the shaving mirror. He watched himself say, 'Music. Music.' He thought he would never understand.

Easter breakfast was fun. Alex had a tin of toffees with Easter bunnies on the outside. One of them was playing a trumpet and he turned the tin quickly round to look at the others. Dad got his cigarettes just like always, but Mum had wrapped them in a piece of paper with yellow flowers on it. Dad gave Mum a special grin and put the packet beside his plate.

Margaret told Alex he could have some of her bath salts for his bath that night. Mum was happy with her Easter egg and said she could get fat if she ate it all by herself. So to help her not get fat they all ate it with her, after their cereal and toast.

Then Margaret ran off to her room and Mum went after her. Alex looked in and saw them talking and arguing. Something about Margaret's hair and hair ribbon.

He watched Dad shave, then he got dressed in his best clothes that Mum had put out by his bed last night. Dad wore a white shirt and told Mum he wasn't going to wear a tie no matter what. So she left him alone.

Alex and Dad were ready ages before Mum and Margaret and when they left the flat to go to church, Margaret was still fussing about her hair. Mum had all her best clothes on, and tried to look as if she was used to wearing them every day.

The morning was wet but sunny. The pavement was dry in patches and wet where the cracks were. Cars and buses slid by them on the road. Alex saw his parents and Margaret look up and when he looked up too, he saw a plane swoop low towards the airport beyond the high-rise flats. The plane's line of movement was big and strong like the curve of the hill.

Alex liked the church; it was old and warm and pretty, the way a grandmother ought to be. It had been there ever so long before the flats were built, Margaret said. Mum and Dad looked a little shy when they stood inside the big swing doors. They found an empty pew and sat in a row. Mum leaned over and told Margaret something. Margaret took her hands down from her hair and looked sulky.

They knelt down and Alex took his hands away from his face and stared about him. There were grey angels on top of the pillars, one to each pillar in a pattern. White candles moved a little as the door at the back of the church opened to let late people in. The sun shone through red and blue windows, tall as the high-rise flats and pointed like rockets.

Alex felt a quiver in his seat and looked up to where the organ was. Sure enough, the organist was there, moving like a piano player, pulling and pushing knobs like Mum did when she was cooking in a hurry. Alex felt suddenly sorry for the lady in the flat downstairs. She didn't bother with Easter or Christmas. All her days were the same.

The man in white robes came in with the choir boys. They spoke with their movements and Alex's family stood and sat and knelt when all the other people did. It was like a slow dance they were all doing together. But when the man went up the steps to the round pulpit, his face was in a little shadow, so Alex couldn't tell what he said.

Instead he shut his eyes and thought about yesterday's bus, red against the wet dark evening. And he thought about the car slipping over the curve of the hill, and the lights that slanted and leapt when the bus went by them. He thought about the smooth glass of the bath salt bottle, the rough rolling pink granules inside it, and the airplane's strong movement across the sky.

He opened his eyes and sat up. Colour and shape and size and movement had been all round him all the time. He would never have to ask about music any more.

'I see it!' said Alex, then louder, 'I see it!'

Dad and Mum and Margaret tried to stop him, but he went on shouting for joy all through the hymn, 'I see it, I see it! I can see music!'

'Faster than Thought'

REBECCA MOCKFORD (AGED 12)

I ran, I laughed.
I shouted and I smiled.
Racing in the breeze.
Rosy cheeks
And shining eyes,
Hair flowing out behind me,
Skirt pulling at brambles,
A tearing hand.
Socks around my ankles,
Then lying down in the bristly barley
Scratching my chin.
Catching my breath,
Leaping up and haring away until I reached
    the cottage's white gates.
I think...
I wish.
I remember.
As I sit in my wheelchair wondering if I will
    ever be there again.

4
Friend or Foe?

We all enjoy having friends, and it's a horrible thing
when friends turn into enemies. But can we turn
enemies into friends?

The first two stories in this section are included especially for
younger readers. Anna-Magdalena, though inclined to be
bossy, has the knack of making friends. And 'a little give and
take' solves the problem of *The Frightful Food Feud*.

Quarrels and secrets figure in two of the poems I have chosen,
and *Wanda Petronski* shows what can happen when teasing
gets out of hand.

Friends can be just like us, or very different. And the last
three stories show friendships that cross barriers of race and
colour and religion.

Anna-Magdalena Makes a Friend

From *Anna-Magdalena: the Little Girl with the Big Name*

KAY KINNEAR

One Sunday morning Anna-Magdalena, a boy called Jack and four other children were sitting on a rug waiting for Sunday school to begin...

Anna-Magdalena liked Sunday school because her teacher, Mrs Lander, was smiley and kind. Every week she told them interesting stories... There was always something to do after the story, and Anna-Magdalena liked that too.

'Jack, move over,' said Anna-Magdalena to the boy next to her on the rug. 'I haven't got enough room.'

Jack moved himself slowly to give Anna-Magdalena just a very tiny bit more space. Jack was a tall, strong, clever boy and he had firm opinions about things. Anna-Magdalena was a small, strong, clever girl and she also had firm opinions about things. Sometimes Jack and Anna-Magdalena got along well, but more often than not they argued.

Just then Mrs Lander came in with a new little boy. 'This is Neville,' she said. 'He's just moved from the country to live near our church.'

Mrs Lander asked Anna-Magdalena, Jack and the others in the class – Polly, Rajinder, Tommy and Kevin – to say their names one by one. The thin, silent little boy called Neville didn't look at the other children. He stared down at his feet.

'Can you make a place for Neville on the rug, please,' asked Mrs Lander. Nobody moved for a moment. Then Anna-Magdalena cheerfully bumped her small body against Jack and Polly to make space.

'There's room here for Neville,' she called. 'Come and sit here.' Without speaking, Neville folded himself into a small hunched shape beside Anna-Magdalena.

'Now,' said Mrs Lander, 'we'll have a story.' And she told them the story of Noah and his ark.

Anna-Magdalena and the others asked lots of questions about the story. But Neville, the new boy, didn't ask anything.

'Did you like the story, Neville?' asked Anna-Magdalena.

Neville slowly looked up from his feet and gave the very smallest of nods.

Mrs Lander clapped her hands and said, 'Now, we'll be doing Noah's ark pictures *next* week, but today we want to finish decorating our new folders!'

She turned to Neville. 'We're making folders to keep our pictures in till they're ready to take home. What colour folder would *you* like to make, Neville?'

'Have blue,' urged Anna-Magdalena. '*Mine's* blue.'

Neville didn't say anything, but he gave the very smallest of nods.

The children went over to the work table and Anna-Magdalena chose a light blue folder for Neville. Then she found her own folder and looked at it carefully. It was pretty, she thought. The tree she had drawn on the folder was leaning a bit, but the bird was very good. It was as big as the tree. She took a crayon and began to colour the bird.

While she was colouring, she noticed Neville standing beside her holding his blue folder.

'Shall I help you, Neville?' asked Anna-Magdalena. Without waiting for an answer, she took the folder and pressed down the top flap. 'Now it's ready,' she said. 'You can do patterns on it. You can do fish. Or birds. Or trees. Or flowers. Or what do you like?'

Neville looked at Anna-Magdalena, but he didn't say anything.

Anna-Magdalena made a decision. 'Who's got the flower stencil?' she asked. Rajinder passed it down the table.

'Neville's having flowers,' said Anna-Magdalena, drawing three times round the flower stencil onto Neville's folder. 'There you are. All you've got to do is colour,' said Anna-Magdalena, handing Neville a crayon.

Mrs Lander asked Neville gently, 'Is that all right, Neville?'

He nodded the very smallest of nods and began to colour slowly.

'Don't you ever talk?' asked Jack.

'He doesn't have to,' said Anna-Magdalena, firmly defending her new friend.

'He probably can't get a word in edgeways with you two chatter-boxes,' said Mrs Lander and she gave Neville a friendly pat on the shoulder.

After Sunday school Anna-Magdalena met her mum and their friend Gerald outside the church. She told them about the folders they'd been making and then all about Neville, her new friend.

'He doesn't talk,' said Anna-Magdalena. 'He doesn't do anything, so I help him. I helped him make his folder.'

'That's nice of you, Mags,' said her mum, 'but give him time to settle in.'

Gerald picked up Anna-Magdalena to give her a piggyback ride to his car. He said to her, 'One day, maybe Neville will surprise you.'

A week later, on the next Sunday morning, Anna-Magdalena met Neville going into the church hall.

'H'lo, Neville, you can sit by me today,' she said, smiling.

Neville gave the very smallest of nods.

When Mrs Lander arrived they talked about the story of Noah and the ark. Every child could remember something – about the rain, the boat, the food, the animals or the rainbow. Jack and Anna-Magdalena, of course, could remember lots of things.

Then Mrs Lander asked Neville, 'Do you remember the story, Neville?'

Neville gave the very smallest of nods, but he didn't say anything.

When they moved to the work table to make Noah's ark pictures, Mrs Lander gave each child a big piece of paper. Then she put some stiff cardboard shapes to draw round onto the middle of the table. There were animal shapes, a boat shape, and several people shapes.

'I'll do my picture,' said Anna-Magdalena to Neville who was next to her, 'then I'll help you do yours.'

Anna-Magdalena waited to see the very smallest of nods, but even though she carefully watched there wasn't a nod. In fact, she thought that maybe Neville shook his head to say 'no' but she wasn't sure.

Neville took a stack of animal shapes and looked at them. He looked at the elephant and put it back on the table. He looked at the giraffe and the tiger and put them back on the table. He put back the lion, the monkey and the bear. Some of the other children began to watch Neville putting all the shapes down.

'I want to have *lots* of lions and tigers and bears in my picture,' said Jack.

'It's s'posed to be only two of each animal,' Anna-Magdalena pointed out. Then turning to Neville, she said, 'You wait and I'll help you.'

But Neville took no notice of Anna-Magdalena. At the bottom of the stack of animals he found a cow and a pig. He took the two shapes and drew neatly round them. Then, pushing the animal shapes aside, he began to draw by himself. Without any shapes to help, he drew two lambs. He drew two chickens. He drew two goats and two ducks.

Neville never looked up. He drew around the boat shape for the ark. Then he drew a sort of ramp, for the animals to get into the boat. Then he drew one cat sitting on the ark and another on the ramp. Finally he drew wavy lines along the bottom of the boat for the water.

Jack leaned over the table to look at Neville's drawing. 'That's a good picture,' he said admiringly.

Anna-Magdalena leaned over to look too. Then all the children leaned over to see Neville's picture.

'That's a lovely picture, Neville,' said Mrs Lander. 'You've picked all the farm animals to draw, haven't you? Because you've lived on a farm, you know just what they look like.'

Neville gave a little nod.

Then Mrs Lander turned to the rest of the class. 'This month it's our turn to display our pictures on the walls of the church hall, so *all* of your pictures will be put up for people to see.'

Then she held up a little magazine. 'One more thing,' she added, smiling, 'the very best picture of all will be printed in our church magazine with your name beside it.'

'Neville's,' cried Anna-Magdalena. 'Neville's is the best picture.'

'Neville, Neville,' joined in Jack. That's nice of Jack, thought Anna-Magdalena, because his picture was probably the next best one. Then all the other children joined in and said that Neville's picture should be chosen.

Turning to the silent little boy, Mrs Lander asked, 'Would you like your picture in the magazine, Neville?'

Neville gave not the very smallest of nods, not even a medium-sized nod, but a very big nod indeed.

Anna-Magdalena tugged at Neville's sleeve. 'My picture's gone a bit wrong, Neville,' she said. 'Will you help me do a new one?'

Neville stared at her. Then his face broke into a huge smile. It was the first Neville smile that anyone had ever seen.

The class was even more surprised when Neville opened his mouth and said to Anna-Magdalena, 'Yes, I'll help you.' And he gave the very biggest nod that anyone had ever seen.

The Frightful Food Feud

BRIAN SIBLEY

Once upon a time – a very long time ago – there were two towns. One was called Aralia and the other was called Zedonia. Each town stood on a hill and between the hills ran a wide river crossed by a fine old stone bridge.

Because there were no walls or gates to the towns, the people could come and go as they pleased and lived in peace and harmony with each other.

The Aralians grew fruit and vegetables while the people of Zedonia kept cows and chickens. Every day, people from Aralia crossed the bridge to Zedonia with barrowloads of firm white potatoes, crisp green lettuces, fat brown onions and sweet red apples.

And every day, people from Zedonia crossed the bridge to Aralia with buckets of creamy milk, trays of large speckled eggs, golden butter and cheeses the size of cartwheels.

Nobody paid for anything, but everybody always had everything they needed.

One day the King of Zedonia's Chancellor thought of something he hadn't thought of before.

'Your Majesty,' he asked, 'why do we give the Aralians milk and cream and butter and cheese and eggs, when all we ever get from them is a few strawberries?'

'They're jolly good strawberries!' replied the King, who was having his tea at the time. 'Besides, they give us a lot of other things, too – like cabbages and potatoes.'

'Potatoes!' snorted the Chancellor. 'Any fool can grow a few potatoes!'

Taking another strawberry, the King asked what he should do about it.

'Tell them we will not go on being exploited!' replied the Chancellor. 'Demand that they double the amount of everything they give us!'

The Queen of Aralia was so worried when she got the King of Zedonia's message that she sent for her Prime Minister.

'If you give the Zedonians what they're asking for,' the Prime Minister told her, 'we will have to go hungry ourselves. But if they don't get what they want, they may try to take it by force! Then there would have to be a WAR!'

'Unthinkable!' said the Queen. 'We've never had a war!'

'But if we *did*,' said the Prime Minister, 'the Zedonians could simply march across the bridge and attack us! We must *destroy* it without delay!'

'Oh, dear,' sighed the Queen. 'I suppose we don't have any choice, but I will miss having cream with my strawberries...'

That night, a hooded figure carried a large barrel of explosives down the hill from Aralia, leaving a trail of gunpowder as he went. The Prime Minister (for that is who it was) placed the barrel in the middle of the bridge, then hurried back to the town. He lit the gunpowder and put his fingers in his ears. A spark hissed and fizzed away into the darkness, and then...

'What was that?' asked the King of Zedonia in a terrible panic.

'It's WAR!' said the Chancellor. 'Obviously the Aralians were trying to blow up the town! It's lucky they only blew up the bridge! Next time it might be our homes and shops and schools – even *the Palace!* We must defend ourselves!'

'How?' asked the King, turning rather pale.

'We must build a wall! And we must begin AT ONCE!'

'Oh, dear,' sighed the King, 'I suppose we don't have any choice, but I will miss having strawberries with my cream...'

As soon as it was morning, the Chancellor began supervising the building. Everyone had to help: carrying wheelbarrows full of sand, mixing cement, breaking rocks, digging foundations, putting up scaffolding and laying stones.

Day and night they worked, and as the wall around Zedonia grew higher and higher, the people of Aralia grew more and more worried.

'But why are they building a wall?' asked the Queen of Aralia anxiously.

'It is obvious,' replied the Prime Minister. 'They are getting ready to launch an All Out Offensive against us!'

'But we will be defenceless!' moaned the Queen.

'Not if *we* also build a wall, just like theirs – only higher and stronger!'

So they did.

'Why are the Aralians building a wall that is even higher than ours?' demanded the King of Zedonia.

'I imagine,' the Chancellor replied darkly, 'it is so that they can stand on the battlements and fire things at us.'

'Fire things?' squeaked the King.

'Arrows, stones, cannon-balls, the usual things...'

'B-B-But,' stuttered the King, 'we'll all be killed!'

'Not if we build our wall HIGHER!' replied the Chancellor triumphantly.

So they did.

'The Zedonians' wall is even higher than ours,' said the Queen of Aralia peering over the top of her own wall.

'Not for long!' replied the Prime Minister, 'I have given the order to make our wall EVEN HIGHER! And we'll build buttresses and ramparts and towers and turrets!'

So they did.

And that's how both towns went on, until they finally ran out of stones. But by that time, the walls were so high that no one in Zedonia could see the town of Aralia, and no one in Aralia could see the town of Zedonia.

Everyone felt safer, although sometimes the people of Aralia wished they had something to pour over their strawberries and sometimes the people of Zedonia wished they had something to dip in their cream.

Many years went by. Then, one morning, the Queen of Aralia got something of a surprise.

'Mashed potato for breakfast!' she grimaced, angrily pushing her plate away. '*What* is the meaning of this?'

'I'm afraid there is something of a food shortage at present, ma'am,' explained the Prime Minister.

'But we grow every type of fruit and vegetable there is!'

'Unfortunately, we are having problems with the rain.'

'Nonsense!' laughed the Queen. 'It hasn't rained for months!'

'*That*, ma'am, is the problem!' the Prime Minister explained. 'There is a drought; the plants and trees are dying and food is getting scarce. We do still have a few sacks of potatoes, ma'am, so you won't go completely hungry – at least, not for a week or so...'

'Deary me,' muttered the Queen, 'if only we hadn't fallen out with Zedonia, we could have asked them for help.'

'What is this supposed to be?' asked the King of Zedonia, pointing at his plate.

'Cheese, your Majesty,' replied the Chancellor.

'But there's hardly enough here to put in a mouse-trap!'

'Regrettably true, your Majesty. It's due to drought, you see; the grass has dried up and the cows can't make milk. We have one or two cheeses left, but when they've gone, well...' his voice trailed helplessly away.

'This is terrible!' stormed the King. 'What a nuisance we're not still on friendly terms with Aralia; we could have asked them to help us.'

'I have a plan, ma'am,' said the Prime Minister of Aralia. 'We will INVADE Zedonia! And to do that, we will build a bridge!'

The Queen looked astonished. 'I thought we blew up a bridge so that the Zedonians *couldn't* invade *us*, and now we are going to build a bridge so that we *can* invade *them*?'

'Correct, ma'am; that is what is known as politics! What is especially cunning about this plan,' the Prime Minister went on, unrolling a diagram, 'is that we'll build the bridge from the top of our wall to the top of theirs and then lower ourselves down on ropes!'

'Did you say invade Aralia?' asked the King of Zedonia.

'Absolutely, your Majesty!' replied the Chancellor with great enthusiasm. 'And this we will do by means of a tunnel! We simply dig down, beneath the walls, under the river and come up in the middle of Aralia!'

☆

The Queen of Aralia looked puzzled. 'But how will the bridge be held up?'

'It's all rather technical,' said the Prime Minister, referring to his diagram. 'Pulleys, cantilevers, rods, poles, perches – that sort of thing...'

'I suppose you know what you're doing,' sighed the Queen. 'I must say it would be nice to have cream with my strawberries again.'

'Unfortunately, ma'am, at the moment, there *aren't* any strawberries!'

The King of Zedonia scratched his head. 'But how will you know when you're under the middle of Aralia?'

'Couldn't be simpler, your Majesty,' said the Chancellor waving vaguely at a plan. 'It's all a question of latitudes, longitudes, meantimes and meridians!'

'Then you'd better start digging,' said the King. 'I must say it would be nice to have strawberries with my cream again.'

'You forget, your Majesty,' snapped the Chancellor, 'there *isn't* any cream!'

So the people of Aralia started building their bridge. They fixed up scaffolding, screwed brackets to the walls, tied ropes to towers and lowered planks from the battlements, until it reached across the valley to the walls of Zedonia.

Meanwhile the people of Zedonia started digging their tunnel to Aralia. They burrowed this way and that, shovelling and scratching and scraping at the earth until they decided they were directly beneath Aralia.

One morning, several days later, the Queen of Aralia climbed up to the top of the wall in order to try out the bridge.

At about the same time, the King of Zedonia got down on his hands and knees and began to crawl into the long, winding, dirty tunnel.

'This way, your Majesty,' called the Chancellor. 'Mind your head!'

'It's terribly – ouch! – dark in here!' said the King, stopping to rub his head. 'How much further is it?'

'One more shovelful, your Majesty, and up we'll come in the middle of Aralia!'

One more shovelful, and up they came!

'This isn't the middle of Aralia!' shouted the King, feeling rather muddy. 'This is the middle of the river!'

'Oh, but it can't be, your Majesty,' answered the Chancellor, 'rivers are wet!'

'Not during a drought, they're not!' bellowed the King. 'We didn't need to dig a tunnel, we could have...' The King stopped short. There was a strange creaking noise. He looked up and saw the bridge swaying to and fro. There, wobbling along it, was the Queen of Aralia followed by the Prime Minister.

Suddenly there was a terrible snapping of ropes and a splintering of wood! The Queen of Aralia and her Prime Minister landed – PLOP! – in the mud right next to the King of Zedonia and his Chancellor.

When they got over their surprise, the King and Queen asked each other what they were doing. Both said they were on their way to ask the other for help. Sensibly, neither of them mentioned the word 'invade'!

'You know,' said the Queen of Aralia, 'we were stupid to build those walls!'

'True,' replied the King of Zedonia. 'I can't even remember why we built them!'

'*We* can!' interrupted the Prime Minister and the Chancellor.

'Be quiet!' shouted the King of Zedonia.

'Yes,' added the Queen of Aralia, 'we've had enough of your foolishness!'

SPLISH! Something very like a spot of rain fell out of the sky! SPLASH! Then came another spot! SPLOSH! And another! It began as a shower, but soon it was a torrential downpour.

The King and Queen looked at each other and smiled. They laughed and shook hands. Then they started dancing about in the rain, while the Chancellor and the Prime Minister looked on in horror.

'I've had an idea!' said the King of Zedonia.

'So have I!' said the Queen of Aralia.

'Let's knock these walls down!!' they both said together.

So the people of Aralia and Zedonia took picks and hammers and mallets and axes and crowbars and knocked down the two great walls. And with all the stones they built a fine new bridge across the river which was soon flowing through the valley once more.

When the bridge was finished, they built a stone archway at either end. But they didn't put up any gates, because they wanted to make sure the people were free to come and go as they pleased.

In Aralia, the plants and trees soon began to grow again. In Zedonia, the cattle found lots of nice new grass to chew on. Everything got back to normal.

Very soon, people started crossing the bridge from Aralia with sweet green peas, dark purple plums, juicy yellow pears, round white cauliflowers and baskets of strawberries for the people of Zedonia.

And, on the way, they would pass people from Zedonia crossing the bridge with cool fresh milk, golden yellow butter, large brown eggs, mild crumbly cheese and jugs of thick cream for the people of Aralia.

And that is how the people of both towns managed to live happily ever after!

'My Hard Repair Job'

From *When I Dance*

JAMES BERRY

In the awful quarrel
we had, my temper burnt
our friendship to cinders.
How can I make it whole again?

This way, that way
that time, this time,
I pick up the burnt bits,
trying to change them back.

Wanda Petronski

From *The Hundred Dresses*
ELEANOR ESTES

Wanda Petronski. Most of the children in Room 13 didn't have names like that. They had names easy to say, like Thomas, Smith, or Allen. There was one boy named Bounce, Willie Bounce, and people thought that was funny but not funny in the same way that Petronski was.

Wanda didn't have any friends. She came to school alone and went home alone. She always wore a faded blue dress that didn't hang right. It was clean, but it looked as though it had never been ironed properly. She didn't have any friends, but a lot of girls talked to her. They waited for her under the maple trees on the corner of Oliver Street. Or they surrounded her in the school yard as she stood watching some little girls play hopscotch on the worn hard ground.

'Wanda,' Peggy would say in a most courteous manner, as though she were talking to Miss Mason or to the principal perhaps. 'Wanda,' she'd say, giving one of her friends a nudge, 'tell us. How many dresses did you say you had hanging up in your closet?'

'A hundred,' said Wanda.

'A hundred!' exclaimed all the girls incredulously, and the little girls would stop playing hopscotch and listen.

'Yeah, a hundred, all lined up,' said Wanda. Then her thin lips drew together in silence.

'What are they like? All silk, I bet,' said Peggy.

'Yeah, all silk, all colours.'

'Velvet too?'

'Yeah, velvet too. A hundred dresses,' repeated Wanda stolidly. 'All lined up in my closet.'

Then they'd let her go. And then before she'd gone very far, they couldn't help bursting into shrieks and peals of laughter.

A hundred dresses! Obviously the only dress Wanda had was the blue one she wore every day. So what did she say she had a hundred for? What a story!

Peggy was not really cruel. She protected small children from bullies. And she cried for hours if she saw an animal mistreated. If anybody had said to her, 'Don't you think that is a cruel way to treat Wanda?' she would have been very surprised. Cruel? What did the girl want to go and say she had a hundred dresses for? Anybody could tell that was a lie. Why did she want to lie? And she wasn't just an ordinary person, else why would she have a name like that? Anyway, they never made her cry.

As for Maddie, Peggy's friend, this business of asking Wanda every day how many dresses and how many hats and how many this and that she had was bothering her. Maddie was poor herself. She usually wore somebody's hand-me-down clothes. Thank goodness, she didn't live up on Boggins Heights or have a funny name... But suppose Peggy and all the others started in on her next! She wasn't as poor as Wanda perhaps, but she was poor. Of course she would have more sense than to say a hundred dresses. Still she would not like them to begin on her. Not at all! Oh dear! She did wish Peggy would stop teasing Wanda Petronski.

Thinking about Wanda and her hundred dresses all lined up in the closet, Maddie began to wonder who was going to win the drawing and colour contest. For girls, this contest consisted of designing dresses, and for boys, of designing motor boats. Probably Peggy would win the girls' medal. Peggy drew better than anyone else in the room. At least that's what everybody thought. You should see the way she could copy a picture in a magazine or some film star's head. You could almost tell who it was. Oh, Maddie did hope Peggy would win. Hope so? She was sure Peggy would win. Well, tomorrow the teacher was going to announce the winners. Then they'd know.

☆

The next day it was drizzling. Maddie and Peggy hurried to school under Peggy's umbrella. Naturally on a day like this they didn't wait for Wanda Petronski on the corner of Oliver Street, the street that far, far away, under the railroad tracks and up the hill, led to Boggins Heights. Anyway they weren't taking chances on being late today, because today was important.

'Do you think Miss Mason will surely announce the winners today?' asked Peggy.

'Oh, I hope so, the minute we get in,' said Maddie, and added, 'Of course you'll win, Peg.'

'Hope so,' said Peggy eagerly.

The minute they entered the classroom they stopped short and gasped. There were drawings all over the room, on every ledge and window sill, tacked to the tops of the blackboards, spread over the bird charts, dazzling colours and brilliant lavish designs, all drawn on great sheets of wrapping paper.

There must have been a hundred of them all lined up!

These must be the drawings for the contest. They were! Everybody stopped and whistled or murmured admiringly.

As soon as the class had assembled Miss Mason announced the winners. Jack Beggles had won for the boys, she said, and his design of an outboard motor boat was on exhibition in Room 12, along with the sketches by all the other boys.

'As for the girls,' she said, 'although just one or two sketches were submitted by most, one girl – and Room 13 should be very proud of her – this one girl actually drew one hundred designs – all different and all beautiful. In the opinion of the judges, any one of her drawings is worthy of winning the prize. I am happy to say that Wanda Petronski is the winner of the girls' medal. Unfortunately Wanda has been absent from school for some days and is not here to receive the applause that is due her. Let us hope she will be back tomorrow. Now, class, you may file around the room quietly and look at her exquisite drawings...'

While the class was circling the room, the monitor from the principal's office brought Miss Mason a note. Miss Mason read it several times and studied it thoughtfully for a while. Then she clapped her hands and said, 'Attention, class. Everyone back to his seat.'

When the shuffling of feet had stopped and the room was still and quiet, Miss Mason said, 'I have a letter from Wanda's father that I want to read to you.'

Miss Mason stood there a moment and the silence in the room grew tense and expectant. The teacher adjusted her glasses slowly and deliberately. Her manner indicated that what was coming – this letter from Wanda's father – was a matter of great importance. Everybody listened closely as Miss Mason read the brief note:

'Dear Teacher: My Wanda will not come to your school any more. Jake also. Now we move away to big city. No more holler Polack.*
No more ask why funny name. Plenty of funny names in the big city. Yours truly.

Jan Petronski.'

That night Maddie could not get to sleep. She thought about Wanda and her faded blue dress and the little house she had lived in. And she thought of the glowing picture those hundred dresses made – all lined up in the classroom.

At last Maddie sat up in bed and pressed her forehead tight in her hands and really thought. This was the hardest thinking she had ever done. After a long, long time she reached an important conclusion.

She was never going to stand by and say nothing again.

If she ever heard anybody picking on someone because they were funny looking or because they had strange names, she'd speak up. Even if it meant losing Peggy's friendship. She had no way of making things right with Wanda, but from now on she would never make anybody else so unhappy again. Finally, all tired out, Maddie fell asleep.

* Wanda Petronski was Polish and 'Polack' is an insulting name for Polish people.

'Secrets'

CORAL RUMBLE

I love secrets when they belong to me,
When all my friends crowd round
And whisper quietly.

I love secrets when they belong to friends
Who say that they can't share them,
But tell me in the end.

I love secrets when they belong to Mum,
They twinkle brightly in her eyes
And promise me some fun.
I love secrets when they belong to Dad
Because he teases me with clues
And nearly drives me mad.

But I hate secrets when they snigger and they lie,
When they belong to someone else
Who wants to make me cry.

My White Brother

From *The Land of the Beaver*
ELIZABETH GEORGE SPEARE

*Matt's father builds a log cabin deep in the heart of Indian
country. Then he goes off to fetch the rest of the family, leaving
Matt in charge. He's gone so long that Matt begins to wonder if
he will ever come back. Things look bad until Matt makes friends
with Attean, an Indian boy, and learns new ways to survive.
When the Indians decide to move away from the white settlers,
they want Matt to go with them. But this is the land his father
has cleared. He cannot leave, he can only wait and hope.*

Every morning, in spite of himself, Matt kept an eye out for Attean.
When four days had gone by he decided there was little chance that
he would see his friend again. Doubtless the Indians had already left
the village and were on their way north. So when he saw Attean
coming through the woods with his dog at his heels he ran across
the clearing to meet him, not bothering to hide his relief and
pleasure.

'You think different?' Attean asked quickly. 'You go with us?'

Matt's eagerness died away. 'No,' he said unhappily. 'Please try to
understand, Attean. I must wait for my father.'

Attean nodded. 'I understand,' he said. 'My grandfather
understand too. I do same for my father if he still live.'

The two boys stood looking at each other. There was no
amusement and no scorn in Attean's eyes. How very strange, Matt

134

thought. After all the brave deeds he had dreamed of to win this boy's respect, he had gained it at last just by doing nothing, just by staying here and refusing to leave.

'My grandfather send you gift,' Attean said now. He unstrapped from his back a pair of snowshoes. They were new, the wood smooth and polished, the netting of deerhide woven in a neat design. Before Matt could find words, Attean went on.

'My grandmother send gift,' he said. He took from his pouch a small birch basket of maple sugar. Late in the season like this, Matt knew, sugar was scarce and dear to the Indians.

'Thank you,' he said. 'Tell your grandmother that when you come back I'll help gather more sap for her.'

Attean was silent. 'Not come back,' he said then.

'In the spring, I mean, when the hunt is over.'

'Not come back,' Attean repeated. 'Not live in village again. Our people find new hunting ground.'

'But this is your home!'

'My people hunters. My grandfather say many white men come soon. Cut down trees. Make house. Plant corn. Where my people hunt?'

What could Matt answer to this? He had only one argument to offer. 'Your grandfather wants you to learn to read,' he reminded Attean. 'I haven't been much of a teacher. But when my family comes it will be different. My mother will teach you to read, and to write too.'

'What for I read? My grandfather mighty hunter. My father mighty hunter. They not read.'

'Your grandfather wants you to be able to understand treaties,' Matt insisted.

'We go far away. No more white man. Not need to sign paper.'

An uncomfortable doubt had long been troubling Matt. Now, before Attean went away, he had to know. 'This land,' he said slowly, 'this place where my father built his cabin. Did it belong to your grandfather? Did he own it once?'

'How one man own ground?' Attean questioned.

'Well, my father owns it now. He bought it.'

'I not understand.' Attean scowled. 'How can man own land? Land same as air. Land for all people to live on. For beaver and deer. Does deer own land?'

How could you explain, Matt wondered, to someone who did not want to understand? Somewhere in the back of his mind there was a sudden suspicion that Attean was making sense and he was not. It was better not to talk about it. Instead he asked, 'Where will you go?'

'My grandfather say much forest where sun go down. White man not come so far.'

To the west. Matt had heard his father talk about the west. There was good land there for the taking. Some of their neighbours in Quincy had chosen to go west instead of buying land in Maine. How could he tell Attean that there would be white men there too? Still, they said there was no end of land in the west. He reckoned there must be enough for both white men and Indians. Before he could think what to say, Attean spoke again.

'I give you gift,' he said. 'Dog like you. I tell him stay with you.'

'You mean you're not taking him with you?'

'No good for hunt,' Attean said. 'Walk slow now. Good for stay here with *medabe* – with white brother.'

Attean's careless words did not deceive Matt. He knew very well how Attean felt about that no-good dog that followed him everywhere he went.

And Attean had said white brother!

Matt could not find the words he needed, but he knew there was something he must do. He had to have a gift for Attean. And he had nothing to give, nothing at all that belonged to him. *Robinson Crusoe?* What could that mean to a boy who would never now learn to read it?

He did have one thing. At the thought of it, something twisted tight in his stomach. But it was the only thing he had that could possibly match the gifts Attean had given him.

'Wait here,' he told Attean. He went into the cabin and took down the tin box. The watch was ticking away inside it. He had never forgotten to wind it, even when he was too tired to notch a stick. Now he lifted it out and held it in his hand, the way he had held it when his father had given it to him, as though it were a fragile bird's egg. His father would never understand. Before he could think about it another minute, Matt hurried back to where Attean stood waiting.

'I have a gift for you,' he said. 'It tells the time of day. I'll show you how to wind it up.'

Attean held the watch even more carefully. There was no mistaking that he was pleased and impressed. Probably, Matt thought, Attean

136

would never learn to use it. The sun and the shadows of the trees told him all he needed to know about the time of day. But Attean knew that Matt's gift was important.

'Fine gift,' he said. He put the watch very gently into his pouch. Then he held out his hand. Awkwardly the two boys shook hands.

'Your father come soon,' Attean said.

'I hope you get the biggest moose in Maine,' Matt answered.

Attean turned and walked into the woods. The dog sprang up to follow him. Attean motioned him back and uttered one stern order. Puzzled, the dog sank down and put his chin between his paws. As Attean walked away, he whined softly, but he obeyed. Matt knelt down and put his hand on the dog's head.

'I, Too'

LANGSTON HUGHES

I, too, sing America.

I am the darker brother,
They send me to eat in the kitchen
When company comes,
But I laugh,
And eat well,
And grow strong.

Tomorrow,
I'll sit at the table
When company comes.
Nobody'll dare
Say to me,
'Eat in the kitchen,'
Then.

Besides,
They'll see how beautiful I am
And be ashamed –

I, too, am America.

Sisters Under the Skin

From *Kiesha*

MILLIE MURRAY

Kiesha's family comes from the West Indies. So does Janeese's,
though her grandmother is Indian. The two girls are best friends,
but that doesn't mean they agree about white boyfriends.
'Mama Tiny' is Kiesha's grandmother.

The morning sun burned through my flower-patterned cotton curtains, its rays washing over my body like healing ointment. I woke up feeling a bit depressed...

I thought about Janeese telling me yesterday that she would go out with a white boy – I just don't understand her... It's funny, you know, people the world over always seem to fall into the same trap. How a person dresses, or what car they drive, or where they live, or how good-looking they are, or how much money they have are what attract people to each other. The list could go on and on. I can't say that I don't go by those things – I'm just as bad...

I got up and drew the curtains. The flowers in the garden were being gently blown by the cool morning breeze. 'I think I'll go and see Janeese today, I don't think she's doing anything special,' I said to myself, looking through the window. I began to sort through my wardrobe for what to put on. Hmmm, I wonder if I should walk to Janeese's house.

When I got downstairs Mum was hoovering the hall. 'Morning, Mum.'

'Morning, Kiesha. Glad to see that a good night's sleep has done you good.'

'Oh, Mum. I must be better looking for it, after all, it was my beauty sleep.'

Mum laughed. 'You're a nut case. Go on, go and get something to eat.'

'Morning, Mama Tiny.' I breezed into the kitchen.

'Marnin, chile. Waan yur breakfast now?' she asked.

'Yes please.'

Mama Tiny put a bowlful of cornmeal porridge in front of me. I suddenly didn't fancy anything to eat and pushed it away.

'No thanks, Mama Tiny.'

'What happen, chile, it too sweet?'

'No, I just don't want it,' I said, turning up my nose.

'Yu don't know how lucky yu is. Come yu mus eat it,' she said, pushing the bowl back to me.

I sighed. What a drag. I had a spoonful and just stirred the porridge in the bowl to make it look as though I had tried. Honestly, Mama Tiny thinks I'm a baby. There wasn't any point saying anything, she would probably go on and on.

I got up from the table and said, 'I've finished, Mama Tiny,' making a quick exit so that she couldn't collar me.

'Mum, is it all right if I go to Janeese's house?'

She turned the Hoover off. 'Okay, for a little while. Don't be too long now.'

As I was about to knock on Janeese's door it opened.

'I saw you coming up the road,' she smiled.

'I was going to phone you, but I didn't think you were doing anything today, so I thought I'd just come round.'

'That's all right. Come in.'

We went into the front room. It was a bit overcrowded with furniture, the two two-seater settees taking up a lot of room. There was quite a big record collection in the corner, LPs stacked on top of one another. 'Whose are those, Janeese?' I pointed to them.

'Oh, my dad's. His favourite is Paul Robeson.'

'Who? I've never heard of him,' I said.

'He's really got a deep voice. He's good, though,' Janeese said.

The telly was under the window, with the video underneath it. At the side were loads of video tapes.

'Who watches all those?' I asked.

'Who do you think? Neal. He's a video freak.'...

We sat quietly for a moment and then I just had to ask her. 'Janeese, do you still think that you would say yes to going out with a white boy?'

'Oh, Kiesha, you're not still going on about that, are you?' She leaned back against the settee, folded her arms and closed her eyes. 'Kiesha,' she said, sounding a bit fed up. 'People are forever going to pick on other people for one thing or another. If it's not colour, it's religion, or because you're poor or you're a woman. The story of people trying to keep other people down will always be going on and on. Do you know, in the West Indies, the lighter skinned you are the better job prospects and marriage ties and the best of everything you get. If your hair is straight and your features are too, well, you've no problem getting anything you want.'

'That's not true, Janeese, and you know it and if those things did ever happen it's only because the slave owners kept telling us that's how life goes, after they made all the women pregnant. Anyway, you're only saying that to get out of answering truthfully and that...'

Janeese sat up. 'No, I'm not. Okay then, perhaps I would have to seriously think about having a white boyfriend, but what I said about the West Indies is true. In America it's the same, even in this country,' she pointed to the floor. 'Listen, even white people, who started this discrimination thing off, discriminate against each other, Irish, French. Look at the Second World War, it was mainly white people killing off each other. They're mad people and even us blacks are beginning to pick up their bad ways.'

'It's only because they drummed it into us in the first place, I keep telling you,' I mumbled.

I was getting really mad. I wanted to shake Janeese and call her a traitor and all sorts of names. My fists were clenched and I could feel the anger inside. I felt a hand on my shoulder – it was Janeese.

'Keisha, I know you're angry, we all get like that over these things. I'm just about fed up with this fighting over colour, when will it end? That's why I said that I would go out with a white boy, just to be defiant. My dad hates white people. I can understand, he has been through a lot with them and it wasn't good stuff. My mum tries to

talk to him about his hatred and he goes mad. We near enough
have it in our house twenty-four hours a day. We don't talk to our
neighbours for that reason. It wasn't Dad's fault, they started it, and
I don't know who's right and who's wrong. But Keisha, I don't want
to live like that, hating people all my life, because the thing about
hating people – and I've seen it with my dad – is that it starts to
affect you and destroys you. That's one of the major reasons our
family is splitting up, because of hate.'

'What – hating white people?'

'No, not just that, but my dad, it seems, hates everyone who
doesn't agree with him, and he can never see that perhaps he might
be wrong. But the funny thing is it's the men in this situation who
don't talk to one another, but the women do. It's crazy.'

'Well, I know I hate policemen.'

'Well, yeah, that's a different thing altogether. You know, I think if
women had all the jobs that men have the world would be a better
place. How about mainly women policemen? Ohh, that sounds really
funny, women policemen, ha, ha.'

'Yeah, what about women firemen?'

'No, no, Kiesha, what about women gasmen?' laughed Janeese.

We were both laughing now. 'Janeese, Janeese, what about a
woman Prime Minister?'

We both stopped laughing. 'What about one?' she said, looking at
me from the side of her eyes.

'Oh, I forgot. Well, she's like a man anyway. I mean, women who
are women.' I grinned.

'Okay, how about Kiesha Tashana Ferell for Prime Minister?'
shouted Janeese.

'Hurrah, long live Kiesha, hurrah for me!'

We both rolled about on the settee laughing.

'Oh, Kiesha, you'll always be my friend, won't you?'

I sensed the pleading in her voice. 'Oh course, wild horses
wouldn't drag me away from you. Listen, when we leave school we
can share a flat together, and when we get married we can live next
door to one another.'

'Yeah, that'll be great.'

'Janeese, how many children do you want?' I asked her.

'Hmm, this many.' She held up ten fingers.

'Oh no, you're joking, how are you going to feed them all?'

She laughed. 'I'm going to marry a manager of a supermarket and we'll get our food cheap.'

'Why don't you be a bit more ambitious and marry someone who owns a supermarket?'

'Yeah, that's a good idea, but,' she said, eyeing me, 'what if he's a West Indian Indian?' She smiled.

'A West Indian Indian, what's that?' I screwed up my eyes. 'Hmm, I'd have to think about that one.'

Janeese jumped up and started searching the drawers of the cabinet in the corner of the room. She came back to the settee with a photo album. 'Guess who this woman is.'

She handed me a photo of an Indian woman whose long hair trailed down her back, outside a beautiful detached house surrounded by trees and flowers. It looked hot wherever she was.

'I don't know, who is she?'

'She's my grandmother, that's who she is.'

I held the photo up closer to my eyes to get a really good look. 'She looks like your mum. Look at her hair, she looks like an Indian lady. Her skin is right dark and all.'

'There we go back to colour again. In Trinidad, there are so many different races living side by side, every one is mixed up. I think that the world over will soon be like that, I mean, it's becoming that way now. Then who will hate who? We'll all be related to each other.'...

Janeese put her arm around my shoulder and I put mine around her. We sat there for a while, just hugging each other. I felt so close to her at that moment, she was really like how I imagined a sister would be...

'Being Black'

RACHEL GILLIES (AGED 11)

I am black and you are white
You say I'm wrong and you are right
I'm just the same as you and you
I do the same I do, I do

To you I'm just a passer-by
And you still hate me, tell me why
I'm just the same as him and him
Every bone and every limb

Don't call me coloured it's not true
I am not green and I'm not blue
I'm just the same as them and them
I'm not a tiger or a wren

Let's not fight and let's be friends
Let's shake hands and make amends
I'm just the same as you and you
I do the same I do, I do

The Fight

From *The Twelfth Day of July*

JOAN LINGARD

*Sadie and Tommy are Protestants; Kevin and Brede McCoy are
Catholics. They live in Belfast, in separate streets very near to
each other. Midnight sorties into forbidden territory have the spice
of danger. For the 'Prods' and the 'Micks' do not mix – they hate.
They hate because their parents hate – and they don't think
much about why. But friendship begins to grow, across the divide,
and the night of the fight brings home the terrible cost of hate.*

It was late by the time Brede had cleared up and put the little ones to
bed. When she shook the crumbs out of the tablecloth into the yard
she saw that there was a little light left in the sky.

'I think I'll just take a wee walk,' said Kevin.

'You'll do no such thing,' said Mr McCoy. 'At this time of night!'

'I said I'd see Brian.'

'If you go out you'll get into trouble. I know you. So stay in.'

Brede picked up a book, though tonight she found it difficult to
read. She felt almost as restless as Kevin for once, and wanted to
be out in the night air. The mood of the city had reached out and
touched her. Kevin sat slumped in a chair swinging one foot,
Mr McCoy watched the television.

When the programmes finished, he yawned and said he was going
to bed.

'Don't be long yourselves.'

'We'll be up in a minute,' said Kevin.

Kevin and Brede sat without speaking. Their father usually fell asleep quickly. After a few minutes Kevin tiptoed out of the room. He came back smiling.

'He's away with the angels. Making enough racket to keep the whole street awake. Come on.'

He caught Brede's hand and she went with him. Their father was snoring, Kevin was right. The noise of it followed them out through the hall on to the pavement.

A fresh breeze was blowing up. With the wind in their faces they ran through the streets to Kate's father's scrapyard. It was there that they had arranged to meet Kate and Brian.

Brian was sitting behind the steering-wheel of a battered old car with Kate curled up on the passenger seat beside him.

'There you are!' she cried. 'We'd almost given you up.'

Kevin had a look round the yard examining the old pieces of bent iron and smashed machinery. He liked junk. You never knew what you were going to turn up next.

'Let's get out of here,' said Kate, who saw enough of the junkyard. 'I'm cold with all that hanging about waiting for the two of you.'

'Aye, let's go,' said Kevin.

They fell into line. Kate linked arms with Brede, the two boys walked a little apart from them. They knew where they were going without a word being said. It was as if they were being drawn by a magnet. A few other children tagged on behind.

On the fringe of their area they paused a moment.

'Now don't go attracting any attention,' Kevin warned them. 'Just walk quiet and keep your mouths shut.'

They turned into the main road. There was not much traffic on it now. They had a clear view across it.

'Well, well,' said Kevin softly. 'Our friends are waiting for us.'

There, on the opposite pavement, were Sadie and her brother and several other children. Catholic and Protestant faced one another, with only a strip of road separating them.

For a moment there was silence. They could hear the hum of the city traffic in the distance, but they were only concerned with what was going to happen here, in this street. This is what they had been waiting for all week: to stand face-to-face, on either side of the road.

The Fight

One or two shivered, either with fear or the thrill of expectation. But none moved away. It was as if a magnet held them there irresistibly.

The moment of quiet passed. Now the voices were raised, soft and taunting to begin with.

'Dirty Micks!'

'Filthy ould Prods!'

Tempers flared. The voices grew louder.

'Kick the Pope!'…

No one knew who threw the first stone. One seemed to come from each side simultaneously.

It was as if a whistle had been blown. Suddenly children appeared from every direction; they came swarming out of side streets, yelling, cheering, booing. Their hands scoured the ground for any ammunition they could find, large stones, small ones, pieces of wood, half-bricks. They advanced on to the road. The gap between the two sides narrowed.

Sadie was in the front line. Her face glowed, and her heart thudded with excitement. She felt as though a fever possessed her. And then for a second she paused, a yell trapped at the back of her throat. She had seen Brede's face. Brede stood behind the Catholics, not shouting, or throwing, just standing.

At that moment a brick flew high over the heads of the crowd. Sadie saw Brede duck. But she was too late; the brick caught her full on the side of the head.

Brede went down and disappeared amongst the swirling bodies of the Catholics.

'Brede!' roared Sadie.

Brede was hurt. Brede… why Brede? Inside Sadie felt cold. There was no fever now, no excitement only a desperate need to get across and find out what had happened to the fallen girl. With another roar Sadie surged forward.

'Come back, Sadie,' someone yelled behind her. 'They'll murder you.'

Sadie fought through the lines, hauling children out of her way. She felt hands trying to grasp her, but the strength in her body was so great they could not stop her. She reached the group gathered round Brede's body.

A boy caught hold of her roughly.

'Leave her be,' said Kevin McCoy quietly, looking up from where he knelt beside his sister.

Sadie knelt beside him.

'Is she bad?'

'Think so.'

Brede lay still, her arms sprawled at her sides, her eyes closed. There was blood on her head.

The sound of a police siren screamed further along the road. Children flew to right and left, dropping their ammunition as they ran. By the time the police car arrived the street was almost empty. Only four children remained.

Tommy crossed the road to join Sadie and Kevin. He squatted beside them, staring down at Brede.

'Stupid,' he said. 'Stupid, stupid, stupid!'

The car doors slammed; two policemen got out and came towards them.

'Now then, what's been going on?'

'We'll need an ambulance,' said Kevin.

An ambulance was summoned, and arrived within minutes with its blue light flashing. The other three children stood back to allow the men to lift Brede on to a stretcher. They covered her with a blanket and carried her into the ambulance.

Sadie, Tommy and Kevin went into the back of the police car. They swept through the late-night streets behind the ambulance, watching its flashing light, listening to its wail. The sound made Sadie shudder.

At the hospital the lights were bright and blinding. Brede was taken away; doors closed behind her.

The waiting-room was warm, but Sadie could not stop shivering. Kevin took a bar of chocolate from his pocket and broke it into three pieces. They ate in silence, sitting side by side on a bench.

After a few minutes a police officer appeared to take down their statements. He shook his head.

'Why can't you kids keep to your own sides of the road?'

'Will she die?' Sadie burst out, unable to control the question any longer.

'We don't know yet.'

The door opened, and in came Mr McCoy looking white and shaken. He began to shout when he saw Kevin.

'I can't trust you kids an inch. I knew you'd end up in trouble. And there's your ma in Tyrone...'

'Come on,' said the police officer to Sadie and Tommy. 'I'll get someone to take you home.'

'Can't we wait and see how she is?' asked Tommy.

'Your parents will be worrying about you. Don't you think you've caused enough trouble for one night? But I'll see if there's any news before you go.'

Sadie looked back at Kevin. 'I hope she'll be all right.'

Kevin nodded.

They left him with his father. As soon as the door closed they heard Mr McCoy starting to shout again. They waited in the corridor whilst the policemen went to enquire.

'If I got my hands on the one that did it!' said Tommy.

'Does it matter?' said Sadie wearily.

'You mean it could just as easily have been me?'

'Aye. Or me.'

5

Shaping Up to Life

Sometimes something happens – or a decision is made – that changes everything. A challenge comes, and we begin to take charge of our own lives, to grow up. That is why I have chosen this next group of stories. To make it more fun, the stories from long ago – extracts from famous classics – are all mixed in with ones from today: an extract from *The Railway Children* comes first, then another story about Ramona, a piece from *Little Women*, and so on.

The children in these stories all find themselves in tough situations: David is on the run; Pollyanna, an orphan; Katy Carr has been paralysed by an accident; the 'little princess' has lost her fortune; Jody's pet fawn has been killed...

But out of hard times there comes something good.

The Terrible Secret

From *The Railway Children*

E. NESBIT

They were not railway children to begin with. I don't suppose they
had ever thought about railways except as a means of getting to the
Pantomime, Zoological Gardens, and Madame Tussaud's. They were
just ordinary suburban children, and they lived with their Father and
Mother in an ordinary red-brick-fronted villa, with coloured glass in
the front door, a tiled passage that was called a hall, a bath-room
with hot and cold water, electric bells, french windows, and a good
deal of white paint, and 'every modern convenience', as the house-
agents say.

There were three of them. Roberta (Bobbie) was the eldest. Of
course, Mothers never have favourites, but if their Mother *had* had a
favourite, it might have been Roberta. Next came Peter, who wished
to be an Engineer when he grew up; and the youngest was Phyllis,
who meant extremely well.

*Things can go wrong, even for the happiest family. One dreadful day some
strangers called and Father was taken away. No one would say why. The
family moved to the country, where they could live more cheaply.*

When they first went to live at Three Chimneys, the children had
talked a great deal about their Father, and had asked a great many
questions about him, and what he was doing and where he was and
when he would come home. Mother always answered their questions

152

as well as she could. But as the time went on they grew to speak less of him. Bobbie had felt almost from the first that for some strange miserable reason these questions hurt Mother and made her sad. And little by little the others came to have this feeling, too, though they could not have put it into words.

One day, when Mother was working so hard that she could not leave off even for ten minutes, Bobbie carried up her tea to the big bare room that they called Mother's workshop. It had hardly any furniture. Just a table and chair and a rug. But always big pots of flowers on the window-sills and on the mantelpiece. The children saw to that. And from the three long uncurtained windows the beautiful stretch of meadow and moorland, the far violet of the hills, and the unchanging changefulness of cloud and sky.

'Here's your tea, Mother-love,' said Bobbie; 'do drink it while it's hot.'

Mother laid down her pen among the pages that were scattered all over the table, pages covered with her writing, which was almost as plain as print, and much prettier. She ran her hands into her hair, as if she were going to pull it out by handfuls.

'Poor dear head,' said Bobbie, 'does it ache?'

'No – yes – not much,' said Mother. 'Bobbie, do you think Peter and Phil are *forgetting* Father?'

'*No*,' said Bobbie, indignantly. 'Why?'

'You none of you ever speak of him now.'

Bobbie stood first on one leg and then on the other. 'We often talk about him when we're by ourselves,' she said.

'But not to me,' said Mother. 'Why?'

Bobbie did not find it easy to say why.

'I – you – ' she said and stopped. She went over to the window and looked out.

'Bobbie, come here,' said her Mother, and Bobbie came.

'Now,' said Mother, putting her arm round Bobbie and laying her ruffled head against Bobbie's shoulder, 'try to tell me, dear.'

Bobbie fidgeted.

'Tell Mother.'

'Well, then,' said Bobbie, 'I thought you were so unhappy about Daddy not being here, it made you worse when I talked about him. So I stopped doing it.'

'And the others?'

'I don't know about the others,' said Bobbie. 'I never said anything about *that* to them. But I expect they felt the same about it as me.'

'Bobbie dear,' said Mother, still leaning her head against her, 'I'll tell you. Besides parting from Father, he and I have had a great sorrow – oh, terrible – worse than anything you can think of, and at first it did hurt to hear you all talking of him as if everything were just the same. But it would be much more terrible if you were to forget him. That would be worse than anything.'

'The trouble,' said Bobbie, in a very little voice – 'I promised I would never ask you any questions, and I never have, have I? But – the trouble – it won't last always?'

'No,' said Mother, 'the worst will be over when Father comes home to us.'

'I wish I could comfort you,' said Bobbie.

'Oh, my dear, do you suppose you don't? What should I do without you – you and the others? Do you think I haven't noticed how good you've all been, not quarrelling nearly as much as you used to – and all the little kind things you do for me – the flowers, and cleaning my shoes, and tearing up to make my bed before I get time to do it myself?'

Bobbie *had* sometimes wondered whether Mother noticed these things.

'That's nothing,' she said, 'to what – '

'I *must* get on with my work,' said Mother, giving Bobbie one last squeeze. 'Don't say anything to the others.'

That evening in the hour before bedtime instead of reading to the children Mother told them stories of the games she and Father used to have when they were children and lived near each other in the country – tales of the adventures of Father with Mother's brothers when they were all boys together. Very funny stories they were, and the children laughed as they listened.

'Uncle Edward died before he was grown up, didn't he?' said Phyllis, as Mother lighted the bedroom candles.

'Yes, dear,' said Mother, 'you would have loved him. He was such a brave boy, and so adventurous. Always in mischief, and yet friends with everybody in spite of it. And your Uncle Reggie's in Ceylon – yes, and Father's away, too. But I think they'd all like to think we'd enjoyed talking about the things they used to do. Don't you think so?'

'Not Uncle Edward,' said Phyllis, in a shocked tone; 'he's in Heaven.'

'You don't suppose he's forgotten us and all the old times, because God has taken him, any more than I forget him. Oh, no, he remembers. He's only away for a little time. We shall see him some day.'

'And Uncle Reggie – and Father, too?' said Peter.

'Yes,' said Mother. 'Uncle Reggie and Father, too. Good night, my darlings.'

'Good night,' said everyone. Bobbie hugged her mother more closely even than usual, and whispered in her ear. 'Oh, I do love you so, Mummy – I do – I do – '

When Bobbie came to think it all over, she tried not to wonder what the great trouble was. But she could not always help it. Father was not dead – like poor Uncle Edward – Mother had said so. And he was not ill, or Mother would have been with him. Being poor wasn't the trouble. Bobbie knew it was something nearer the heart than money could be.

'I mustn't try to think what it is,' she told herself; 'no, I mustn't. I *am* glad Mother noticed about us not quarrelling so much. We'll keep that up.'

[But] alas, that very afternoon she and Peter had what Peter called a first-class shindy...

'*I* was using the rake,' said Bobbie.

'Well, I'm using it now,' said Peter.

'But I had it first,' said Bobbie.

'Then it's my turn now,' said Peter. And that was how the quarrel began.

'You're always being disagreeable about nothing,' said Peter, after some heated argument.

'I had the rake first,' said Bobbie, flushed and defiant, holding on to its handle.

'Didn't I tell you this morning I meant to have it? Didn't I, Phil?'

Phyllis said she didn't want to be mixed up in their rows. And instantly, of course, she was.

'If you remember, you ought to say.'

'Of course, she doesn't remember – but she might say so.'

'I wish I'd had a brother instead of two whiny little kiddy sisters,' said Peter. This was always recognized as indicating the high-water mark of Peter's rage.

Bobbie made the reply she always made to it.

'I can't think why little boys were ever invented,' and just as she said it she looked up, and saw the three long windows of Mother's workshop flashing in the red rays of the sun. The sight brought back those words of praise:

'You don't quarrel like you used to do.'

'*Oh!*' cried Bobbie, just as if she had been hit, or had caught her finger in a door, or had felt the hideous sharp beginning of toothache.

'What's the matter?' said Phyllis.

Bobbie wanted to say: 'Don't let's quarrel. Mother hates it so,' but though she tried hard, she couldn't. Peter was looking too disagreeable and insulting.

'Take the horrid rake, then,' was the best she could manage. And she suddenly let go her hold on the handle. Peter had been holding on to it too, firmly and pullingly, and now that the pull the other way was suddenly stopped, he staggered and fell over backwards, the teeth of the rake between his feet.

'Serve you right,' said Bobbie, before she could stop herself.

Peter lay still for half a moment – long enough to frighten Bobbie a little. Then he frightened her a little more, for he sat up – screamed once – turned rather pale, and then lay back and began to shriek, faintly but steadily. It sounded exactly like a pig being killed a quarter of a mile off.

Mother put her head out of the window, and it wasn't half a minute after that she was in the garden kneeling by the side of Peter, who never for an instant ceased to squeal.

'What happened, Bobbie?' Mother asked.

'It was the rake,' said Phyllis. 'Peter was pulling at it, so was Bobbie, and she let go and he went over.'

'Stop that noise, Peter,' said Mother. 'Come. Stop at once.'

Peter used up what breath he had left in a last squeal and stopped.

'Now,' said Mother, 'are you hurt?'

'If he was really hurt, he wouldn't make such a fuss,' said Bobbie, still trembling with fury; 'he's not a coward!'

'I think my foot's broken off, that's all,' said Peter huffily, and sat up. Then he turned quite white. Mother put her arm round him.

'He *is* hurt,' she said; 'he's fainted. Here, Bobbie, sit down and take his head on your lap.'

Then Mother undid Peter's boots. As she took the right one off, something dripped from his foot on to the ground. It was red blood. And when the stocking came off there were three red wounds in Peter's foot and ankle, where the teeth of the rake had bitten him, and his foot was covered with red smears.

'Run for water – a basinful,' said Mother, and Phyllis ran. She upset most of the water out of the basin in her haste, and had to fetch more in a jug.

Peter did not open his eyes again till Mother had tied her handkerchief round his foot, and she and Bobbie had carried him in and laid him on the brown wooden settle in the dining-room. By this time Phyllis was halfway to the Doctor's.

Mother sat by Peter and bathed his foot and talked to him, and Bobbie went out and got tea ready, and put on the kettle.

'It's all I can do,' she told herself. 'Oh, suppose Peter should die, or be a helpless cripple for life, or have to walk with crutches, or wear a boot with a sole like a log of wood!'...

The Doctor came and looked at the foot and bandaged it beautifully, and said that Peter must not put it to the ground for at least a week.

'He won't be lame, or have to wear crutches or a lump on his foot, will he?' whispered Bobbie, breathlessly, at the door.

'My aunt! No!' said Dr Forrest; 'he'll be as nimble as ever on his pins in a fortnight. Don't you worry, little Mother Goose.'

It was when Mother had gone to the gate with the Doctor to take his last instructions and Phyllis was filling the kettle for tea, that Peter and Bobbie found themselves alone.

'He says you won't be lame or anything,' said Bobbie.

'Oh, course I shan't, silly,' said Peter, very much relieved all the same.

'Oh, Peter, I *am* so sorry,' said Bobbie, after a pause.

'That's all right,' said Peter, gruffly.

'It was *all* my fault,' said Bobbie.

'Rot,' said Peter.

'If we hadn't quarrelled, it wouldn't have happened. I knew it was wrong to quarrel. I wanted to say so, but somehow I couldn't.'

'Don't drivel,' said Peter. 'I shouldn't have stopped if you *had* said it. Not likely. And besides, us rowing hadn't anything to do with it. I might have caught my foot in the hoe, or taken off my fingers in the chaff-cutting machine or blown my nose off with fireworks. It would have been hurt just the same whether we'd been rowing or not.'

'But I knew it was wrong to quarrel,' said Bobbie, in tears, 'and now you're hurt and – '

'Now look here,' said Peter, firmly, 'you just dry up. If you're not careful you'll turn into a beastly little Sunday-school prig, so I tell you.'

'I don't mean to be a prig. But it's so hard not to be when you're really trying to be good.'

The time went slowly, slowly.

'I do wish there was something to read,' said Peter, 'I've read all our books about fifty times over.'

'I'll go to the Doctor's,' said Phyllis; 'he's sure to have some.'

'Only about how to be ill, and about people's nasty insides, I expect,' said Peter.

'Perks* has a whole heap of magazines that came out of trains when people are tired of them,' said Bobbie. 'I'll run down and ask him.'

So the girls went their two ways.

Bobbie found Perks busy cleaning lamps.

'And how's the young gent?' said he.

'Better, thanks,' said Bobbie, 'but he's most frightfully bored. I came to ask if you'd got any magazines you could lend him.'

'There, now,' said Perks, regretfully, rubbing his ear with a black and oily lump of cotton waste, 'why didn't I think of that, now? I was trying to think of something as 'ud amuse him only this morning, and I couldn't think of anything better than a guinea-pig. And a young chap I know's going to fetch that over for him this tea-time.'

'How lovely! A real live guinea-pig! He will be pleased. But he'd like the magazines as well.'

'That's just it,' said Perks. 'I've just sent the pick of 'em to Snigson's boy – him what's just getting over the pewmonia. But I've lots of illustrated papers left.'

He turned to the pile of papers in the corner and took up a heap six inches thick.

'There!' he said. 'I'll just slip a bit of string and a bit of paper round 'em.'

He pulled an old newspaper from the pile and spread it on the table, and made a neat parcel of it.

'There,' said he, 'there's lots of pictures, and if he likes to mess 'em about with his paint-box or coloured chalks or what not, why let him. *I* don't want 'em.'

'You're a dear,' said Bobbie, took the parcel, and started. The papers were heavy, and when she had to wait at the level-crossing while a train went by, she rested the parcel on the top of the gate. And idly she looked at the printing on the paper that the parcel was wrapped in.

Suddenly she clutched the parcel tighter and bent her head over it. It seemed like some horrible dream. She read on – the bottom of the column was torn off – she could read no farther.

She never remembered how she got home. But she went on tiptoe to her room and locked the door. Then she undid the parcel and read that printed column again, sitting on the edge of her bed, her hands and feet icy cold and her face burning. When she had read all there was, she drew a long, uneven breath.

'So now I know,' she said.

What she had read was headed, 'End of the Trial. Verdict. Sentence'.

The name of the man who had been tried was the name of her father. The verdict was 'Guilty'. And the sentence was 'Five years' Penal Servitude'.

'Oh, Daddy,' she whispered, crushing the paper hard, 'it's not true – I don't believe it. You never did it! Never, never, never!'

There was a hammering at the door.

'What is it?' said Bobbie.

'It's me,' said the voice of Phyllis; 'tea's ready, and a boy's brought Peter a guinea-pig. Come along down.'

And Bobbie had to.

*A great friend of the children who works at the station.

The Quarrel

From *Ramona and her Mother*
BEVERLY CLEARY

*It can be upsetting when parents quarrel. But it doesn't always
lead to divorce! Quarrels can happen even in close and loving
families like the Quimbys in this story. Beezus (Beatrice) is
Ramona's big sister.*

As soon as Ramona stepped through the back door, she knew
something was wrong. There was a chill about the house, and it had
the faint mustiness of a place that had been closed and unoccupied
all day. There was no welcoming fragrance of simmering meat and
vegetables. The tiny light on the Crock-Pot was dark, the pot cold.

'Oh, no!' cried Mrs Quimby, noticing.

'What's wrong?' asked Mr Quimby, coming in from the hall where
he had gone to turn up the thermostat of the furnace.

'Wrong!' Mrs Quimby lifted the lid of the electric casserole on
the kitchen counter. 'Someone forgot to plug in the Crock-Pot this
morning, that's what's wrong.'

The family gathered to peer in at the cold vegetables and raw
meat.

'I'm starving!' wailed Beezus.

'Me, too,' said Ramona.

'I thought you turned it on,' said Mrs Quimby to her husband as
she shoved the plug into the socket. The stew could cook overnight
and be warmed up for the next evening.

'Don't look at me,' said Mr Quimby to his wife. 'I thought you turned it on.' There was an edge to his voice.

For some reason his remark annoyed Mrs Quimby. 'I suppose you think turning on a Crock-Pot is woman's work.' The edge in her voice matched the edge in his.

'Not exactly,' said Mr Quimby, 'but now that you mention it – '

'Don't forget the time you forgot to fork the potatoes you put in to bake and they exploded,' his wife reminded him.

Ramona stifled a laugh at that memory. Her father had looked so surprised the evening the potatoes exploded – *poof!* – when he had opened the oven door.

Mr Quimby was not going to be drawn into a discussion of past baked potatoes. 'Why not just throw the stuff into the frying pan and cook it?' he asked. His idea of cooking was to toss everything into a pan and stir until done. Sometimes he invented interesting dishes with ground meat and eggs, zucchini and cheese. Other times the family tried to be good sports at dinner.

'Because you can't fry stewing meat.' Mrs Quimby sounded annoyed as she looked into the cupboard and the refrigerator. 'It's too tough. You know that. Did you bring groceries?'

'No. I thought we were having stew for dinner,' answered Mr Quimby. Crossly, Ramona thought. 'I didn't see anything on the grocery list.'

Picky-picky, the cat, rubbed against Mrs Quimby's legs, telling her how hungry he was. 'Scat,' said Mrs Quimby.

Picky-Picky went to Beezus, not Ramona. He did not like Ramona, had never liked her because she was too noisy.

'I'm practically dying of hunger,' said Beezus as she picked up the old cat and rubbed her cheek against him.

'Me, too,' said Ramona.

'You girls are no help,' Mrs Quimby told her daughters. 'We have a couple of eggs, not enough for an omelette, two strips of bacon, three carrots, and some tired old lettuce. That's it.' She looked at her husband.

'I could make carrot salad,' suggested Beezus, as if carrot salad might smooth things over.

'We could have pancakes,' said Mr Quimby, 'with half a strip of bacon apiece.'

'Not a very nutritious meal,' said Mrs Quimby, 'but better than starvation.' She reached for a mixing bowl while Beezus, who had dropped Picky-picky and washed her hands, began to grate carrots onto a sheet of waxed paper. Ramona leaned against the counter to watch. She wanted to make sure her sister did not grate her fingers into the salad.

'Ramona, don't just stand there,' said Mr Quimby as he laid the bacon in a frying pan. 'Get busy and set the table. As my grandmother used to say, "Every kettle must rest on its own bottom," so do your part.'

Ramona made a face as she reached for the place mats. 'Daddy, I bet your grandmother didn't really say all the things you say she said.'

'If she did, she must have been a dreadful bore,' said Mrs Quimby, who was beating batter as if she were angry with it.

Mr Quimby looked hurt. 'You didn't know my grandmother.'

'If she went around spouting wisdom all the time, I can't say I'm sorry.' Mrs Quimby was on her knees, dragging the griddle from behind the pots and pans in the bottom of the cupboard.

Ramona paused in laying the silverware to make sure there was no blood on the carrots. She felt the muscles of her stomach tighten as they always tightened when her mother was cross with her father.

'My grandmother was a wonderful woman,' said Mr Quimby. 'She had a hard life out there in the country, but she was good to us kids and we learned a lot from her.'

'Well, my grandmother wasn't so bad herself.' With an angry sounding crash the griddle knocked over two pans and a double boiler as Mrs Quimby yanked it from the cupboard. 'And I learned a lot from her.'

Ramona and Beezus exchanged an anxious look.

'Just what did you learn from your grandmother?' asked Mr Quimby. 'As far as I could see, all she ever did was gad around and play bridge.'

Ramona and Beezus exchanged another look. Were their parents quarrelling? Really quarrelling? Yes, the sisters' eyes agreed. Both girls were worried...

'Are you sure those pancakes are done?' asked Mr Quimby as his wife slid the pancake turner under them. 'They don't look done to me.'

'They bubbled in the middle before I turned them,' said Mrs Quimby, 'and they look done to me.'

Mr Quimby took the pancake turner from his wife. Using it as a weapon, he slashed each pancake in the centre. Ramona and Beezus exchanged a shocked look. Their father had slashed their mother's pancakes! He had gone too far. Frightened, they watched raw batter ooze from four gashes in the pancakes. Their father was right. The cakes were not done. Now what would their mother do?

Mrs Quimby was furious. She snatched back the pancake turner, scooped up the oozing cakes, and tossed them into the garbage.

'You didn't need to do that.' Mr Quimby looked amused. He had won. 'You could have turned them again and let them finish cooking.'

'And I suppose your grandmother made absolutely perfect pancakes,' said Mrs Quimby in a voice stiff with anger.

Mr Quimby looked calm and even more amused. 'As a matter of fact, she did,' he said. 'Brown and lacy, cooked all the way through, and with crisp edges.'

'The best pancakes you ever ate,' stated Mrs Quimby in a voice that made Ramona silently pray. Mother, be nice again. Please, please be nice again.

'Right,' said Mr Quimby. 'Light enough to melt in your mouth.'

Be quiet, Daddy, prayed Ramona. You'll make things worse.

'Oh – you!' Mrs Quimby gave Mr Quimby a swat on the seat of his pants with the pancake turner before she threw it on the counter. 'Bake them yourself since you learned so much from that noble grandmother of yours!'

Ramona and Beezus stood frozen with shock. Their mother had hit their father with a pancake turner. Ramona wanted to fly at her mother, to strike her and cry out, You hit my daddy! She dared not.

Mr Quimby tucked a dish towel in his belt for an apron and calmly ladled batter onto the griddle while his wife stalked into the living room and sat down with the newspaper. If only he wouldn't whistle so cheerfully as he deftly turned the cakes and drained the bacon.

'Dinner is served,' Mr Quimby announced as he set a platter of hot cakes and bacon on the table and pulled the dish towel from his belt. Silently Mrs Quimby joined the family...

Ramona felt all churned up inside, as if she didn't know whether to cry or to burst out of the house shouting, My mother and father had a fight!

'Please pass the butter.' Mrs Quimby might have been speaking to a stranger.

'May I please have the syrup?' Mr Quimby asked politely.

The evening was quiet. Mr Quimby dozed in front of the television set. Mrs Quimby took a shower and went to bed to read. Beezus did her homework in her room. Ramona tried to draw a monster eating a mouthful of people, but she could not make the picture on paper match the one in her imagination. Her monster looked as if he were eating paper dolls instead of real people. The house was unnaturally quiet. The television droned on. Both girls went to bed without being told.

Unhappy thoughts kept Ramona awake. What if her mother and father did not love one another anymore? What if they decided to get a divorce like her friend Davy's parents? What would happen to her? Who would take care of her? Beezus was closer to being a grown-up, but what about Ramona? She wanted to cry but could not. She felt too tight inside to cry. Tears teetered on her eyelashes but would not give her the relief of falling.

Finally Ramona could stand her fear and loneliness no longer. She slipped out of bed and tiptoed into her sister's room.

'Ramona?' Beezus too was awake.

'I can't go to sleep,' whispered Ramona.

'Neither can I,' said Beezus. 'Come on, get in bed with me.'

This invitation was what Ramona had been hoping for. Gratefully she slipped beneath the covers and snuggled against her sister. 'Do you think they'll get a divorce?' she whispered. 'They won't talk to each other.'

'Of course not,' said Beezus. 'At least I don't think so.'

'Who would take care of me if they did?' Ramona felt she had to have the answer from someone. 'I'm still little.'

In the morning, a few seconds after she awoke and found herself in her sister's bed, a dull, unhappy feeling settled over Ramona. Her parents had quarrelled. She dreaded facing them at breakfast. She did not know what to say to them. Beezus looked unhappy, too. Getting dressed took longer than usual, and when they finally went into the kitchen, they were surprised to see their parents sharing the morning paper as they ate breakfast together.

'Good morning, girls,' said Mr Quimby with his usual cheerfulness.

'There is oatmeal on the stove.' Mrs Quimby smiled fondly at her daughters. 'Did you sleep well?'

Beezus was suddenly angry. 'No, we didn't!'

'No, we didn't,' echoed Ramona, encouraged by her sister's anger. How could her mother expect them to sleep well when they were so worried?

Startled, both parents laid down the newspaper.

'And it's all your fault,' Beezus informed them.

'What on earth are you talking about?' asked Mrs Quimby.

Beezus was near tears. 'Your big fight, that's what.'

Ramona blinked back tears, too. 'You wouldn't even talk to each other. And you hit Daddy!'

'Of course we were speaking,' said Mrs Quimby. 'Where did you get the idea we weren't? We were just tired is all. We had one of those days when everything seemed to go wrong.'

So did I, thought Ramona.

'I went to bed and read,' continued Mrs Quimby, 'and your father watched television. That was all there was to it.'

Ramona felt almost limp with relief. At the same time she was angry with her parents for causing so much worry. 'Grown-ups aren't supposed to fight,' she informed them.

'Oh, for heaven's sake,' said Mrs Quimby. 'Why not?'

Ramona was stern. 'Grown-ups are supposed to be perfect.'

Both her parents laughed...

Ramona refused to smile. 'Don't you ever do it again.'

The Telegram

From *Little Women*
LOUISA M. ALCOTT

*Meg, Jo, Beth and Amy are the 'little women' of this story.
Their father is away at the war and their mother, Mrs March
(Marmee), has a struggle to make ends meet. Hannah helps in
the house and looks after the girls. Laurie is the boy next door,
living alone with his wealthy grandfather.*

'November is the most disagreeable month in the whole year,' said
Margaret, standing at the window one dull afternoon, looking out
at the frost-bitten garden.

'That's the reason I was born in it,' observed Jo, pensively, quite
unconscious of the blot on her nose.

'If something very pleasant should happen now, we should think
it a delightful month,' said Beth, who took a hopeful view of everything, even November.

'I dare say; but nothing pleasant ever *does* happen in this family,'
said Meg, who was out of sorts...

'Two pleasant things are going to happen right away' [said Beth];
Marmee is coming down the street, and Laurie is tramping through
the garden as if he had something nice to tell.'

In they both came, Mrs March with her usual question, 'Any
letter from father, girls?' and Laurie to say, in his persuasive way,
'Won't some of you come for a drive?'

'Can I do anything for you, Madam Mother?' asked Laurie,

166

leaning over Mrs March's chair, with the affectionate look and tone he always gave her.

'No, thank you, except call at the office, if you'll be so kind, dear. It's our day for a letter, and the penny postman hasn't been. Father is as regular as the sun but there's some delay on the way, perhaps.'

A sharp ring interrupted her and, a minute after, Hannah came in with a letter.

'It's one of them horrid telegraph things, mum,' she said, handling it as if she was afraid it would explode, and do some damage.

At the word 'telegraph,' Mrs March snatched it, read the two lines it contained, and dropped back into her chair as white as if the little paper had sent a bullet to her heart. Laurie dashed downstairs for water, while Meg and Hannah supported her, and Jo read aloud in a frightened voice, –

'MRS MARCH: –
Your husband is very ill. Come at once.
S. HALE,
Blank Hospital, Washington.'

How still the room was as they listened breathlessly! how strangely the day darkened outside! and how suddenly the whole world seemed to change, as the girls gathered about their mother, feeling as if all the happiness and support of their lives was about to be taken from them. Mrs March was herself again directly; read the message over, and stretched out her arms to her daughters, saying, in a tone they never forgot, 'I shall go at once, but it may be too late; oh, children, children! help me to bear it!'

For several minutes there was nothing but the sound of sobbing in the room, mingled with broken words of comfort, tender assurances of help, and hopeful whispers, that died away in tears. Poor Hannah was the first to recover, and with unconscious wisdom she set all the rest a good example; for, with her, work was the panacea for most afflictions.

'The Lord keep the dear man! I won't waste no time a cryin', but git your things ready right away; mum,' she said, heartily, as she wiped her face on her apron, gave her mistress a warm shake of the hand with her own hard one, and went away to work, like three women in one.

'She's right; there's no time for tears now. Be calm, girls, and let me think.'

They tried to be calm, poor things, as their mother sat up, looking pale, but steady, and put away her grief to think and plan for them.

'Where's Laurie?' she asked presently, when she had collected her thoughts, and decided on the first duties to be done.

'Here, ma'am; oh, let me do something!'...

'Send a telegram saying I will come at once. The next train goes early in the morning; I'll take that.'

'What else? The horses are ready; I can go anywhere – do anything,' he said, looking ready to fly to the ends of the earth.

'Leave a note at Aunt March's. Jo, give me that pen and paper.'

Tearing off the blank side of one of her newly-copied pages, Jo drew the table before her mother, well knowing that money for the long, sad journey must be borrowed, and feeling as if she could do anything to add a little to the sum for her father...

Everything was arranged by the time Laurie returned with a note from Aunt March, enclosing the desired sum, and a few lines repeating what she had often said before, that she had always told them it was absurd for March to go into the army, always predicted that no good would come of it, and she hoped they would take her advice next time. Mrs March put the note in the fire, the money in her purse, and went on with her preparations, with her lips folded tightly, in a way which Jo would have understood if she had been there.

The short afternoon wore away; all the other errands were done, and Meg and her mother busy at some necessary needlework, while Beth and Amy got tea, and Hannah finished her ironing with what she called a 'slap and a bang,' but still Jo did not come. They began to get anxious; and Laurie went off to find her, for no one ever knew what freak Jo might take into her head. He missed her, however, and she came walking in with a very queer expression of countenance, for there was a mixture of fun and fear, satisfaction and regret in it, which puzzled the family as much as did the roll of bills she laid before her mother, saying, with a little choke in her voice, 'That's my contribution towards making father comfortable, and bringing him home!'

'My dear, where did you get it! Twenty-five dollars! Jo, I hope you haven't done anything rash?'

'No, it's mine honestly; I didn't beg, borrow, nor steal it. I earned it; and I don't think you'll blame me, for I only sold what was my own.'

As she spoke, Jo took off her bonnet, and a general outcry arose, for all her abundant hair was cut short.

'Your hair! Your beautiful hair!' 'Oh, Jo, how could you? Your one beauty.' 'My dear girl, there was no need of this.' 'She don't look like my Jo any more, but I love her dearly for it!'

As every one exclaimed, and Beth hugged the cropped head tenderly, Jo assumed an indifferent air, which did not deceive any one a particle, and said, rumpling up the brown bush, and trying to look as if she liked it, 'It doesn't affect the fate of the nation, so don't wail, Beth. It will be good for my vanity; I was getting too proud of my wig. It will do my brains good to have that mop taken off; my head feels deliciously light and cool, and the barber said I could soon have a curly crop, which will be boyish, becoming, and easy to keep in order. I'm satisfied; so please take the money, and let's have supper.'

'Tell me all about it, Jo; *I* am not quite satisfied, but I can't blame you, for I know how willingly you sacrificed your vanity, as you call it, to your love. But, my dear, it was not necessary, and I'm afraid you will regret it, one of these days,' said Mrs March.

'No I won't!' returned Jo, stoutly, feeling much relieved that her prank was not entirely condemned.

'What made you do it?' asked Amy, who would as soon have thought of cutting off her head as her pretty hair.

'Well, I was wild to do something for father,' replied Jo, as they gathered about the table, for healthy young people can eat even in the midst of trouble. 'I hate to borrow as much as mother does, and I knew Aunt March would croak; she always does, if you ask for a ninepence. Meg gave all her quarterly salary towards the rent, and I only got some clothes with mine, so I felt wicked, and was bound to have some money, if I sold the nose off my face to get it.'

'You needn't feel wicked, my child, you had no winter things, and got the simplest, with your own hard earnings,' said Mrs March, with a look that warmed Jo's heart.

'I hadn't the least idea of selling my hair at first, but as I went along I kept thinking *what* I could do, and feeling as if I'd like to dive into some of the rich stores and help myself. In a barber's window I saw tails of hair with the prices marked; and one black tail, longer, but not so thick as mine, was forty dollars. It came over me all of a sudden that I had one thing to make money out of, and, without stopping to think, I walked in, asked if they bought hair, and what they would give me for mine.'

'I don't see how you dared to do it,' said Beth, in a tone of awe...

'Didn't you feel dreadfully when the first cut came?' asked Meg, with a shiver.

'I took a last look at my hair while the man got his things, and that was the end of it. I never snivel over trifles like that; I will confess though, I felt queer when I saw the dear old hair laid out on the table, and felt only the short, rough ends on my head. It almost seemed as if I'd an arm or a leg off. The woman saw me look at it, and picked out a long lock for me to keep. I'll give it you, Marmee, just to remember past glories by; for a crop is so comfortable I don't think I shall ever have a mane again.'

Mrs March folded the wavy, chestnut lock, and laid it away with a short grey one in her desk. She only said 'Thank you, deary,' but something in her face made the girls change the subject...

No one wanted to go to bed, when, at ten o'clock, Mrs March put by the last finished job, and said, 'Come, girls.' Beth went to the piano and played the father's favourite hymn; all began bravely, but broke down one by one till Beth was left alone, singing with all her heart, for to her music was always a sweet consoler.

'Go to bed, and don't talk, for we must be up early, and shall need all the sleep we can get. Good-night, my darlings,' said Mrs March, as the hymn ended, for no one cared to try another.

They kissed her quietly, and went to bed as silently as if the dear invalid lay in the next room. Beth and Amy soon fell asleep in spite of the great trouble, but Meg lay awake thinking the most serious thoughts she had ever known in her short life. Jo lay motionless, and her sister fancied that she was asleep, till a stifled sob made her exclaim, as she touched a wet cheek, –

'Jo, dear, what is it? Are you crying about father?'

'No, not now.'

'What then?'

'My – my hair,' burst out poor Jo, trying vainly to smother her emotion in the pillow.

It did not sound at all comical to Meg, who kissed and caressed the afflicted heroine in the tenderest manner.

'I'm not sorry,' protested Jo, with a choke. 'I'd do it again tomorrow, if I could. It's only the vain, selfish part of me that goes and cries in this silly way. Don't tell any one, it's all over now. I thought you were asleep, so I just made a little private moan for my one beauty.'

God of Green Pastures

From *I am David*

ANNE HOLM

*David has escaped from a concentration camp into a world he
has never known. The man in the camp who helped him said he
must go north, to Denmark. But how will he find his way?*

There was not much traffic up on the road, only an occasional car
passing by, and the lowest branches of the trees were within easy
reach to climb. David picked two oranges so as to have one in
reserve. Then he found a comfortable place to sit on a flat rock and
settled down to his breakfast. A little bit of bread, water – fresh and
clear, not muddy and tasteless like the water in the camp – and then
an orange to finish with.

But he had better be on his way; if *they* had begun to search for
him, he must get away quickly. They had no photographs they could
recognize him by – that was a point in his favour. He stood up and as
he stumbled over a loose stone his compass went flying over the edge
of the rock where he had been sitting. Before he could put his hand
out to catch it it was too late.

All he could do was to follow it with his eyes until it disappeared
into the sea so far below that he could not even hear the plop.

The sea was very deep under the rocks, and David knew he would
never find it again. He sat for a long time staring at the place where it
had disappeared. He was lost now. Now he *would* go round in circles
and keep coming back to the same place. And *they* would find him.

He had had so little. Now he had nothing; nothing at all to safeguard his freedom.

'God!' he said softly. 'Oh, God!'

He did not know why. It was what the men sometimes said in the camp when they were most in despair. But as for himself, he had no God.

And no compass either. Freedom was precious, and he had nothing to defend it with.

Then David decided that he must have a God: it might help. But which God should he choose? It was important to find the right one. If only he had listened more carefully to what the men had talked about in the camp! He had been interested only in learning new words. If he had asked more questions, he would have learnt a lot more.

What gods did he know of? The one the Jews had made so many demands to in return for his help? And what had David to give? Nothing! And if you were not a Jew, perhaps you had no right to choose him. The God of the Catholics seemed to leave things to a woman called Mary. Not that David had anything against women, but as he knew so little about them it might be better to choose one who looked after things himself. Johannes should have taught him something about God. Instead, he had only told him about a man, also called David, who had lived a long time ago. David dug into his memory: when he thought hard he could recall many of the things Johannes had said. Was not there something about a god, too, in that story about David? Something in rather difficult words – he had always liked new words that were long and strange: he enjoyed finding out what they meant.

Suddenly it came back to him. That other David had said of his God, 'He maketh me to lie down in green pastures, He leadeth me beside the still waters.'

He was the one he would choose!

Clutching his orange tightly, he first looked round to make sure there was no one who could overhear him, and then said in a low voice, 'God of the green pastures and the still waters, I am David and I choose you as my God! But you must please understand that I can't do anything for you, because I've always been in a wicked place where no one could think or learn or get to know anything, and I know nothing about what people ought to do for their God. But the

173

David Johannes used to talk about knew that even if he couldn't see you, you were there and were stronger than any men. I pray you will help me so that *they* won't catch me again. Then perhaps I can gradually find out about you so that I can do something in return. And if you know where Johannes is now, will you please thank him for me for going with me to Salonica, and tell him that now I'm free I can think about him again. I am David. Amen.'

Perhaps it was a mistake to say 'amen' because that's what Catholics did, but David knew it was a holy word, and if you did not have an ending God would not know when you had finished your prayer.

He felt a sense of relief and added strength just as he had the morning he had determined to go on living. He was glad he had thought of it: a god would be a lot better than a compass... though, of course, it would have been nice to have both.

The 'Glad' Game

From *Pollyanna*
ELEANOR H. PORTER

*Eleven-year-old Pollyanna is alone in the world, apart from
Aunt Polly whom she has never met till this moment. But there
is a game her father has taught her, that helps her cheerfully to
face even the direst of difficulties. Nancy – Aunt Polly's hired girl
– is the first to share a secret that will change not only the
frosty aunt, but everyone Pollyanna meets.*

Miss Polly Harrington did not rise to meet her niece. She looked up
from her book, it is true, as Nancy and the little girl appeared in the
sitting-room doorway, and she held out a hand with 'duty' written
large on every coldly extended finger.

'How do you do, Pollyanna? I – ' She had no chance to say more.
Pollyanna had fairly flown across the room and flung herself into
her aunt's scandalized, unyielding lap.

'Oh, Aunt Polly, Aunt Polly, I don't know how to be glad enough
that you let me come to live with you,' she was sobbing. 'You don't
know how perfectly lovely it is to have you and Nancy and all this
after you've had just the Ladies' Aid!'

'Very likely – though I've not had the pleasure of the Ladies' Aid's
acquaintance,' rejoined Miss Polly, stiffly, trying to unclasp the small,
clinging fingers, and turning frowning eyes on Nancy in the doorway.

'Nancy, that will do. You may go. Pollyanna, be good enough, please,
to stand erect in a proper manner. I don't know yet what you look like.'

Pollyanna drew back at once, laughing a little hysterically.

'No, I suppose you don't; but you see I'm not very much to look at, anyway, on account of the freckles. Oh, and I ought to explain about the red gingham and the black velvet basque with white spots on the elbows. I told Nancy how Father said – '

'Yes; well, never mind now what your father said,' interrupted Miss Polly crisply. 'You had a trunk, I presume?'

'Oh, yes, indeed, Aunt Polly. I've got a beautiful trunk that the Ladies' Aid gave me. I haven't got so very much in it – of my own, I mean. The barrels haven't had many clothes for little girls in them lately; but there were all Father's books, and Mrs White said she thought I ought to have those. You see, Father – '

'Pollyanna,' interrupted her aunt again sharply, 'there is one thing that might just as well be understood right away at once; and that is, I do not care to have you keep talking of your father to me.'

The little girl drew in her breath tremulously.

'Why, Aunt Polly, you – you – mean – ' She hesitated, and her aunt filled the pause.

'We will go upstairs to your room. Your trunk is already there, I presume. I told Timothy to take it up – if you had one. You may follow me, Pollyanna.'...

Eagerly Pollyanna's small feet pattered behind her aunt. Still more eagerly her big blue eyes tried to look in all directions at once, that no thing of beauty or interest in this wonderful house might be passed unseen. Most eagerly of all her mind turned to the wondrously exciting problem about to be solved; behind which of all these fascinating doors was waiting now her room – the dear, beautiful room, full of curtains, rugs and pictures, that was to be her very own? Then, abruptly, her aunt opened a door and ascended another staircase.

There was little to be seen here. A bare wall rose on either side. At the top of the stairs wide reaches of shadowy space led to far corners where the roof came almost down to the floor, and where were stacked innumerable trunks and boxes. It was hot and stifling too. Unconsciously Pollyanna lifted her head higher – it seemed so hard to breathe. Then she saw that her aunt had thrown open a door at the right.

'There, Pollyanna, here is your room, and your trunk is here, I see. Have you your key?'

Pollyanna nodded dumbly. Her eyes were a little wide and frightened.

Her aunt frowned.

'When I ask a question, Pollyanna, I prefer that you should answer aloud – not merely with your head.'

'Yes, Aunt Polly.'

'Thank you; that is better. I believe you have everything that you need here,' she added, glancing at the well-filled towel-rack and water-pitcher. 'I will send Nancy up to help you unpack. Supper is at six o'clock,' she finished, as she left the room and swept downstairs.

For a moment after she had gone Pollyanna stood quite still, looking after her. Then she turned her wide eyes to the bare wall, the bare floor, the bare windows. She turned them last to the little trunk that had stood not so long before in her own little room in the far-away Western home. The next moment she stumbled blindly toward it and fell on her knees at its side, covering her face with her hands.

Nancy found her there when she came up a few minutes later.

'There, there, you poor lamb,' she crooned, dropping to the floor and drawing the little girl into her arms. 'I was just a-fearin' I'd find you like this, like this.'

Pollyanna shook her head.

'But I'm bad and wicked, Nancy – awful wicked,' she sobbed. 'I just can't make myself understand that God and the angels needed my father more than I did.'

'No more they did, neither,' declared Nancy stoutly.

'Oh-h! – *Nancy!*' The burning horror in Pollyanna's eyes dried the tears.

Nancy gave a shamefaced smile and rubbed her own eyes vigorously.

'There, there, child, I didn't mean it, of course,' she cried briskly. 'Come, let's have your key and we'll get inside this trunk and take out your dresses in no time, no time.'

Somewhat tearfully Pollyanna produced the key.

'There aren't very many there, anyway,' she faltered.

'Then they're all the sooner unpacked,' declared Nancy.

Pollyanna gave a sudden radiant smile.

'That's so! I can be glad of that, can't I?' she cried.

Nancy stared...

'You don't seem ter see any trouble bein' glad about everythin',' she said.

Pollyanna laughed softly.

'Well, that's the game, you know, anyway.'

'The – *game*?'

'Yes; the 'just being glad' game.'

'Whatever in the world are you talkin' about?'

'Why, it's a game. Father told it to me, and it's lovely,' rejoined Pollyanna. 'We've played it always, ever since I was a little, little girl. I told the Ladies' Aid, and they played it – some of them.'

'What is it? I ain't much on games, though.'

Pollyanna laughed again, but she sighed, too; and in the gathering twilight her face looked thin and wistful.

'Why, we began it on some crutches that came in a missionary barrel.'

'*Crutches!*'

'Yes. You see I'd wanted a doll, and Father had written them so; but when the barrel came the lady wrote that there hadn't any dolls come in, but the little crutches had. So she sent 'em along as they might come in handy for some child, some time. And that's when we began it.'

'Well, I must say I can't see any game about that, about that,' declared Nancy, almost irritably.

'Oh, yes; the game was to just find something about everything to be glad about – no matter what twas,' rejoined Pollyanna earnestly. 'And we began right then – on the crutches.'

'Well, goodness me! I can't see anythin' ter be glad about – gettin' a pair of crutches when you wanted a doll!'

Pollyanna clapped her hands.

'There is – there is,' she crowed. 'But *I* couldn't see it, either, Nancy, at first,' she added, with quick honesty. 'Father had to tell it to me.'

'Well, then, suppose *you* tell *me*,' almost snapped Nancy.

'Goosey! Why, just be glad because you *don't – need – 'em!*' exulted Pollyanna triumphantly. 'You see it's just as easy – when you know how!'

'Well, of all the queer doin's!' breathed Nancy, regarding Pollyanna with almost fearful eyes.

'Oh, but it isn't queer – it's lovely,' maintained Pollyanna enthusiastically. 'And we've played it ever since. And the harder 'tis, the more fun 'tis to get 'em out; only – only – sometimes it's almost too hard – like when your father goes to heaven, and there isn't anybody but a Ladies' Aid left.'

'Yes, or when you're put in a snippy little room 'way at the top of the house with nothin' in it,' growled Nancy.

Pollyanna sighed... 'I've got so used to playing it. It's a lovely game. F-Father and I used to like it so much,' she faltered. 'I suppose though, it – it'll be a little harder now, as long as I haven't anybody to play it with. Maybe Aunt Polly will play it, though,' she added, as an afterthought.

'My stars and stockings! – *her!*' breathed Nancy, behind her teeth. Then, aloud, she said doggedly: 'See here, Miss Pollyanna, I ain't sayin' that I'll play it very well, and I ain't sayin' that I know how, anyway; but I'll play it with ye, after a fashion – I just will, I will!'

'Oh, Nancy!' exulted Pollyanna, giving her a rapturous hug. 'That'll be splendid! Won't we have fun?'

'Er – maybe,' conceded Nancy, in open doubt. 'But you mustn't count too much on me, ye know. I never was no case fur games, but I'm a-goin' ter make a most awful old try on this one. You're goin' ter have someone ter play it with, anyhow,' she finished, as they entered the kitchen together.

Pollyanna ate her bread and milk with good appetite; then, at Nancy's suggestion, she went into the sitting-room, where her aunt sat reading.

Miss Polly looked up coldly...

'Pollyanna, it's quite time you were in bed. You have had a hard day, and tomorrow we must plan your hours and go over your clothing to see what it is necessary to get for you. Nancy will give you a candle. Be careful how you handle it. Breakfast will be at half-past seven. See that you are down to that. Good night.'

Quite as a matter of course, Pollyanna came straight to her aunt's side and gave her an affectionate hug.

'I've had such a beautiful time, so far,' she sighed happily. 'I know I'm going to just love living with you – but then, I knew I should before I came. Good night,' she called cheerfully, as she ran from the room...

☆

Fifteen minutes later, in the attic room, a lonely little girl sobbed into the tightly clutched sheet:

'I know, Father-among-the-angels, I'm not playing the game one bit now – not one bit; but I don't believe even you could find anything to be glad about sleeping all alone 'way off up here in the dark – like this. If only I was near Nancy or Aunt Polly, or even a Ladies' Aider, it would be easier!'

Downstairs in the kitchen, Nancy, hurrying with her belated work, jabbed her dish-mop into the milk pitcher, and muttered jerkily:

'If playin' a silly-fool game – about bein' glad you've got crutches when you want dolls – is got ter be – my way – o' bein' that rock o' refuge – why, I'm a-goin' ter play it – I am, I am!'

The Christmas Mittens

From *Cowboy Jess*

GERALDINE McCAUGHREAN

Cowboy Jess has made firm friends with Sweet Rain,
a Sioux Indian girl. So when he hears the townsfolk talk
of a plan to drive a railroad right across 'injun' lands,
Jess comes up with a plan of his own...

No one quite knew where Jess Ford had sprung from. That is to say,
they knew where they had found him, but not the reason for him
being there or where he rightly should have been at the time. He
was found as a baby, sleeping soundly inside a raccoon hat. One
cold spring morning a cowboy out rounding up strays found him,
between the tracks of four wagon wheels, by a burned-out camp-fire,
beside the Sweetwater River crossing. It was just as if he'd been
overlooked and left behind. The raccoon fur was all spangled with
dew, like diamonds, but the only other riches found on this particular
wayfarer were a brass pocket watch and two lead pencils.

People reckoned he was an orphan even before he got mislaid, 'cos
no one came back looking for him, and even the most absent-minded
mothers and fathers generally notice losing a thing like a child. They
called him *Jess*, after the cowboy who found him, and *Ford* after the
place where he got found.

Jess picked out the softest, silkiest pair of fur mittens on sale in the
town store, and paid for them with a fistful of dollars. The storekeeper

raised her eyebrows in astonishment. 'A Christmas present?' she said.

'Sort of,' said Jess. Around him were piles of tinned food and sacks of meal; tools, bullets and clothes. There were bolts of calico, ferocious knives, pots, pans and brooms. Jess had spent an hour trying to find the perfect present, but in the end he chose the mittens: the best in the shop.

'Of course after the *railroad* comes to town, I shall have a much larger choice,' the storekeeper boasted, as she wrapped the mittens in red paper.

'Yes! Imagine!' exclaimed Jess. 'The railroad!'

There was great excitement in Sundown at the news. The barber told his customers, the men told the ladies, the ladies told the children, the children told each other: 'Have you heard? The railroad's coming to Sundown!'

There were two maps pinned up outside the newspaper office, so everyone could see what was planned. One was a map of the town, showing where the station would be: the sidings, the stockyards, the railroad office. Dirty fingermarks soon made a black smudge over the spot where the trains would pull in.

'I'll get a job as a guard,' said Hobo Hill.

'I'll get a job as a fireman,' said Matt Bunt.

'I'll get a job as a porter,' said Jemima Coolidge. (She had the muscles for it, too.)

'I'll ride the train out of here one day,' said Ma Stapley's little boy. 'And go to the big city, and be president.'

The other map showed Paradise County. Two dotted lines ran across it, straight as rulers. The railroad had not yet decided which route the line would take after Sundown. Route B went through the desert by way of Coney Creek. Route A went across the Squash River and straight on.

'But that's Sioux territory,' said Jess out loud.

'That won't worry the railroad company,' said Pat Bodger cheerfully. 'They've plenty of lines through injun country.'

'But what...'

'If the injuns don't like it, the army jest drive 'em out!'

Jess backed off the sidewalk and mounted his horse [Destiny]. Suddenly he did not feel so very thrilled about the railroad coming to town. He rode directly out to Mitten Rock and left his hat there, pinned down with a rock. That was the sign agreed with Sweet Rain, the sign that meant, 'Let's talk.'

Sure enough, two days later, she appeared out of nowhere. He was driving young cattle in closer to the ranch, because there was snow in the air. And Sweet Rain just rode up, wearing his hat. She gave it back. 'You want to see me?' she said.

She was wearing a thick doeskin dress, long boots and a blanket clutched over her hair and shoulders. But Jess could see that the fist holding the blanket was purple with cold. He was really pleased he had chosen the mittens. He pulled the red paper packet out of his saddlebag. 'A Christmas present.'

'We don't keep Christmas,' she said.

'No,' said Jess. 'But I do. Anyway, I never thanked you properly for getting Destiny back from the army.'

When she saw the mittens, she did not hide her delight. 'They're wonderful! Warm and wonderful! Thank you!'

'But I have some bad news, too...'

He did not want to tell her about the railroad. He did not even want to think about that great steel track ploughing through this hunting ground, that fishing place, those burial grounds sacred to Sweet Rain and the other Sioux. But he did tell her.

Her cold face grew even paler than before. Pale and hard. 'You white men. You won't rest till you drive us off our fathers' lands.'

'Not me! I don't want it! I'm determined they won't build that way. Believe me! I'll find some way to stop them!'

Sweet Rain looked down at the mittens, and began to pull them off.

'Don't,' said Jess. 'Not yet! Give me a chance. If I can't stop them, you can give me back the mittens. Next spring. Deal?'

'I must go and tell this news to the tribe,' was all she said. Clutching the blanket tight around her face with a gloved hand, she turned her back on Jess and rode away.

All through Christmas, Jess tried to think of a way to make the railroad choose the other, desert route. He could argue with them, but he knew he would lose. He could start up a campaign, but he knew just how many people in Sundown were so afraid of the Sioux as to gladly see them driven off their land. No, he would have to tackle the problem some other way.

There were pies and punch and puddings at the ranch house.

There was snow on the range. There were carols at the church, and all the cowboys sang the Cowboys' Hymn. But as Jess sat there, in the Christmas candlelight, all he could think of was those railroad engines. They were waiting, like black monsters in their sheds, to hurtle across the countryside and plough up Sioux territory.

Doctor Luke was late for the carol service. He squeezed in beside Jess, apologising. 'The Gomez child has a fever. I had to pay her a visit.'

Quite suddenly, the pew was half empty, as the ladies on the far side of Doctor Luke all huddled away from him, like chickens from a fox. 'Never fear, ladies,' he soothed them. 'It was nothing catching.' He winked at Jess. 'If I'd said it was smallpox, I could have emptied the church in ten seconds, you know... Are you all right, Jess?'

'Yes,' said Jess decidedly. *'Yes, yes, yes, yes, yes!* At least I will be, if you'll help me!'

'Shshshsh!' said the ladies fiercely. The choir was starting to sing.

The first good weather brought the railroad's Chief Surveyor to Sundown. He wanted a guide to the local countryside, and Jess volunteered at once. But the Sheriff swore in a couple of armed deputies as well, 'in case those Sioux make trouble'.

'They're no danger right now,' said Jess mysteriously.

They rode out as far as the Squash River. The melting snows had turned it into a rushing torrent.

'That's no problem,' said the Surveyor with a confident sneer. 'I've built bridges over far bigger rivers.'

They rode between the striped rocks of Blind Canyon. *'This* is no problem,' said the Surveyor with a haughty sniff. 'I've built bridges over canyons twice as wide.'

'But isn't the desert route easier?' asked Jess eagerly.

'Steam engines need water, sonny,' said the Surveyor, as if to a little child. 'And railroad tracks don't rest happily on sand.'

So on they rode, through the pretty Sioux countryside, and though the deputies kept a lookout all the while, they did not see a single Indian. Not one.

'That's the Sioux burial ground,' Jess pointed out. 'This is where their shamans have visions. These trees are where the young men cut the wood for their bows.'

'Good,' said the Surveyor grimly. 'When we rip it all out, they may move on. Passengers don't like Indians living alongside the track. We like to shift them if we can.'

The deputies nodded, in agreement, but Jess could feel his temper growing like a fire inside him. He took several deep breaths and kept silent.

Still no Sioux showed themselves. It was as if the countryside was deserted already. Then Sweet Rain's village came in sight. It lay right in the path of the proposed railroad.

'You won't want to go any closer,' said Jess.

'What's those pieces of yellow cloth hung up in the trees? said Deputy Hobo.

'A warning to strangers,' said Jess.

'And what's that smell? said Deputy Matt.

'They're burning herbs to keep off disease,' said Jess.

'But where in the blue blazes is everyone?' Hobo burst out at last. At any moment, he expected savage Sioux to leap out of the trees and ambush him.

'All inside their tents, of course,' said Jess casually. 'Either they're sick, or they're looking after the sick. Myself, I think I'll ride round, if it's all the same with you, gentlemen. I don't care to get too close to smallpox.'

'SMALLPOX?'

The Surveyor dropped his theodolyte. Deputy Hobo pulled his bandanna up over his nose. Deputy Matt turned his horse round then and there. The wind blowing up from the village brought the faint sound of groaning and sobbing.

'But are you *certain* it's smallpox?' the Surveyor asked Jess a fifth time, as they galloped back across the Squash River ford.

'You'd have to ask Doctor Luke in town,' said Jess. 'It might only be measles. Or typhus.'

So the Surveyor asked Sundown's town doctor if he knew what ailed the Indian population up beyond the Squash River.

Doctor Luke snatched a white gauze mask out of the drawer of his desk and put it on. Only his eyes frowned back at the Surveyor. 'Well, smallpox, of course! The land out there is riddled with it. The trees, the river. The land where they bury their dead, of course. But most anywhere they've set down. Their sheep, too, naturally. Their horses... Fortunately the Sioux don't come to the likes of me for doctoring. And if you have been in contact with them, gentlemen, I fear I *may* have to place you in quarantine for a few weeks…'

He turned his blue eyes on Jess and one of them flickered shut – almost as if he were winking.

An excited crowd of Sundowners pressed around the Surveyor at the bar of the Silver Dollar Saloon, to see what this clever man from back East had decided about the future of their town.

'Simple, yes,' the Surveyor was saying grandly. 'I've built railroads over deserts *far* dryer than that one. That's why I've decided on Route B – through the desert and past Coney Creek…'

Jess took off his hat to wipe his brow with relief. He looked at the battered old hat: he must go and post it at Mitten Rock, as a signal to Sweet Rain that the plan had worked. He wanted to see her, too. He wanted to congratulate her on the show. Fancy her being able to persuade the whole tribe to join in the charade!

He tried to imagine them all crouching inside their tents, peeping out through the seams, groaning and grinning and watching for the white men to hurry away. It made Jess smile himself to think of it.

He did leave his hat at Mitten Rock. But no Sweet Rain appeared. After a week, he said to his horse, 'I'd best get out there again, Destiny. Maybe my hat blew away.' But he was half afraid, as he rode Destiny out towards the strange wind-carved, hand-shaped landmark, that he might find his hat still in place, and the fur mittens beside them that he had given her for Christmas. Perhaps he was just too much of a white man to keep the friendship of a Sioux maiden.

But when he got to the rock, Sweet Rain had not returned his gloves. She had simply answered his gift with a Christmas present of her own. At least the children of her tribe had done.

For Mitten Rock was painted with a hundred colourful figures, animals, stars, patterns, handprints, flowers… All around the base, as high as the tallest child could reach, the rock was decorated. Jess thought it was the best Christmas present he had ever received.

Even if the month was March, and the grass on the range was already bright with spring flowers.

Katy's Lessons

From *What Katy Did*

SUSAN COOLIDGE

At thirteen, Katy is the eldest of Dr Carr's six motherless children.
She is full of fun and constantly in 'scrapes'. One day, disobeying
Aunt Izzie, she goes to swing in the barn – and the swing breaks.
Katy is badly hurt, and it seems like the end of everything –
until Cousin Helen visits...

If anybody had told Katy, that first afternoon, that at the end of a
week she would still be in bed, and in pain, and with no time fixed
for getting up, I think it would have almost killed her. She was so
restless and eager, that to lie still seemed one of the hardest things
in the world. But to lie still and have her back ache all the time was
worse yet...

Then there came a time when Katy didn't even ask to be allowed
to get up. A time when sharp, dreadful pain, such as she never
imagined before, took hold of her. When days and nights got all
confused and tangled up together, and Aunt Izzie never seemed to
go to bed. A time when Papa was constantly in her room. When
other doctors came and stood over her, and punched and felt her
back, and talked to each other in low whispers. It was all like a long,
bad dream, from which she couldn't wake up...

By-and-by the pain grew less, and the sleep quieter. Then, as the
pain became easier still, Katy woke up as it were – began to take
notice of what was going on about her, to put questions.

'How long have I been ill?' she asked one morning.

'It is four weeks yesterday,' replied Papa.

'Four weeks!' said Katy. 'Why, I didn't know it was so long as that. Was I very sick, Papa?'

'Very, dear. But you are a great deal better now.'...

'Can I get up again and go downstairs at once?'

'Not yet, I'm afraid,' said Dr Carr, trying to speak cheerfully.

Katy didn't ask any more questions then. Another week passed, and another. The pain was almost gone... But still the once active limbs hung heavy and lifeless, and she was not able to walk, or even stand alone.

'My legs feel so queer,' she said one morning, 'they are just like the Prince's legs which were turned to black marble in the Arabian Nights. What do you suppose is the reason, Papa? Won't they feel natural soon?'

'Not soon,' answered Dr Carr. Then he said to himself: 'Poor child, she had better know the truth.' So he went on, aloud, 'I am afraid, my darling, that you must make up your mind to stay in bed a long time.'

'How long?' said Katy, looking frightened. 'A month more?'

'I can't tell exactly how long,' answered her father. 'The doctors think, as I do, that the injury to your spine is one which you will outgrow by-and-by, because you are so young and strong. But it may take a good while to do it. It may be that you will have to lie here for months, or it may be more. The only cure for such a hurt is time and patience. It is hard, darling' – for Katy began to sob wildly – 'but you have hope to help you along. Think of poor Cousin Helen, bearing all these years without hope!'

'Oh, Papa,' gasped Katy, between her sobs, 'doesn't it seem dreadful, that just getting into the swing for a few minutes should do so much harm? Such a little thing as that!'

'Yes, such a little thing!' repeated Dr Carr, sadly. 'And it was only a little thing, too, forgetting Aunt Izzie's order about the swing. Just for the want of the small 'horse-shoe nail' of Obedience, Katy.'

Years afterwards, Katy told somebody that the six longest weeks of her life were those which followed this conversation with Papa. Now that she knew there was no chance of getting well at once, the days dragged dreadfully. Each seemed duller and dismaller than the day before. She lost heart about herself, and took no interest in anything...

☆

The first thing which broke in upon this sad state of affairs, was a letter from Cousin Helen, which Papa brought one morning and handed to Aunt Izzie.

'Helen tells me she's going home this week,' said Aunt Izzie, from the window, where she had gone to read the letter…

'Oh, Aunt Izzie,' cried Katy, 'is Cousin Helen coming this way when she goes home? Oh, do make her stop! If it's just for one day, do ask her! I want to see her so much! I can't tell you how much! Won't you? Please! Please, dear Papa!'

She was almost crying with eagerness.

'Why, yes, darling if you wish it so much,' said Dr Carr…

For the next week Katy was feverish with expectation. At last Cousin Helen came. This time Katy was not on the steps to welcome her, but after a little while Papa brought Cousin Helen in his arms, and sat her in a big chair beside the bed.

'How dark it is!' she said, after they had kissed each other and talked for a minute or two. 'I can't see your face at all. Would it hurt your eyes to have a little more light?'

'Oh, no!' answered Katy. 'It don't hurt my eyes, only I hate to have the sun come in. It makes me feel worse somehow.'

'Push the blind open a little bit then, Clover,' and Clover did so.

'Now I can see,' said Cousin Helen.

It was a forlorn-looking child enough which she saw lying before her. Katy's face had grown thin, and her eyes had red circles about them from continual crying. Her hair had been brushed twice that morning by Aunt Izzie, but Katy had run her fingers impatiently through it, till it stood out above her head like a frowsy bush. She wore a calico dressing-gown, which, though clean, was particularly ugly in pattern; and the room, for all its tidiness, had a dismal look, with the chairs set up against the wall, and a row of medicine-bottles on the chimney-piece.

'Isn't it horrid?' sighed Katy, as Cousin Helen looked around. 'Everything's horrid. But I don't mind so much now that you've come. Oh, Cousin Helen, I've had such a dreadful, *dreadful* time!'

'I know,' said her cousin, pityingly. 'I've heard all about it, Katy, and I'm so very sorry for you! It's a hard trial, my poor darling.'

'But how do *you* do it?' cried Katy. 'How do you manage to be so

189

sweet and beautiful and patient, when you're feeling badly all the time and can't do anything, or walk, or stand?' Her voice was lost in sobs.

Cousin Helen didn't say anything for a little while. She just sat and stroked Katy's head.

'Katy,' she said at last, 'has Papa told you that he thinks you are going to get well by-and-by?'

'Yes,' replied Katy, 'he did say so. But perhaps it won't be for a long, long time. And I wanted to do so many things. And now I can't do anything at all!'

'What sort of things?'

'Study, and help people, and become famous. And I wanted to teach the children. Mamma said I must take care of them, and I meant to. And now I can't go to school or learn anything myself. And if I ever do get well, the children will be almost grown up, and they won't need me.'

'But why must you wait till you get well?' asked Cousin Helen, smiling.

'Why, Cousin Helen, what can I do lying here in bed?'

'A good deal. Shall I tell you, Katy, what it seems to me that I should say to myself if I were in your place?'

'Yes, please!' cried Katy, wonderingly.

'I should say this: "Now Katy Carr, you wanted to go to school and learn to be wise and useful and here's a chance for you. God is going to let you go to *his* school – where he teaches all sorts of beautiful things to people..."'

'What are the lessons?' asked Katy, getting interested, and beginning to feel as if Cousin Helen were telling her a story.

'Well, there's the lesson of Patience. That's one of the hardest studies. You can't learn much of it at a time, but every bit you get by heart, makes the next bit easier. And there's the lesson of Cheerfulness. And the lesson of Making the Best of Things.'

'Sometimes there isn't anything to make the best of,' remarked Katy, dolefully.

'Yes, there is, always! Everything in the world has two handles. Didn't you know that? One is the smooth handle. If you take hold of it the thing comes up lightly and easily, but if you seize the rough handle, it hurts your hand and the thing is hard to lift. Some people always manage to get hold of the wrong handle.'

'Is Aunt Izzie a "thing"?' asked Katy. Cousin Helen was glad to hear her laugh.

'Yes – Aunt Izzie is a *thing* – and she has a nice pleasant handle too, if you just try to find it. And the children are "things", also, in one sense. All their handles are different. You know human beings aren't made just alike, like red flower-pots. We have to feel and guess before we can make out just how other people go, and how we ought to take hold of them. It is very interesting; I advise you to try it. And while you are trying, you will learn all sorts of things which will help you to help others.'

'If I only could!' sighed Katy. 'Are there any other studies in the school, Cousin Helen?'

'Yes, there's the lesson of Hopefulness. That class has ever so many teachers. The Sun is one. He sits outside the window all day, waiting a chance to slip in and get at his pupil. He's a first-rate teacher, too. I wouldn't shut him out, if I were you.'

'Do you really think I could be nice and sweet and patient, and a comfort to people?'

'I am sure you can, if you try.'

'But what would you do first?' asked Katy, who, now that her mind had grasped a new idea, was eager to begin.

'Well – first I would open the blinds, and make the room look a little less dismal. Are you taking all those medicines in the bottles now?'

'No – only that big one with the blue label.'

'Then you might ask Aunt Izzie to take away the others. And I'd get Clover to pick a bunch of fresh flowers every day for your table. By the way, I don't see the little white vase.'

'No – it got broken the very day after you went away; the day I fell out of the swing,' said Katy, sorrowfully.

'Never mind, pet, don't look so doleful. I know the tree those vases grow upon, and you shall have another. Then, after the room is made pleasant, I would have all my lesson-books fetched up, if I were you, and I would study a couple of hours every morning.'

'Oh!' cried Katy, making a wry face at the idea.

Cousin Helen smiled. 'I know,' said she, 'it sounds like dull work learning geography and doing sums up here all by yourself. But I think if you make the effort you'll be glad by-and-by. You won't lose so much ground, you see – won't slip back quite so far in your education. And then, studying will be like working at a garden, where things don't grow easily. Every flower you raise will be a sort of triumph, and you will value it twice as much as a common flower which has cost no trouble.'

'Well,' said Katy, rather forlornly, 'I'll try. But it won't be a bit nice studying without anybody to study with me. Is there anything else, Cousin Helen?'

Just then the door creaked, and Elsie timidly put her head into the room.

'Oh, Elsie, run away!' cried Katy. 'Cousin Helen and I are talking. Don't come just now.'

Katy didn't speak unkindly, but Elsie's face fell, and she looked disappointed. She said nothing, however, but shut the door and stole away.

Cousin Helen watched this little scene without speaking. For a few minutes after Elsie was gone, she seemed to be thinking.

'Katy,' she said at last, 'you were saying just now, that one of the things you were sorry about was that while you were ill you could be of no use to the children. Do you know, I don't think you have that reason for being sorry?'

'Why not?' said Katy, astonished.

'Because you *can* be of use. It seems to me that you have more of a chance with the children now than you ever could have had when you were well, and flying about as you used. You might do almost anything you liked with them.'

'I can't think what you mean,' said Katy, sadly. 'Why, Cousin Helen, half the time I don't even know where they are, or what they are doing. And I can't get up and go after them, you know.'

'But you can make your room such a delightful place, that they will want to come to you! Don't you see, a sick person has one splendid chance – she is always on hand. Everybody who wants her knows just where to go. If people love her, she gets naturally to be the heart of the house.

'Once make the little ones feel that your room is the place of all others to come to when they are tired, or happy, or grieved, or sorry about anything, and that the Katy who lives there is sure to give them a loving reception – and the battle is won...'

Just then Dr Carr came in.

'Oh, Papa, you haven't come to take Cousin Helen, have you?' cried Katy.

'Indeed I have,' said her father. 'I think the big invalid and the little invalid have talked quite long enough. Cousin Helen looks tired.'

For a minute, Katy felt just like crying. But she choked back the tears. 'My first lesson in Patience,' she said to herself, and managed to give a faint, watery smile as Papa looked at her.

'That's right, dear,' whispered Cousin Helen, and she bent forward to kiss her. 'And one last word, Katy. In this school, to which you and I belong, there is one great comfort, and that is that the Teacher is always at hand. He never goes away.'

The Last Doll

From *A Little Princess*
FRANCES HODGSON BURNETT

*Motherless Sara Crewe has been sent home from India to
Miss Minchin's school in England. Because her father is rich,
Sara is treated like a little princess. Then news comes that Sara's
father is dead and her fortune lost. She is poor – a little princess
no longer. Emily is the doll Sara's father bought for her – more
friend than doll. Becky is the scullery maid and general drudge,
whom Sara has always treated kindly.*

'Tell Sara to come to my room,' Miss Minchin had said to her sister.
'And explain to her clearly that I will have no crying or unpleasant
scenes.'

'Sister,' replied Miss Amelia, 'she is the strangest child I ever saw.
She has actually made no fuss at all. You remember she made none
when Captain Crewe went back to India. When I told her what had
happened, she just stood quite still and looked at me without making
a sound. Her eyes seemed to get bigger and bigger, and she went
quite pale. When I had finished, she still stood staring for a few
seconds, and then her chin began to shake, and she turned round
and ran out of the room and upstairs. Several of the other children
began to cry, but she did not seem to hear them or to be alive to
anything but just what I was saying. It made me feel quite queer not
to be answered; and when you tell anything sudden and strange, you
expect people will say *something* – whatever it is.'

Nobody but Sara herself ever knew what had happened in her room after she had run upstairs and locked her door. In fact, she herself scarcely remembered anything but that she walked up and down, saying over and over again to herself in a voice which did not seem her own:

'My papa is dead! My papa is dead!'

Once she stopped before Emily, who sat watching her from her chair, and cried out wildly:

'Emily! Do you hear? Do you hear – papa is dead! He is dead in India – thousands of miles away.'

When she came into Miss Minchin's sitting-room in answer to her summons, her face was white and her eyes had dark rings around them. Her mouth was set as if she did not wish it to reveal what she had suffered and was suffering. She did not look in the least like the rose-coloured butterfly who had flown about from one of her treasures to the other in the decorated schoolroom. She looked instead a strange, desolate, almost grotesque little figure.

She had put on, without Mariette's help, the cast-aside black-velvet frock. It was too short and tight, and her slender legs looked long and thin, showing themselves from beneath the brief skirt. As she had not found a piece of black ribbon, her short, thick, black hair tumbled loosely about her face and contrasted strongly with its pallor. She held Emily tightly in one arm, and Emily was swathed in a piece of black material.

'Put down your doll,' said Miss Minchin. 'What do you mean by bringing her here?'

'No,' Sara answered. 'I will not put her down. She is all I have. My papa gave her to me.'

She had always made Miss Minchin feel secretly uncomfortable, and she did so now. She did not speak with rudeness so much as with a cold steadiness with which Miss Minchin felt it difficult to cope – perhaps because she knew she was doing a heartless and inhuman thing.

'You will have no time for dolls in future,' she said. 'You will have to work and improve yourself and make yourself useful.'

Sara kept her big, strange eyes fixed on her, and said not a word.

'Everything will be very different now,' Miss Minchin went on. 'I suppose Miss Amelia has explained matters to you.'

'Yes,' answered Sara. 'My papa is dead. He left me no money. I am quite poor.'

'You are a beggar,' said Miss Minchin, her temper rising at the recollection of what all this meant. 'It appears that you have no relations and no home, and no one to take care of you.'

For a moment the thin, pale little face twitched, but Sara again said nothing.

'What are you staring at?' demanded Miss Minchin sharply. 'Are you so stupid that you cannot understand? I tell you that you are quite alone in the world, and have no one to do anything for you, unless I choose to keep you here out of charity.'

'I understand,' answered Sara, in a low tone; and there was a sound as if she had gulped down something which rose in her throat. 'I understand.'

'That doll,' cried Miss Minchin, pointing to the splendid birthday gift seated near – 'that ridiculous doll, with all her nonsensical, extravagant things – I actually paid the bill for her!'

Sara turned her head toward the chair.

'The Last Doll,' she said. 'The Last Doll.' And her little mournful voice had an odd sound.

'The Last Doll, indeed!' said Miss Minchin. 'And she is mine, not yours. Everything you own is mine.'

'Please take it away from me, then,' said Sara. 'I do not want it.'

If she had cried and sobbed and seemed frightened, Miss Minchin might almost have had more patience with her. She was a woman who liked to domineer and feel her power, and as she looked at Sara's pale little steadfast face and heard her proud little voice, she quite felt as if her might was being set at naught.

'Don't put on grand airs,' she said. 'The time for that sort of thing is past. You are not a princess any longer. Your carriage and your pony will be sent away – your maid will be dismissed. You will wear your oldest and plainest clothes – your extravagant ones are no longer suited to your station. You are like Becky – you must work for your living.'

To her surprise, a faint gleam of light came into the child's eyes – a shade of relief.

'Can I work?' she said. 'If I can work it will not matter so much. What can I do?'

'You can do anything you are told,' was the answer. 'You are a

sharp child, and pick up things readily. If you make yourself useful I
may let you stay here. You speak French well, and you can help with
the younger children.'

'May I?' exclaimed Sara. 'Oh, please, let me! I know I can teach
them. I like them, and they like me.'

'Don't talk nonsense about people liking you,' said Miss Minchin.
'You will have to do more than teach the little ones. You will run
errands and help in the kitchen as well as in the schoolroom. If you
don't please me, you will be sent away. Remember that. Now go.'

Sara stood still just a moment, looking at her. In her young soul
she was thinking deep and strange things. Then she turned to leave
the room.

'Stop!' said Miss Minchin. 'Don't you intend to thank me?'

Sara paused, and all the deep, strange thoughts surged up in her
breast.

'What for?' she said.

'For my kindness to you,' replied Miss Minchin. 'For my kindness
in giving you a home.'

Sara made two or three steps toward her. Her thin little chest
heaved up and down, and she spoke in a strange, unchildishly fierce
way.

'You are not kind,' she said. 'You are *not* kind, and it is *not* a
home.' And she had turned and run out of the room before
Miss Minchin could stop her or do anything but stare after her
with stony anger.

She went up the stairs slowly, but panting for breath, and she
held Emily tightly against her side.

'I wish she could talk,' she said to herself. 'If she could speak –
if she could speak!'

She meant to go to her room and lie down on the tiger-skin,
with her cheek upon the great cat's head, and look into the fire and
think and think and think. But just before she reached the landing
Miss Amelia came out of the door and closed it behind her, and stood
before it, looking nervous and awkward. The truth was that she felt
secretly ashamed of the thing she had been ordered to do.

'You – you are not to go in there,' she said.

'Not go in?' exclaimed Sara, and she fell back a pace.

'That is not your room now,' Miss Amelia answered, reddening a
little.

Somehow, all at once, Sara understood. She realized that this was the beginning of the change Miss Minchin had spoken of.

'Where is my room?' she asked, hoping very much that her voice did not shake.

'You are to sleep in the attic next to Becky.'

Sara knew where it was. Becky had told her about it. She turned, and mounted up two flights of stairs. The last one was narrow, and covered with shabby strips of old carpet. She felt as if she were walking away and leaving far behind her the world in which that other child, who no longer seemed herself, had lived. This child, in her short, tight old frock, climbing the stairs to the attic, was quite a different creature.

When she reached the attic door and opened it, her heart gave a dreary little thump. Then she shut the door and stood against it and looked about her.

Yes, this was another world. The room had a slanting roof and was whitewashed. The whitewash was dingy and had fallen off in places. There was a rusty gate, an old iron bedstead, and a hard bed covered with a faded coverlet. Some pieces of furniture too much worn to be used downstairs had been sent up. Under the skylight in the roof, which showed nothing but an oblong piece of dull grey sky, there stood an old battered red footstool. Sara went to it and sat down. She seldom cried. She did not cry now. She laid Emily across her knees and put her face down upon her and her arms around her, and sat there, her little black head resting on the black draperies not saying one word, not making one sound.

And as she sat in this silence there came a low tap at the door – such a low, humble one that she did not at first hear it, and, indeed, was not roused until the door was timidly pushed open and a poor tear-smeared face appeared peeping round it. It was Becky's face, and Becky had been crying furtively for hours and rubbing her eyes with her kitchen apron until she looked strange indeed.

'Oh, miss,' she said under her breath. 'Might I – would you allow me – jest to come in?'

Sara lifted her head and looked at her. She tried to begin to smile, and somehow she could not. Suddenly – and it was all through the loving mournfulness of Becky's streaming eyes – her face looked more like a child's not so much too old for her years. She held out her hand and gave a little sob.

'Oh, Becky,' she said. 'I told you we were just the same – only two little girls – just two little girls. You see how true it is. There's no difference now. I'm not a princess any more.'

Becky ran to her and caught her hand, and hugged it to her breast, kneeling beside her and sobbing with love and pain.

'Yes, miss, you are,' she cried, and her words were all broken. 'Whats'ever 'appens to you – whats'ever – you'd be a princess all the same – an' nothin' couldn't make you nothin' different.'

Jody Grows Up

From *The Yearling*

MARJORIE KINNAN RAWLINGS

*For Jody, growing up in the backwoods of Florida in the early
1900s, life is lonely on his father's farm – until he adopts a
motherless fawn called Flag. For a year the two are inseparable.
But then Flag begins to destroy the newly planted crops on which
the family depends. It is Flag's life or theirs. When the fawn is
shot Jody feels that his injured father (Penny) has betrayed him.
He runs away...*

Flag was dead. He would never run to him again. Jody tortured
himself with saying the words.

'Flag's dead.'

They were as bitter as alum-root tea.

He had not yet probed the deepest pain.

He said aloud, 'Pa went back on me.'

It was a sharper horror than if Penny had died of the snake-bite.
He rubbed his knuckles over his forehead. Death could be borne.
Fodder-wing had died and he was able to bear it. Betrayal was
intolerable. If Flag had died, if bear or wolf or panther had slipped in
on him, he would have grieved with a great grief, but he could have
endured it. He would have turned to his father, and his father would
have comforted him. Without Penny, there was no comfort anywhere.
The solid earth had dissolved under him. His bitterness absorbed his
sorrow, and they were one.

The sun dropped below the tree-tops...

Darkness filled both land and water. A hoot owl cried in the thicket near him. He shivered. The night wind stirred and was chill. He heard a rustling that might be leaves moving ahead of the wind, or small creatures passing. He was not afraid. It seemed to him that if a bear came, or a panther, he might touch it and stroke it and it would understand his grief. Yet the night sounds about him made his flesh creep. It would be good to have a camp-fire. Penny could start a fire even without his tinder-horn, in the way the Indians did, but he had never been able to do it. If Penny were here, there would be a blazing fire, and warmth and food and comfort. He was not afraid. He was only desolate. He pulled the moss over him and cried himself to sleep.

The sun awakened him, and the red-winged blackbirds chattering in the reeds. He stood up and pulled the long strands of moss from his hair and clothing. He was weak and dizzy. Now that he was rested, he knew that he was hungry. The thought of food was torture...

A fresh wave of loneliness swept over him. He had lost Flag and he had lost his father, too. The gaunt little man he had last seen crouched in pain in the kitchen doorway, calling for help to stand, was a stranger. He pushed out his dug-out and took up his paddle and headed for the open waters. He was out in the world, and it seemed to him that he was alien here, and alone, and that he was being carried away into a void. He paddled for the location where he had seen the steamer pass. Living was no longer the grief behind him, but the anxiety ahead. Leaving the mouth of the creek behind him, he found the wind freshening. Out from the shelter of the land a brisk breeze was blowing. He ignored the gnawing in his belly and paddled desperately. The wind caught the dug-out and slewed it around. He could not keep it headed. The waves were mounting. Their soft lapping changed to a hissing. They began to break over the bow of the canoe. When it swung sideways they washed in and it tipped and rolled. There was an inch of water across the bottom. There was no vessel of any sort in sight.

He looked back. The shore had receded alarmingly. Ahead of him, the open water seemed to stretch without an end. He turned about in a panic and paddled madly for the shore... He headed for an opening that must be the end of the Salt Springs run. When he reached it, it was a blind opening in the shore that led only into swamp. The mouth of the run was nowhere to be found.

He was trembling from his exertion and from his fear. He told himself that he was not lost, for the river ran north out of Lake George and came at the end to Jacksonville, and he had only to follow it. But it was so wide, and the shore line was so confusing – He rested a long time, then began to paddle slowly north, close to the thick-cypressed land, following the endless curves and bays and indentations. The gnawing in his stomach was an acute pain. He began to have a feverish vision of the usual Baxter table. He saw slices of ham steaming, brown and dripping in their own juice. He smelled the sweet savour. He saw tawny biscuits and dark-crusted cornbread and swimming bowls of cow-peas, with squares of white bacon floating among them. He smelled fried squirrel so definitely that the saliva ran in his mouth. He tasted the warm foam of Trixie's milk. He could have fought with the dogs for their pan of cold grits and gravy.

This, then, was hunger. This was what his mother had meant when she had said, 'We'll all go hungry.' He had laughed, for he had thought he had known hunger, and it was faintly pleasant. He knew now that it had been only appetite. This was another thing. The thing was terrifying…

He worked his way north along the shore line all day. In the late afternoon he was sick at his stomach from the heat of the sun, but there was nothing to vomit but the river water he had drunk. A cabin showed ahead among trees and he pulled into it hopefully. It was deserted. He prowled inside, like a hungry 'coon or 'possum. There were cans on a dusty shelf, but all were empty. In a jar he found a cupful of musty flour. He mixed it with water and ate the paste. It was flavourless, even in his hunger, but it stopped the pain in his stomach. There were birds and squirrels in the trees and he tried to hit them with stones, but he only drove them all away. He was feverish and exhausted and the flour in his belly made him sleepy. The cabin offered shelter, and he made a pallet of some rags, from which the roaches scurried. He slept a drugged, nightmare-ridden sleep.

In the morning he was again conscious of acute hunger, and the cramps were sharp-nailed fingers that twisted his entrails. He found some last year's acorns that the squirrels had buried and ate them so ravenously that the hard, unchewed pieces were fresh knives in his contracting stomach. A lethargy settled on him, and he could scarcely force himself to take up his paddle. If the current had not been with him, he decided he could have gone no farther. He covered only a short distance during the morning. In the afternoon, three boats passed in mid-stream. He stood up and waved his arms and shouted. They paid no attention to his cries. When they had passed from sight, he was torn unwillingly with sobbing. He decided to cut out away from the shore to intercept the next vessel. The wind had died. The water was calm. The glare from it burned his face and neck and bare arms. The sun was scalding. His head throbbed. Black spots alternated before his eyes with bobbing golden balls. A thin humming whined in his ears. The humming snapped.

All that he knew when he opened his eyes was that it was dark and he was being lifted up.

A man's voice said, 'He ain't drunk. It's a boy.'

Another said, 'Lay him in the bunk there. He's sick. Tie his dug-out behind.'

Jody looked up. He lay in a bunk on what must be the mailboat. A lamp flickered on the wall. A man leaned over him.

'What's the matter, young un? We near about run you down in the dark.'

He tried to answer but his lips were swollen.

A voice called from above, 'Try him on somethin' to eat.'

'You hungry, boy?'

He nodded. The boat was now in motion. The man in the cabin clattered at the galley-stove. Jody saw a thick cup thrust in front of him. He lifted his head and clutched at it. The cup held cold soup, thick and greasy. For a mouthful or two it had no taste at all. Then the saliva ran in his mouth and his whole being reached out for it, and he bolted it so ravenously that he choked on bits of meat and potato.

The man said curiously, 'How long since you et?'

'I don't know.'

'Hey, Cap, the young un don't even know when he et last.'

'Give him plenty but feed him slow. Don't give him too much or he'll puke in my bunk.'

The cup came back again, and biscuits with it. He tried to control himself, but he trembled when the man waited too long before feedings. The third cupful tasted infinitely better than the first, then further food was refused him.

The man said, 'Where'd you come from?'...

'Baxter's Island.'

'Never heard of no Baxter's Island in this river.'

The mate spoke up.

''Tain't a real island, Cap. It's a place off in the scrub. 'Bout fifteen miles up the road from here.'

'Then you want to get off here, boy… You got folks?'

Jody nodded.

'They know where you was goin'?'

He shook his head.

'Runnin' away, eh? Well, if I was a scrawny little big-eyed boy like you, I'd stay home. Nobody but your folks'll bother with a little ol' shirt-tail boy like you. Swing him down to the dock, Joe.'

Brawny arms lifted him down.

'Turn his dug-out a loose. Catch it, boy. Let's go.'

The whistle blew. The side-wheels churned. The mail-boat chugged up-stream. The wake boiled after her… Jody crouched on his heels, holding the bow of the dug-out. There was no place left to go, but Baxter's Island.

He dropped into the canoe and took up his paddle. He paddled across to the west shore. He tethered the dug-out to a stake. He looked back across the river... His throat tightened. The world had discarded him. He turned and walked slowly up the road. He was weak, and conscious again of hunger, but the night's food had renewed him. The nausea was gone, and the pain.

He walked west without plan. There was no other direction in which to go. Baxter's Island drew him like a magnet. There was no reality but the clearing. He trudged on. He wondered if he dared go home. Probably they would not want him. He had caused them a great deal of trouble. Perhaps if he walked into the kitchen, his mother would drive him out as she had driven Flag. He was no good to anybody. He had prowled and played and eaten recklessly. They had put up with his impudence and his appetite. And Flag had destroyed the better part of the year's living. Almost certainly, they would feel they were better off without him, and he would not be welcome.

He loitered along the road. The sun was strong. The winter was over. He thought hazily that it must now be April. Spring had taken over the scrub, and the birds were mating and singing in the bushes. Only he, in all the world, was homeless... His head began to ache. He told himself that he did not mean to go home. He would only go to the spring, and go down between the cool dark banks, and lie a little while in the running water... He turned down the trail to Silver Glen. The steep bank dropped to the ribbon of creek that ran south of the great spring itself, and had a kindred source. He ached in all his bones. He was so thirsty that his tongue seemed glued to the roof of his mouth. He stumbled down the bank and fell flat beside the cool shallow water and drank. The water bubbled over his lips and nose. He drank until his belly was swollen. He felt sickened and rolled over on his back and closed his eyes. The nausea passed and he was drowsy. He lay in a stupor of weariness. He hung suspended in a timeless space. He could go neither forward nor back. Something was ended. Nothing was begun.

In the late afternoon, he roused. He sat up... There was no comfort anywhere.

There was Penny. A wave of home-sickness washed over him so that it was suddenly intolerable not to see him. The sound of his father's voice was a necessity. He longed for the sight of his stooped shoulders as he had never, in the sharpest of his hunger, longed for food. He clambered to his feet and up the bank and began to run down the road and the clearing, crying as he ran. His father might not be there. He might be dead. With the crops ruined, and his son gone, he might have packed up in despair and moved away and he would never find him.

He sobbed, 'Pa – Wait for me.'

The sun was setting. He was in a panic that he would not reach the clearing before dark. He exhausted himself, and was obliged to slow down to a walk. His flesh quivered. His heart pounded. He had to stop entirely and rest. Darkness overtook him half a mile from home. Even in the dusk, landmarks were familiar. The tall pines of the clearing were recognizable, blacker than the creeping night. He came to the slat fence. He felt his way along it. He opened the gate and went into the yard. He passed around the side of the kitchen stoop and stepped up on it. He crept to the window on bare silent feet and peered in.

A fire burned low on the hearth. Penny sat hunched beside it, wrapped in quilts. One hand covered his eyes. Jody went to the door and unlatched it and stepped inside. Penny lifted his head.

'Ory?'

'It's me.'

He thought his father had not heard him.

'It's Jody.'

Penny turned his head and looked at him wonderingly, as though the gaunt ragged boy with sweat and tear-streaks down the grime, with hollow eyes under matted hair, were some stranger to whom he expected that he state his business.

He said, 'Jody.'

Jody dropped his eyes.

'Come close.'

He went to his father and stood beside him. Penny reached out for his hand and took it and turned it over and rubbed it slowly between his own. Jody felt drops on his hand like a warm rain.

'Boy – I near about give you out.'

Penny felt along his arm. He looked up at him.

'You all right?'

He nodded.

'You all right – You ain't dead nor gone. You all right.' A light filled his face. 'Glory be.'

It was unbelievable, Jody thought. He was wanted.

He said, 'I had to come home.'

'Why, sure you did.'

'I ain't meant what I said. Hatin' you...'

The light broke into the familiar smile.

'Why, sure you ain't. "When I was a child, I spake as a child."'

Penny stirred in his chair.

'They's rations in the safe. In the kettle there. You hungry?'

'I ain't et but once. Last night.'

'Not but once? Then now you know. Ol' Starvation...' His eyes shone in the firelight as Jody had pictured them. 'Ol' Starvation – he's got a face meaner'n ol' bear Slewfoot, ain't he?'

'It's fearful.'

'There's biscuits there. Open the honey. There's due to be milk in the gourd.'

Jody fumbled among the dishes. He ate standing, wolfing down the food. He dipped into a dish of cooked cow-peas with his fingers, scooping them into his mouth. Penny stared at him.

He said, 'I'm sorry you had to learn it that-a-way.'

'Where's Ma?'

'She's drove the wagon to the Forresters to trade for seed-corn. She figgered she'd try to plant a part of a crop again. She carried the chickens, to trade. It hurted her pride turrible, but she was obliged to go.'

Jody closed the door of the cabinet.

He said, 'I should have washed. I'm awful dirty.'

'There's warm water on the hearth.'

Jody poured water in the basin and scrubbed his face and arms and hands. The water was too dark even for his feet. He threw it out of the door and poured more, and sat on the floor and washed his feet.

Penny said, 'I'd be proud to know where you been.'

'I been on the river. I aimed to go to Boston.'

'I see.'

He looked small and shrunken inside the quilts.

Jody said, 'How you makin' it, Pa? You better?'

Penny looked a long time into the embers on the hearth.

He said, 'You just as good to know the truth. I ain't scarcely worth shootin'.'

Jody said, 'When I get the work done, you got to leave me go fetch ol' Doc to you.'

Penny studied him.

He said, 'You've done come back different. You've takened a punishment. You ain't a yearlin' no longer. Jody...'

'Yes, sir.'

'I'm going to talk to you, man to man. You figgered I went back on you. Now there's a thing ever' man has got to know. Mebbe you know it already. 'Twa'n't only me. 'Twa'n't only your yearlin' deer havin' to be destroyed. Boy, life goes back on you.'

Jody looked at his father. He nodded.

Penny said, 'You've seed how things goes in the world o' men. You've knowed men to be low-down and mean. You've seed ol' Death at his tricks. You've messed around with ol' Starvation. Ever' man wants life to be a fine thing, and a easy. 'Tis fine, boy, powerful fine, but 'tain't easy. Life knocks a man down and he gets up and it knocks him down again. I've been uneasy all my life.'

His hands worked at the folds of the quilt.

'I've wanted life to be easy for you. Easier'n 'twas for me. A man's heart aches, seein' his young uns face the world. Knowin' they got to get their guts tore out, the way he was tore. I wanted to spare you, long as I could. I wanted you to frolic with your yearlin'. I knowed the lonesomeness he eased for you. But ever' man's lonesome. What's he to do then? What's he to do when he gets knocked down? Why, take it for his share and go on.'

Jody said, 'I'm 'shamed I runned off.'

Penny sat upright.

He said, 'You're near enough growed to do your choosin'. Could be you'd crave to go to sea, like Oliver. There's men seems made for the land, and men seems made for the sea. But I'd be proud did you choose to live here and farm the clearin'. I'd be proud to see the day when you got a well dug, so's no woman here'd be obliged to do her washin' on a seepage hillside. You willin'?'

'I'm willin'.'

'Shake hands.'

Misfits

NAN HUNT

*A Yowie, so the Australian dictionary says, is 'an ape-like man,
two to two-and-a-half metres tall, believed by some to roam in
certain parts of Australia, especially in southern New South
Wales': a misfit in today's world. Greg is a misfit too –
on the run from the Home where no one trusts him.
Greg and the Yowie meet as a bushfire passes. The encounter
is certainly good for the Yowie. And the trust of this shy creature
is good for Greg too – though it costs him dear.*

It was a Yowie. She was very young, and she was crying. Greg
couldn't believe his eyes. He had been so sure that in all the
blackened forest he was the only creature still alive. The hole in
the rocks had been full of wet moss when he crawled into it and
as the fire swept over him he had dug with his hands to try to hide,
as echidnas do, in a crypt of earth. When his lungs protested at the
smoke-laden air, he had turned face down and breathed through
the damp Musci until it too succumbed to dehydration. It was then
Greg knew how an emerging cicada felt and knew that when the
skin along his back split open he would die. He fought the panic
that screamed at him to run. Clutching handfuls of drying moss
and with clenched teeth, he stayed where he was.

And he was alive!

The fire had left its scattered candle-ends of fuel and rushed on
to feast at a fresh table. Greg shuddered at the sounds of greedy

feeding gradually receding. He uncurled from his shelter and lifted his head.

And there she was. A Yowie. He watched her hobbling across the still-smoking ground, holding out her blistered hands, and saw the burnt patches on her hide where the brown silky hair was singed.

Before the fire, he would have thrown stones at her because she was alien, or chased her with wild shouts, but the fire made everything different. He was years older than the Greg who had run away from the institution where nobody trusted him and everyone treated him as Bad News. He hadn't counted on a bushfire when he planned his escape. He would have to make a new plan. No matter what, though, he wasn't going back. He'd rather die.

The Yowie sat down and tried to bite the spike out of her foot. She tried to move it with her nails, but her burnt hands were too tender. She made little moaning noises of frustration and pain. Greg felt stirrings of pity. They had a bond, he and this young creature who was neither ape nor human. They had survived the fire. He came out from under the rock and squatted in front of her. She blinked and made a defensive escape movement, but the spike hampered her. They looked at each other, human and humanoid, without moving, hardly breathing. Then she held up her foot. The boy took it in his hands, feeling the tough sole, the young bones beneath the skin. She made no sound as the splinter came out under his coaxing fingers, but when blood flowed, she licked the wound like a dog, holding her foot between her wrists.

Greg looked at the valley. It was naked, black mourning ribbons hanging from once-green trees. The rocks ached with heat. Fire still raged in tree stumps and underground roots. The forest that had sheltered the Yowie was a Nothing Place. He couldn't just leave her, in spite of the instinct that told him to look after himself. There would be no food or shelter where the fire had raged. All the roads ran along the ridges and the fire was heading uphill, blazing a trail. He got to his feet, pointed, and moved away. The Yowie remained sitting on the ground, sucking her foot and watching him with anxious eyes.

'Where's your mother?' Greg asked, exasperated. 'What happened to the rest of you?'

The Yowie stared, rocking backwards and forwards. Greg went back to her, turned his back and squatted down. She moved quickly, adjusting her body to his. She rode piggyback, leaning against him, silent and trusting.

His whole concentration bent on survival, the boy had no time to think of what would happen when they reached a road. He threaded his way between blackened sticks – the charcoal etching lines and smudges on skin and clothing, desperately seeking immortality – careful where he put his feet, trying to remember bush skills from endless boring television programmes. The Yowie was asleep. He had felt the difference in weight from buoyancy to dependency, and her trust sustained and cheered him. Time had disappeared into smoke, the ache of stretched muscles becoming part of the burden, the only thing of any importance the next step... the next step... the next step.

There was a great shout from the firefighters when Greg and his burden crunched over the crumbling bracken and twigs through the twilight of smoke. The men were bearded and streaked with stubble and ash, stubborn but weary with the long fight, but it seemed to them an encouraging thing that two live beings should come out of the dead bushland. Greg did not know that he and the Yowie were so blackened that the difference in them was hardly visible. 'Her hands are burnt,' he said simply.

'First aid box on the seat of the first fire truck,' one man said. 'Can you cope?'

'Sure,' said Greg. 'Thanks.' He moved towards the truck, hearing the shout behind him as another switch in the wind took the fire in a different direction and the men responded automatically to the new danger. He did what he could for the Yowie and wrapped her in an old shirt.

A police car pulled up, the driver staring at Greg, who stared back.

'Where did they spring from?' the policeman asked one of the firemen.

'Just walked out of the bush. Will you take charge of them?'

'Going further up, but I'll fix something.' He got out and flagged down an empty stock transport and talked to the driver. The truckie sounded disgruntled and reluctant, but eventually got out and went to the back of the truck to open the gate. The cop walked back to Greg.

'You can't stay here, son. The truck will take you to Richmond and you'll be taken care of there. You live around here? Why weren't you evacuated with the others? What happened to your clothes? Parents?'

'Dead,' Greg said flatly, and life was so empty that his eyes filled with tears.

'Sorry. Look, we'll sort that out later. Hop up in the truck.'

Greg was too tired not to do what he was told. The truck stank of sheep. The boards that made the flooring of the top deck were down and secured to the sides, so there was plenty of space. Greg sat with his back to the cabin, the Yowie beside him. The driver shut the tailgate and went back to his cab. The jerk as the vehicle moved hardly registered on the boy.

The policeman used his radio to report the finding of the runaway.

'You should have hung onto him, he'll get away again.'

'He's safe. Got him locked up in a sheep truck, a red International. See that someone meets him at Richmond, OK?'

In the cabin of the truck the three men stared ahead through the smoke. The old bushman who had hitched a lift spoke slowly. 'Looked like a young Yowie. Must've been smoked out of the valleys further south. They're terribly shy.'

'Go on. Pull the other leg! Cousins to the bunyip, eh?'

'Never seen a bunyip. Saw a couple of Yowies out the back of Porters oh, forty years ago now. Just on dusk. Came within a few yards of the camp. One minute there, the next just melted into the bush. Hunted round but couldn't find them. Found their tracks next morning. It wasn't a dream. Harmless creatures, best left alone.'

'Some of those anthro-something or others would be glad to get their hands on it. Maybe you'd better hang onto it, Bert, might make a buck,' said the other man.

The driver thought it over, excitement rising in him. A better way to make money than carting stock, anyway. He began to plan.

They had to pull up at another patch of fire where tankers blocked the road. The driver got out and went to the back of the vehicle.

'Hey, boy, you wanna leak?'

Greg hadn't thought about it until the man said the words, but it became suddenly urgent. He hopped down from the truck, unzipping his fly.

'Not here! There could be ladies in the car behind, there. Nick across into the bush, and hurry.'

Greg obeyed, and soon heard the driver shouting for him. He ran back and swung up into the truck, and the gate clanged shut behind him. The truck jerked forward.

The Yowie had gone.

To his surprise, Greg was sorry about the Yowie. She had trusted him and it had made him feel good inside. He wondered what she would do. The fire was stopped at the edge of the road but the other side of the highway would go with the first spark. At the next stop he shouted until the driver leaned out.

'You got anything to drink?' The driver passed round a mug of water.

'Thanks,' said the boy, draining it. 'Where's me sister?'

'She's asleep in the dog box. Don't worry about her. She'll be right. I'll take care of her.'

Greg tried to think. Best to go to the town and make a break. With the fires raging, the bush was too populated and he was too exposed. He had forced himself to outstare the cop, hoping he would not be recognized. In a town he could disappear. He went over the steps that could give him a lucky break. Planning the use of each possibility in detail so that when it happened – if it happened – he could act quickly.

The traffic moved half a mile and stopped. In the silence a new sound exploded. The Yowie was keening with fear and rattling on the door of the dog box under the floor of the truck. Greg tried to make reassuring noises to let her know he was there. Anger choked him, as he walked across to where he could shout at the driver. The shout died. He could hear the man boasting of the fortune he would make taking the Yowie round the country shows. Greg gripped the steel of the sides, fighting nausea, feeling the first trickle of sick coming up into his throat, the run of bile before he would have to throw up.

It had been fun in the bush until the fire overtook him. He'd felt clean and free and good. He'd liked himself, because there was no one to put him down. He wanted to keep that feeling. He'd promised himself he'd never go back to the prison of the Home. What would a Yowie do in captivity? All those eyes staring. He knew what sideshows were like. It would be worse than the Home. The Yowie would sicken and go through an agony of deaths before physical death released her.

Nausea retreated and Greg found his voice.

'It's not fair!' he shouted at no one and at everyone. The truck drowned his voice as it jerked forward. 'She's never done you any harm!'

His planning took a new line. Any freedom had to be a freedom for himself and the Yowie. It would be difficult – in a town he could disappear, but with the Yowie he would be too visible.

The truck shuddered into low gear for the steep descent. The valley fell away abruptly from the road that wound round a narrow ledge against a rock wall. This bush was untouched by fire, rivers and waterfalls of tree ferns running down gullies in lighter green than the surrounding eucalypts. Greg tensed. He had to be ready. Getting himself out was the first problem. He worked the pin loose on the tailgate and swung it back, holding it steady. It was a long way to the ground and he didn't dare risk a broken leg or twisted ankle. Then a siren screamed in the distance and the traffic halted to let a fire tender through.

Now?

Greg jumped, the gate crashing back on the steel rails. There was a bend in the highway and smoke made visibility poor. He heard the driver swear, glimpsed him running up the road. From his crouching position beside the truck, Greg opened the dog box and held out his arms. It only took a moment to swing the Yowie over the safety rail.

The traffic began to move again, cautiously. A horn blew behind the truck. The driver returned, had a quick look at the huddle of blankets in the dog box, and climbed back into the cab.

'Blinking kids!' he panted. 'The boy's gone. Couldn't catch him. Just as well I put that Yowie in the dog box or he might have taken it too. Ungrateful young beggar.'

At Richmond the police flagged the red International to a halt.

'You got some freight for us?' the cop said, leaning in the driver's window.

'Oh, the kids? They hopped it up the road a bit. Just went into smoke.' The driver cackled nervously at his own wit.

'What's this, then?' a constable asked, walking round the truck.

'Just an old blanket I keep for me dorg.'

Before he could stop himself, Greg sneezed. When they hauled him out, cramped and filthy, he was silent but exultant. He could still see the Yowie rolling down the hillside after he'd put her down on the other side of the safety fence, into the safety of the valley. As much as he'd ever wanted anything, he'd wanted to go with her.

She had not paused or looked back, but vanished into the freedom of the unburnt forest.

6
Rainbow
Through the Rain

As we begin to learn about life, sadly, we all learn about death too. Often it comes first through the loss of an animal friend or pet. So we can share Kizzy's grief when her beloved horse Joe dies.

When death comes, we want to ask what happens next. Is there a heaven? And what might it be like? The extracts from the Narnia books, *Voyage of the Dawn Treader* and *The Last Battle*, take us to the end of the world and beyond.

The piece from *Beyond the Rainbow* is about the death of a friend. The other stories focus on death within the family – except for the very last, in which young Mary comes to terms with Miz Williams' death, one snowy Christmas time.

But if all this sounds sad and gloomy, you are in for a surprise. For these are stories full of love and a very special hope.

'The Caterpillar'

CHRISTINA ROSSETTI

Brown and furry
Caterpillar in a hurry,
Take your walk
To the shady leaf, or stalk,
    Or what not,
Which may be the chosen spot.
    No toad spy you,
Hovering bird of prey pass by you;
Spin and die,
To live again as butterfly.

Kizzy's Plan

From *The Diddakoi*

RUMER GODDEN

*Half-gypsy, Kizzy Lovell lives with her Gran in the wagon in
Admiral Twiss's orchard. The old horse Joe is her best friend.
Then Gran dies, the wagon is burned, and Kizzy goes to live with
Miss Brooke. The Admiral, who lives at Amberhurst House with
Peters and Nat to help him, makes a home for Joe in
his meadow. But school is misery. Kizzy is a misfit. The children
taunt and bully her, hurting her badly. So, as soon as she
is well again, Kizzy makes a plan...*

'I'm not coming back to school,' Kizzy would have told Clem if she
told anyone, but she knew how to keep secrets which is by not
telling anyone at all...

'Soon as I'm up,' [she said to herself] 'I'll get Joe and Joe and me
will go away.' She could not say 'run' away because Joe could only
plod. She began gathering scraps of food in a carrier bag Miss Brooke
said she could have. She had kept every penny of the pocket money
Miss Brooke gave her, 'to buy sweets or any little thing you want,'
but Kizzy bought nothing. 'Don't you like sweets?' Kizzy did like the
few that had come her way, but buying them meant going to the
village shop, 'where they ask questions'.

There was one question she herself asked Miss Brooke as soon as
her head was better. 'Can I go to the House on Saturday?'

'I expect so – if you keep quiet.'

'I'm always quiet with Joe.'

'Doctor Harwell thinks you can go back to school on Monday.'

To Miss Brooke's surprise Kizzy only nodded, as if it did not matter, yet she must mind, thought Miss Brooke. It must be an ordeal. She looked across at Kizzy's face which seemed – contented, thought Miss Brooke. How could she be contented, this unfathomable child? But Kizzy was far away, far over the Downs on Joe's back. They would walk along at night – when everyone's in bed and no one will see us – and camp in woods and orchards, build a fire; she would collect sticks and pick up old dung for fuel. Why, Joe himself could supply a fire. An old saucepan, thought Kizzy – there was an old one Miss Brooke used for the chickens; she had two so could spare one. I must take matches, planned Kizzy – she had not a flint like Gran's. A blanket, some sacks, a net of hay for Joe – Nat would not miss one – her bag of scraps. I can pick onions and potatoes from people's gardens – she was small enough to get through hedges – p'raps find an egg. Then, when they were far enough away, she would build a house of branches, or find a hollow tree – 'sgood I *am* so small – only first she must be well enough at the weekend to go to Amberhurst House.

She would spend Saturday there, get full of food, stuff myself, thought Kizzy, so it will last, collect and hide all her things. Go again on Sunday and, after lunch, when the Admiral and Peters dozed and Nat went to the Lodge to read the Sunday papers... then put the things on Joe, an' we'll just go, thought Kizzy. She suddenly gave Miss Brooke a beaming smile.

'Kizzy,' said Miss Brooke at breakfast. 'Admiral Twiss telephoned last night.'

Kizzy stopped, a piece of toast halfway to her mouth. 'He didn't say I couldn't come? But I must,' she said. 'I have to see Joe.'

Miss Brooke made a queer sound like a hiccough and put down her cup. It seemed as if she were going to say something but changed her mind. 'As soon as you're ready, we'll go.' Kizzy was too busy with her own plans, hiding the blanket, filling her pockets with matches, bringing out the loaded carrier-bag, 'scraps for Joe,' she said, which was partly true – there were one or two apples. Miss Brooke made another of her queer noises and, queerly too, did not put Kizzy down at the gates but drove her up to the House, which did not suit Kizzy's plans. 'Tell Admiral Twiss I will come if he wants me,' said Miss Brooke as she let Kizzy out.

Why should the Admiral want her? He, Peters, Nat, Kizzy did not
want anybody on Saturdays and Sundays; and why did Miss Brooke
look grave – and as if she were sorry? Why should she be sorry? For
a moment a cold little puzzlement touched Kizzy, then she shook it
off; if Miss Brooke were in trouble she was sorry but this was
Saturday – and tomorrow… With the blanket on her shoulder, the
carrier-bag bumping against her legs, Kizzy set off for the stables,
and stopped.

Usually she went straight to the stables and meadow. Later on she
and Nat would go to the House and have cocoa in the kitchen with
Peters. Usually Kizzy did not see the Admiral till lunch time and not
always then – often he stayed in his workshop – but this morning he
was in the stable yard, waiting. *Waiting for me…* and Kizzy's heart
seemed to skip a beat. He did not call out to her, but waited and, as
she came up to him, she saw the look on his face was the same as
Miss Brooke's, grave and sorry – sorry to sadness.

Then Kizzy was frightened, more frightened than when Mr Blount
had come and taken her to school, or when Peters fetched her and
Gran was dead, when the wagon was burned and the Does talked
about her and Joe, when she dared take Joe to the Admiral, or when
she was sent to Miss Brooke and when the girls caught her on her
way from school. As she looked up at the Admiral, her eyes were
stretched wide with fear. 'Kiz,' said the Admiral. 'It's Joe.'

'Joe?' It came out as a gasp.

Admiral Twiss never dodged, but said things plainly. 'Joe died last
night, Kiz. He is dead.'

Dead. The gravel seemed to tilt under Kizzy's feet, the stable cupola
to run up into the sky. She dropped the blanket and bag. Admiral Twiss
steadied her and brought her to the old mounting block.

'Nat went to give him his hay at seven o'clock and found Joe with
his head hanging, dozing. Nat gave him a pat and held out some
sugar, but Joe did not look at it, then he went down on his knees.
Nat ran and got some beer.'

'Joe – liked – beer.' The words seemed to be torn from Kizzy.

'But, again, he wouldn't look. Then Nat said he rolled over on the
grass and was dead.'

'Was – he – ill?'

'No,' said the Admiral, 'but he was old – and tired. Nat says his
teeth were all worn down which was why we couldn't fatten him,

but Joe died in his own time, Kiz; not many horses do that, and in his meadow on his own grass where he had lived.'

'Show me him,' said Kizzy.

'Show a child a sight like *that*!' Mrs Cuthbert was indignant when she heard. 'Trust a man to do such a thing.'

'You can trust the Admiral,' said Miss Brooke. 'He knows Kizzy wouldn't have believed him else.'

'But to let her see such a sight!'

Joe had not been a sight. When Admiral Twiss took Kizzy to see him, he was lying peacefully in the grass. Kizzy held the Admiral's hand.

Nat came out, took Kizzy's other hand and together the three of them stood looking at the big still body, at Joe's head with the white blaze on his nose, his eyelashes – Nat had closed his eyes – his great legs and mighty hooves that were split and grey – it was a long while since he had worn shoes. His bay coat still shone, Nat had given it many a rubbing; Joe seemed as if he were asleep, but deep deep sleep.

Kizzy went nearer. 'Careful,' said Nat. 'He's getting stiff.'

'Will – will the knacker, the hounds, get him now?'

'They can't,' said Admiral Twiss.

'Can't?' Kizzy's head came up.

'Joe's safe,' said the Admiral, 'because this isn't Joe. He's not here.'

Kizzy broke from him and put her hand to Joe's nose, not touching him. 'He doesn't huff,' she said.

'Of course not. He isn't there.'

Kizzy looked at the Admiral as if weighing what he said and put down her hand again to Joe. 'The warm is gone.'

'Yes.' Admiral Twiss came to her and gently touched Joe's body. 'This is just his old clothes, Kiz. He doesn't need them any more.'

'Where *is* he?'

Mrs Blount might have said, 'In the horses' heaven,' but Admiral Twiss was plainer. 'We don't know. Nobody knows, but I believe we shall find out.'

'When we're dead?'

'Perhaps. It seems to make sense, doesn't it?' said the Admiral. 'If Joe isn't here, he must be somewhere else. Come. We'll leave his body to Nat.'

'Heaven'

LANGSTON HUGHES

Heaven is
The place where
Happiness is
Everywhere.
Animals
And birds sing –
As does
Everything.
To each stone,
'How-do-you-do?'
'Well! And you?'

Aslan's Country

From *The Voyage of the Dawn Treader*
C.S. LEWIS

Edmund and Lucy, two of the four children who first entered
Narnia through the back of the wardrobe in The Lion, the
Witch and the Wardrobe, *have come to Narnia again, with*
their cousin Eustace. They have joined King Caspian, voyaging in
search of his lost friends. With them is Reepicheep, the brave
warrior mouse, whose dream is to go to the End of the World
and beyond to Aslan's Country…

Suddenly there came a breeze from the east, tossing the top of the
wave into foamy shapes and ruffling the smooth water all round
them. It lasted only a second or so but what it brought them in that
second none of those three children will ever forget. It brought both
a smell and a sound, a musical sound. Edmund and Eustace would
never talk about it afterwards. Lucy could only say, 'It would break
your heart.' 'Why,' said I, 'was it so sad?' 'Sad!! No,' said Lucy.

No one in that boat doubted that they were seeing beyond the
End of the World into Aslan's country.

At that moment, with a crunch, the boat ran aground. The water
was too shallow now even for it. 'This,' said Reepicheep, 'is where I
go on alone.'

They did not even try to stop him, for everything now felt as if it
had been fated or had happened before. They helped him to lower
his little coracle. Then he took off his sword ('I shall need it no

more,' he said) and flung it far away across the lilied sea. Where it fell it stood upright with the hilt above the surface. Then he bade them good-bye, trying to be sad for their sakes; but he was quivering with happiness. Lucy, for the first and last time, did what she had always wanted to do, taking him in her arms and caressing him. Then hastily he got into his coracle and took his paddle, and the current caught it and away he went, very black against the lilies. But no lilies grew on the wave; it was a smooth green slope. The coracle went more and more quickly, and beautifully it rushed up the wave's side. For one split second they saw its shape and Reepicheep's on the very top. Then it vanished, and since that moment no one can truly claim to have seen Reepicheep the Mouse. But my belief is that he came safe to Aslan's country and is alive there to this day.

As the sun rose the sight of those mountains outside the world faded away. The wave remained but there was only blue sky behind it.

The children got out of the boat and waded – not towards the wave but southward with the wall of water on their left. They could not have told you why they did this; it was their fate. And though they had felt – and been – very grown up on the *Dawn Treader*, they now felt just the opposite and held hands as they waded through the lilies. They never felt tired. The water was warm and all the time it got shallower. At last they were on dry sand, and then on grass – a huge plain of very fine short grass, almost level with the Silver Sea and spreading in every direction without so much as a molehill.

And of course, as it always does in a perfectly flat place without trees, it looked as if the sky came down to meet the grass in front of them. But as they went on they got the strangest impression that here at last the sky did really come down and join the earth – a blue wall, very bright, but real and solid: more like glass than anything else. And soon they were quite sure of it. It was very near now.

But between them and the foot of the sky there was something so white on the green grass that even with their eagles' eyes they could hardly look at it. They came on and saw that it was a Lamb.

'Come and have breakfast,' said the Lamb in its sweet milky voice.

Then they noticed for the first time that there was a fire lit on the grass and fish roasting on it. They sat down and ate the fish, hungry now for the first time for many days. And it was the most delicious food they had ever tasted.

'Please, Lamb,' said Lucy, 'is this the way to Aslan's country?'

'Not for you,' said the Lamb. 'For you the door into Aslan's country is from your own world.'

'What!' said Edmund. 'Is there a way into Aslan's country from our world too?'

'There is a way into my country from all the worlds,' said the Lamb; but as he spoke his snowy white flushed into tawny gold and his size changed and he was Aslan himself, towering above them and scattering light from his mane.

'Oh, Aslan,' said Lucy. 'Will you tell us how to get into your country from our world?'

'I shall be telling you all the time,' said Aslan. 'But I will not tell you how long or short the way will be; only that it lies across a river. But do not fear that, for I am the great Bridge Builder. And now come; I will open the door in the sky and send you to your own land.'

'Please, Aslan,' said Lucy. 'Before we go, will you tell us when we can come back to Narnia again? Please. And oh, do, do, do make it soon.'

'Dearest,' said Aslan very gently, 'you and your brother will never come back to Narnia.'

'Oh, *Aslan*!!' said Edmund and Lucy both together in despairing voices.

'You are too old, children,' said Aslan, 'and you must begin to come close to your own world now.'

'It isn't Narnia, you know,' sobbed Lucy. 'It's *you*. We shan't meet *you* there. And how can we live, never meeting you?'

'But you shall meet me, dear one,' said Aslan.

'Are – are you there too, Sir?' said Edmund.

'I am,' said Aslan. 'But there I have another name. You must learn to know me by that name. This was the very reason why you were brought to Narnia, that by knowing me here for a little, you may know me better there.'

'And is Eustace never to come back here either?' said Lucy.

'Child,' said Aslan, 'do you really need to know that? Come, I am opening the door in the sky.' Then all in one moment there was a rending of the blue wall (like a curtain being torn) and a terrible white light from beyond the sky, and the feel of Aslan's mane and a Lion's kiss on their foreheads and then – the back bedroom in Aunt Alberta's home in Cambridge.

'Going to Heaven'

EMILY DICKINSON

Going to Heaven!
I don't know when –
Pray do not ask me how!
Indeed, I'm too astonished
To think of answering you!
Going to Heaven!
How dim it sounds!
And yet it will be done
As sure as flocks go home at night
Unto the Shepherd's arm!

Perhaps you're going too!
Who knows?
If you should get there first
Save just a little space for me
Close to the two I lost –
The smallest 'Robe' will fit me
And just a bit of 'Crown' –
For you know we do not mind our dress
When we are going home –

Farewell to Shadowlands

From *The Last Battle*

C.S. LEWIS

The Last Battle *is the final Narnia story. In this extract, the
great battle between King Tirian (helped by Jill and Eustace)
and the forces of evil is over. Aslan has called his people through
the Stable Door and night has fallen for ever on Narnia. The
friends from earlier stories have come to Aslan's country: Digory
and Polly and Frank from* The Magician's Nephew, *Edmund,
Peter, Lucy and Tumnus the Faun from* The Lion, The Witch
and the Wardrobe – *and, of course, Reepicheep, the warrior
mouse from* The Voyage of the Dawn Treader.

They were out of Narnia now and up into the Western Wild which
neither Tirian nor Peter nor even the Eagle had ever seen before.
But the Lord Digory and the Lady Polly had. 'Do you remember? Do
you remember?' they said – and said it in steady voices too, without
panting, though the whole party was now running faster than an
arrow flies.

'What, Lord?' said Tirian. 'Is it then true, as stories tell, that you
two journeyed here on the very day the world was made?'

'Yes,' said Digory, 'and it seems to me as if it were only yesterday.'

'And on a flying horse?' asked Tirian. 'Is that part true?'

'Certainly,' said Digory. But the Dogs barked, 'Faster, faster!'

So they ran faster and faster till it was more like flying than
running, and even the Eagle overhead was going no faster than they.

And they went through winding valley after winding valley and up the steep sides of hills and, faster than ever, down the other sides, following the river and sometimes crossing it and skimming across mountain-lakes as if they were living speed-boats, till at last at the far end of one long lake which looked as blue as a turquoise, they saw a smooth green hill. Its sides were as steep as the sides of a pyramid and round the very top of it ran a green wall: but above the wall rose the branches of trees whose leaves looked like silver and their fruit like gold.

'Farther up and farther in!' roared the Unicorn, and no one held back. They charged straight at the foot of the hill and then found themselves running up it almost as water from a broken wave runs up a rock out at the point of some bay. Though the slope was nearly as steep as the roof of a house and the grass was smooth as a bowling green, no one slipped. Only when they had reached the very top did they slow up; that was because they found themselves facing great golden gates. And for a moment none of them was bold enough to try if the gates would open. They all felt just as they had felt about the fruit – 'Dare we? Is it right? Can it be meant for *us*?'

But while they were standing thus a great horn, wonderfully loud and sweet, blew from somewhere inside that walled garden and the gates swung open.

Tirian stood holding his breath and wondering who would come out. And what came out was the last thing he had expected: a little, sleek, bright-eyed Talking Mouse with a red feather stuck in a circlet on its head and its left paw resting on a long sword. It bowed, a most beautiful bow, and said in its shrill voice:

'Welcome, in the Lion's name. Come farther up and farther in.'

Then Tirian saw King Peter and King Edmund and Queen Lucy rush forward to kneel down and greet the Mouse and they all cried out 'Reepicheep!' And Tirian breathed fast with the sheer wonder of it, for now he knew that he was looking at one of the great heroes of Narnia, Reepicheep the Mouse who had fought at the great Battle of Beruna and afterwards sailed to the World's end with King Caspian the Seafarer. But before he had had much time to think of this he felt two strong arms thrown about him and felt a bearded kiss on his cheeks and heard a well-remembered voice saying:

'What, lad? Art thicker and taller since I last touched thee?'

It was his own father, the good King Erlian: but not as Tirian had seen him last when they brought him home pale and wounded from his fight with the giant, nor even as Tirian remembered him in his later years when he was a grey-headed warrior. This was his father, young and merry, as he could just remember him from very early days when he himself had been a little boy playing games with his father in the castle garden at Cair Paravel, just before bedtime on summer evenings. The very smell of the bread-and-milk he used to have for supper came back to him...

But by now the Mouse was again urging them to come in. So all of them passed in through the golden gates, into the delicious smell that blew towards them out of that garden and into the cool mixture of sunlight and shadow under the trees, walking on springy turf that was all dotted with white flowers. The very first thing which struck everyone was that the place was far larger than it had seemed from outside. But no one had time to think about that for people were coming up to meet the newcomers from every direction...

About half an hour later – or it might have been half a hundred years later, for time there is not like time here – Lucy stood with her dear friend, her oldest Narnian friend, the Faun Tumnus, looking down over the wall of that garden, and seeing all Narnia spread out below. But when you looked down you found that this hill was much higher than you had thought: it sank down with shining cliffs, thousands of feet below them and trees in that lower world looked no bigger than grains of green salt. Then she turned inward again and stood with her back to the wall and looked at the garden.

'I see,' she said at last, thoughtfully. 'I see now. This garden is like the Stable. It is far bigger inside than it was outside.'

'Of course, Daughter of Eve,' said the Faun. 'The farther up and the farther in you go, the bigger everything gets. The inside is larger than the outside.'

Lucy looked hard at the garden and saw that it was not really a garden at all but a whole world, with its own rivers and woods and sea and mountains. But they were not strange: she knew them all.

'I see,' she said. 'This is still Narnia, and, more real and more beautiful than the Narnia down below, just as *it* was more real and more beautiful than the Narnia outside the Stable door! I see... world within world, Narnia within Narnia...'

'Yes,' said Mr Tumnus, 'like an onion: except that as you go in and in, each circle is larger than the last.'

And Lucy looked this way and that and soon found that a new and beautiful thing had happened to her. Whatever she looked at, however far away it might be, once she had fixed her eyes steadily on it, became quite clear and close as if she were looking through a telescope. She could see the whole southern desert and beyond it the great city of Tashbaan: to eastward she could see Cair Paravel on the edge of the sea and the very window of the room that had once been her own. And far out to sea she could discover the islands, island after island to the end of the world, and, beyond the end, the huge mountain which they had called Aslan's country. But now she saw that it was part of a great chain of mountains which ringed round the whole world. In front of her it seemed to come quite close. Then she looked to her left and saw what she took to be a great bank of brightly-coloured cloud, cut off from them by a gap. But she looked harder and saw that it was not a cloud at all but a real land. And when she had fixed her eyes on one particular spot of it, she at once cried out, 'Peter! Edmund! Come and look! Come quickly.' And they came and looked, for their eyes had also become like hers.

'Why!' exclaimed Peter. 'It's England. And that's the house itself – Professor Kirk's old home in the country where all our adventures began!'

'I thought that house had been destroyed,' said Edmund.

'So it was,' said the Faun. 'But you are now looking at the England within England, the real England just as this is the real Narnia. And in that inner England no good thing is destroyed.'

Suddenly they shifted their eyes to another spot, and then Peter and Edmund and Lucy gasped with amazement and shouted out and began waving: for there they saw their own father and mother, waving back at them across the great, deep valley. It was like when you see people waving at you from the deck of a big ship when you are waiting on the quay to meet them.

'How can we get at them?' said Lucy.

'That's easy,' said Mr Tumnus. 'That country and this country – all the *real* countries – are only spurs jutting out from the great mountains of Aslan. We have only to walk along the ridge, upward and inward, till it joins on. And listen! There is King Frank's horn: we must all go up.'

And soon they found themselves all walking together – and a great, bright procession it was – up towards mountains higher than you could see in this world even if they were there to be seen. But there was no snow on those mountains: there were forests and green slopes and sweet orchards and flashing waterfalls, one above the other, going up for ever. And the land they were walking on grew narrower all the time, with a deep valley on each side; and across that valley the land which was the real England grew nearer and nearer.

The light ahead was growing stronger. Lucy saw that a great series of many-coloured cliffs led up in front of them like a giant's staircase. And then she forgot everything else, because Aslan himself was coming, leaping down from cliff to cliff like a living cataract of power and beauty...

Then Aslan said:

'You do not yet look so happy as I mean you to be.'

Lucy said, 'We're so afraid of being sent away, Aslan. And you have sent us back into our own world so often.'

'No fear of that,' said Aslan. 'Have you not guessed?'

Their hearts leaped and a wild hope rose within them.

'There *was* a real railway accident,' said Aslan softly. 'Your father and mother and all of you are – as you used to call it in the Shadowlands – dead. The term is over: the holidays have begun. The dream is ended: this is the morning.'

And as He spoke He no longer looked to them like a Lion; but the things that began to happen after that were so great and beautiful that I cannot write them. And for us this is the end of all the stories, and we can most truly say that they all lived happily ever after. But for them it was only the beginning of the real story. All their life in this world and all their adventures in Narnia had only been the cover and the title page: now at last they were beginning Chapter One of the Great Story which no one on earth has read: which goes on for ever: in which every chapter is better than the one before.

The Night Ben Died

From *Red Sky in the Morning*

ELIZABETH LAIRD

From the moment baby Ben is born, and she knows he is
handicapped, Anna gives him all her love. But Ben does not live
to grow out of babyhood. And when he dies, Anna has to deal
with her own grief and help her sister Katy too.

I think it was Ben's bedroom door banging shut that roused me,
without really waking me up. I half heard Mum's feet pattering
down the stairs, and the buttons on the telephone clicking as she
pressed the numbers. Then her voice, high and desperately afraid,
came floating into my mind, and merged with a dream of hospitals,
and a memory of Ben's birth.

'Dr Randall?' It's Mrs Peacock here. I'm sorry to call you in the
night, but it's Ben. He's not breathing right, and I can't rouse him.
Please, oh can you... I'm so worried... No, my husband's away at
the moment. I'm on my own. Oh thank you, Dr Randall. Fifteen
minutes, you said?'

The receiver clicked down again, and she ran back upstairs and
into Ben's room. I slipped back again into a deep sleep, as reality
and the dream melted into nothingness.

It was probably the cough mixture Mum had given me that
knocked me out completely that night. I didn't hear the doctor
coming, or the sound of him working over Ben's cot, or Mum's
frantic telephone calls to the hotel up north where Dad was staying,
or her first expressions of grief. I knew nothing till 6 o'clock in the

morning, when she crept into my room, and lay down beside me on my bed, and burst into a storm of tears.

She didn't have to tell me what she was crying for. I had woken with a lead weight pressing down on my heart. I knew for sure that Ben was dead, as if God himself had told me. I couldn't cry. I lay there, rigid and dry-eyed, frozen with shock. I couldn't remember his name. I couldn't remember what he looked like. I wondered who this strange woman was, who had come into my room, and was lying on my bed. One word hammered away in my mind, blocking out everything else:

'No! No! No!'

Breakfast was a disgusting idea. The thought of food revolted me. But it was the next thing to do. You get up, you get dressed, then you have your breakfast. Even when there's a death in the house, that's what you do. If you stop doing that, life stops altogether. I managed to drink a cup of tea, and pretended to have some toast. Katy ate a full bowl of cornflakes and asked for more. I had to keep telling myself that she was only nine.

Mum went to the telephone then, and I heard her speak to Granny, and then she went to her room, and I went to mine. The house was uncannily still and quiet.

'This is what it's going to be like,' I thought. 'We'll miss the sound of him first.'

I opened my door, and went quietly along to Ben's room, and slipped inside. The curtains had been drawn, and there was only a dim light coming into the room.

The nurse had moved the cot. It was in the wrong place, alone, in the middle of the room, where he couldn't see the pigeons who were already pecking on the window sill.

'I'll put it right for you,' I whispered, and I pushed it back into place. Then I looked at him.

He was the same. He was himself, asleep. The bedclothes were unnaturally tidy, that was all. One hand lay outside the coverlet, the little fingers curled up, relaxed. The nurse had brushed his hair, and his curls lay smooth as cream silk against his big, blue-veined head.

'Respiratory failure,' Mum had said, on the phone to Granny. I'd been afraid that he would look anguished, choking for breath, in pain, but he didn't. Just restful, and quiet, and happy.

232

My foot kicked against something soft. It was his fluffy rabbit. I picked it up, and tucked it down beside him.

'There you are,' I said. 'There's rabbit.'

My hand brushed against his face. It was cold, quite cold. I knew then. I couldn't pretend any more that he would wake up in a minute, and put out his arms, asking to be lifted. That was the moment when I believed that he was dead. But I knew, even then, that he was still with me, still near, still loving me. His spirit hadn't quite gone away. It lingered on, like a perfume when its wearer has just left the room.

I knelt down then, on the floor beside the cot, and stroked his hand gently, because I was afraid I might disturb him. I talked to him. I told him things. I told him what had happened when I'd first seen him, and how I'd loved him straight away. I told him that he was the best kind of brother and that I'd never wanted him to be different. I told him I'd go on loving him for ever, as long as I lived. I told him he'd be all right.

And then I kissed him, to say goodbye, and the frozen lump in my chest started to melt, and I ran out of his room, and flung myself down on my bed. That's where Dad came to me, later. And when I saw him I found at last that I could cry, and I couldn't stop, and we cried together until there were no tears left...

Two days before the funeral, I found Katy sitting in her wardrobe, where she often goes if she's upset, and she looked so still and woebegone that I felt sorry for her.

'What's the matter with you?' I said.

She said nothing, but held up a little china bambi that Granny had given her when she was three. It was her dearest possession. She always said that if there was a fire and she only had time to grab one thing, she'd go for her bambi.

'What's happening to it?' I said. 'Have you broken it or something?'

She shook her head, so I lay down on the floor and waited. Katy always tells you things in the end. You just have to give her time. She's the sort who can never keep anything secret. Not like me. I often imagine I'm being tortured, and that I'm not telling the names of my fellow revolutionaries. I know I'd be able to keep my trap shut. It's one of my greatest talents.

I got it out of Katy quite quickly. She was feeling awful, because she'd never let Ben touch bambi and he'd often wanted to. He used to point to it, and grizzle, and she'd always snatched it out of reach and run off. Sometimes she'd even teased him with it to make him cry. But now she was so sorry, and she felt so bad about it, and she wanted to give bambi to Ben to take with him. I was shocked at that. It didn't seem decent to me. But then Katy started to cry, and once she started she couldn't stop, and then Dad came in, and asked what the fuss was all about. So I explained it, and he thought for a bit, and then to my surprise, he took Katy's part. He said it was a very nice idea, and he would take her to the undertakers that afternoon, and she could see Ben in the chapel there.

Dad has never been known to refuse Katy anything, at least, not that I can think of. It's the worst thing about him. I don't know why I said I wanted to go too. I suppose it was because I was restless, and thinking about Ben all the time, and I felt drawn to him, as if there was a piece of elastic pulling me.

I hadn't realized that the coffin would be so small, lying there on a big table, in the chapel of rest. It was white, with silver handles, and when Mr Roberts, the undertaker, opened it, and put back the lid, I saw that it was lined with white satin. I felt good about that. It was like a little cot, cosy and comfortable. I looked down at Ben, expecting him to be the same as when I'd seen him last, but he wasn't. He looked kind of pinched, and waxen. But the real change was that now I could see he had gone. His spirit was no longer there, hovering like an invisible sweetness in the air. It had flown away. It was only his shell left in the box, as meaningless now as the chrysalis which the butterfly sloughs off. I was grateful to Katy. I was glad I'd seen him again. I put my arm around her as we looked down at him together. She snuggled into me. I'd hardly ever cuddled her, but I enjoyed it. I felt a rush of affection for her. She looked up at me.

'I'm the youngest now, aren't I, Anna?' she said. I realized then that it had been tough for Katy too. Ben had robbed her of her Mum for two years of her childhood. He'd taken me away too. I'd had no time for her while he had been alive. I gave her shoulders a squeeze.

'Go on then,' I said. 'Where's bambi?'

She pulled it out from under her sweatshirt, gave it a last kiss, stroked its glazed back, and put it down beside Ben.

'Do you think he knows?' she said.

'Yes, of course he does,' I said, and the extraordinary thing was, I felt absolutely sure about it. 'He knows, and he's really pleased, and it was a very nice thing to do.'

The day of the funeral was bright and sunny. It was one of those days in early winter when everything is golden and glowing; and scarlet berries, huge spiders' webs, curled yellow leaves and bulbous brown seed heads make sort of still life pictures everywhere you look. It seemed all wrong to me. I'd imagined the funeral on a dark and gloomy day, with dripping trees, and mist.

It started off badly. I wanted to wear something black, or at least as dark as possible. I chose my clothes carefully. Dad said most people didn't bother with mourning nowadays, but I wanted to wear it. It seemed right to me. But Mum went all funny about it. We had a stupid argument, and then she said.

'You wear what you like then, but I'm going to wear my red coat whatever you say. Ben liked the fur on the collar. He used to stroke it.' And then she cried, and I realized I was being tactless and interfering so I shut up. I thought of offering to lend her my red scarf to go with it, just to show her that I was sorry, but something told me that it wouldn't be a good idea.

The church was full of flowers. It was strangely beautiful, like at a wedding. There were quite a lot of people there, some old friends of Mum's and Dad's and people who lived in our street. Mrs Russell was as near the front as she could get without sitting in the seats reserved for the family. She honestly looked as if she was enjoying herself.

Mr Henderson seemed different when he came in. Sort of solemn, but powerful and in command too. I felt at last that here was someone who understood what was going on. It was like being in a strange new building, and finding someone who's got the keys. Mr Henderson has got keys. I don't mean to the church hall or anything, but keys to secrets about life that he knows how to unlock.

I don't remember everything that happened at the funeral. I just remember the little coffin, shining, bathed in sunlight, speckled in jewel-like colours from the stained glass window, heaped up with white and yellow flowers. And I remember that the words of the service rolled on majestically, like waves breaking on a beach, and I remember that I no longer wanted to curse, and shout 'Where were you, God, the night Ben died?' I felt that somewhere there was a meaning, and one day I would know what it was, and that I was loved, and I had to trust that love, and let Ben go away into its arms, and one day I would go out into it too.

At the end of the service there was a silence, and then the vicar looked round us all, and he smiled, and said with a kind of power and confidence in his voice,

'"Blessed are the pure in heart, for they shall see God."'

I could tell it was a quote from somewhere. The Bible, I suppose. But it described Ben exactly. Pure in heart, that was Ben. It made Mum start crying again, and she clutched Dad's arm, but I found myself nodding, and Katy looked up at me, and she smiled, and I know she felt like I did, that Ben was safe with God.

Friends for Ever

From *Beyond the Rainbow*

CHRISTINE MARION FRASER

Kirsty and Jean become friends in hospital. Both have cancer.
Their holiday together at Jean's home on the island of Sanda is
the happiest of their lives. Mr and Mrs Anderson make Kirsty and
her brother Andy feel very much at home, and a friendship soon
develops with Jean's brothers, Robbie and Jim. The arrival of
Kirsty's father on this 'island of rainbows' completes her joy.

It had been raining, everything looked clean and newly washed, the sea was sparkling, distant islands merged into the mist on the horizon.

Kirsty stood at the window and took a deep breath. Her first morning on Sanda, a wonderful pearly-blue morning filled with light and space and rays of sunshine filtering down from the sky to splash gold on the waves... The birds were singing, a spider's web outside the window glistened with diamond-like dewdrops, a tiny wren was searching for insects in the roof gutters...

And then she saw her first rainbow, shimmering and bright, arched across the great dome of the sky.

She held her breath and as she watched another rainbow appeared, a reflection of the first, fainter than the other but still hazily bright and beautiful.

Kirsty put her hand to her mouth. 'An island of rainbows,' she whispered.

The smell of bacon and eggs came wafting up from the kitchen. Kirsty suddenly felt ravenously hungry and she lost no time getting downstairs. Robbie, Jim, and Andy were already seated at the table, chattering away like long-lost pals.

A large orange and white cat came to wrap itself round Kirsty's legs while a black and white collie dog, not to be outdone, bounded over to take her fingers in his mouth and pull her into the room.

Mrs Anderson turned a hot face from the stove. 'Good morning, Kirsty, you mustn't mind Sam. He thinks he's the boss around here since he retired from the fields. Come away in and sit yourself down. Jean's out feeding the hens but she'll be back in a moment.'

Mr Anderson's big frame darkened the doorway. Stooping, he removed his mud-caked boots and hung his cap on a hook beside a motley collection of ancient jackets. He then went to the sink to give his hands a quick wash.

'We *do* have soap, Alan,' Mrs Anderson laughed.

He had green eyes the same as his daughter and at that moment they were twinkling. 'Waste not, want not,' he replied with a chuckle. 'I'll only get them dirty again later so might as well save the soap till bedtime.'

Jean came rushing in to hurl cold water over her hands before drying them hurriedly on the kitchen towel.

Mrs Anderson had to smile. 'Like father, like daughter, you two are a fine example to set to visitors.'

Jean looked at her father, he gazed back at her and they both grinned at one another and helped themselves to toast.

Kirsty glanced round at all the faces. She liked the Anderson family, they were friendly and funny and very, very natural...

> 'Bless this food and make us good,
> Help us to laugh, love and live,
> and feel compassion to forgive.'

Mrs Anderson had sat down and she was saying grace. The hands of Jean and her father were suspended suddenly above the toast rack. Jean's face was red with suppressed mirth, that of Mr Anderson was no better...

Kirsty giggled. She knew she was going to enjoy her holiday at Croft an Cala.

☆

The highlight of the holiday for both Kirsty and Andy came [one] morning when Jean answered a knock at the door.

'*Dad!*' cried brother and sister in unison, 'what are you doing here?'

Mr McKinnon's blue eyes twinkled. 'That's an odd kind of welcome for a long lost father. Shall I go out and come back in again?'

'You dare!' said Kirsty, running to take his arm and pull him further into the room. 'You're just such a big surprise, that's all. We didn't know you were coming or we would have been at the harbour to meet you.'

'I didn't know I was coming myself until last night. Call it a spur of the moment decision if you like. It's so long since I've seen you both I felt I just had to make the journey to Sanda.'

Placing his hands on Kirsty's shoulders he gazed at her for a long moment. 'You look great, sweetheart, colour in your cheeks, your eyes bright. It's so good to see you back to your old self again.'

'Dad, is everything all right?' Andy asked impatiently, his initial happiness waning as he remembered the dissension that had existed between his parents.

Jean and Mrs Anderson had slipped discreetly from the kitchen, thus giving the McKinnons the freedom to talk openly.

'Everything is perfect,' assured Mr McKinnon happily. 'Your mother and I have been busy and I have a lot to tell you. But first things first, I'd love a cup of tea.'...

Kirsty rushed to put the kettle on. After that she and Andy set out to enjoy their father's visit to the full. He was only staying the one night and every moment was therefore precious. Jean was invited to come along with them and together they wandered Sanda's white beaches, they talked and laughed and had a wonderful time...

A shower of rain made them run to the shelter of the boat cave. Ten minutes later the sun started to appear again and with it came a rainbow, arching across the sky, embracing the rocks and distant islands in its brilliant hues.

'Look, Dad!' cried Kirsty, 'isn't it the loveliest rainbow you ever saw? It's a sign of good luck.'

He ruffled her hair. 'Ay, sweetheart,' he said softly, 'I believe you're right at that.'

Jean's gaze was far away as she watched the sky and softly she recited a verse by the Scottish poet, Iain Frank:

'Let us take hands,
And walk in the sands,
The waves lapping to and fro,
In the evening hour,
After a summer shower,
Let's look beyond the rainbow.'...

Kirsty saw a rainbow as she and Andy were leaving Croft an Cala for the first stage of their journey home. It was a big rainbow, encompassing all the little green and blue islands that shimmered like jewels on the horizon, with the Freshnish Isles caught in the dazzling hues.

'Look, Andy.' Kirsty held her breath. 'It's as if it appeared specially for us.'

They both stared entranced, drinking in their fill of it, knowing it could disappear at any time – there one moment – gone the next.

And then a strange thing happened. They saw Jean, caught as it were, in the shimmering colours. She had just come out of the house and somehow she was there inside the rainbow, a half-real figure touched by the brilliance and light.

'How odd,' breathed Kirsty. 'She's part of it all, part of the sky and the sea and the rainbow.'

The experience shook Kirsty. She wondered what it all meant, if it was a sign of something, something that she didn't understand yet but would in days to come.

Jean came running towards them and suddenly everything was normal again, the rainbow vanished, the islands and the ocean were as they had been before, and Jean was Jean, with nothing different about her at all. The boys appeared and together they all walked down to the harbour where the ferry was just tying up...

For quite some minutes there was a babble of voices as the islanders said their farewells to departing visitors.

Kirsty and Jean briefly embraced, too filled up with the poignancy of the moment to be able to say the things that were in their hearts.

'This is for you.' Jean handed Kirsty a seal-shaped stone she had found on the beach long ago. 'It will remind you of Kalak Mar and the seal people and you will remember Sanda every time you look at it.'

'It's lovely.' Kirsty gazed at the stone, the tears springing once more to her eyes. 'But I don't need to be reminded of Sanda. I'll never forget it nor will I forget how good you and your family were to Andy and me.'

The parting was full of hope and promise. But before long Kirsty and Jean are back in hospital, Jean is very ill, and a final parting is near...

Outside the hospital window the stars were winking in a frosty sky. Kirsty couldn't sleep. She felt sick and heavy, but more than that her heart was sore for Jean who lay so ill in the next bed.

It was quiet and peaceful in the ward. An old lady snored gently in the silence and Jean's erratic breathing seemed hardly to intrude into the dreamings of the night.

In the middle of the ward a tiny glass wind-chime hung from the night-light, glowing with red, green, blue and orange hues.

The colours of the rainbow, thought Kirsty, just like the lovely ones we saw on Sanda. Sanda. She lay back on her pillows, remembering that wonderful holiday, all of them so happy, Jean laughing and running over the fields, playing on the beaches.

Now she was dying and would never run again. Kirsty's eyes blurred. Turning her head she gazed up at the sky, seeing the stars through a veil of tears. One star was bigger and brighter than the rest. Kirsty tried to see it as a symbol of hope.

Her lips moved. 'God,' she whispered, 'Jean is the best friend I ever had, she wanted to do so much with her life, now she'll never see her island again. I hope there will be rainbows in heaven and places as beautiful as Sanda so that she will be happy for all time and never be sick again.' The simple prayer made her feel better. There was a stirring from Jean's bed and her voice came faintly.

'Kirsty, are you awake?'

'Yes, I can't sleep.'

'Kirsty, can I tell you something? I'm afraid, more afraid than I've ever been in my life, yet I'm so tired I'll be glad in a way when it's over. It gets to be like that – you want to cling on but it becomes too much.'

'Oh, Jean,' a sob caught in Kirsty's throat, 'I love you, you were always the strong one, you still are, even now.'

'You're strong too, Kirsty, and I'm so glad we met and became such close friends. It's because we understand one another that I want you to promise me something.'

'Anything, Jean, I'd do anything for you.'

'I want you to tell me that you won't be sad when I die. Remember all the things that Meg told us. Do all the things you said you would do with your life. Just think of me sometimes, and all the things we shared when we were together.'

Kirsty's heart felt as if it were bursting with sorrow. She didn't answer for a moment. Instead she looked up at the enamel rainbow brooch and the little seal stone hanging above her bed.

'Every time I look at my seal stone I'll remember you, Jean.'

'It brought me luck over the years; it will do the same for you. Somehow I feel that it let me meet you. That was good, wasn't it, Kirsty?

'Yes, oh, yes, that was good, Jean, the best thing that ever happened to me.'

'You haven't promised me yet. I need to hear you saying it.'

'I promise,' vowed Kirsty shakily.

Jean sunk into her pillows. 'Is it cold in the ward, Kirsty?'

Kirsty felt hot and feverish and wanted to throw off the blankets. How could Jean feel cold in such a warm, stuffy place? The answer came suddenly to Kirsty. Jean was cold because her weary body had no more strength left to fight.

The night nurse came up just then to see why the girls were awake. 'Please, Nurse,' Kirsty said urgently, 'would you get my Chinese dressing-gown and wrap it round Jean's shoulders. It reminds her of Sanda, she always admired it.'

The nurse took the garment from Kirsty's locker and tucked it round Jean's shoulders. 'Does that feel better?' the nurse asked kindly.

'Lots better,' Jean said softly. 'A cloak of many colours, the turquoise of the sea, the blue of the sky, the crimson of the setting sun...'

Her voice trailed away, the nurse looked at her anxiously, then hurried away to get the night doctor.

The next few hours passed in a blur for Kirsty. She drifted in and out of sleep, so ill herself that she was only vaguely aware of the screens round Jean's bed and the doctors and nurses who came and went all night long.

Then the doctors came to her, though she could only see and hear them through a thick, silent fog that swirled in her head. As if in a dream she heard the voices of Jean's parents and brothers, the sound of their sorrow, the last farewells to a beloved daughter.

In her half-conscious state Kirsty knew that her friend had slipped peacefully away in her sleep and strange visions passed through Kirsty's mind. She and Jean were back on Sanda, wearing shorts and shirts because it was summer. The bees were buzzing in the wild thyme, the larks were singing in the blue sky.

She stood with Jean at the door of Croft an Cala, looking out to sea. Shafts of sunlight were lighting the waves, an enormous rainbow appeared in the sky, and suddenly Jean was in the rainbow, part of the brilliant colours, part of the earth and the sea and the sky.

Kirsty wanted to get inside the rainbow too but Jean wouldn't let her. 'Go back, Kirsty,' she called. 'One day you'll travel beyond the rainbow, but not yet, not yet...'

Kirsty stood alone now at the door of Croft an Cala, her hand upraised in farewell to Jean. 'Goodbye, Jean,' she called. 'Someday we'll meet again... someday...'

Jean had disappeared into a world filled with rainbows, a beautiful world flooded with colour and light and beauty.

Then the visions faded from Kirsty's mind and she was back in the hospital ward, vaguely aware that her mother and father were sitting by her bed, touching her, their eyes filled with love for her.

'Dad'

JULIA WEARN (AGED 11)

Dad was someone who had everything
in the right place –
including his heart.
He never called us little terrors
He always called us the little ones or the kids.
He never hit us, but told us the reasons why
(when we weren't reasonable).

He wore smart shoes,
comfortable trousers.
When you tried his shoes on
they were warm.
But when the time came for him to leave us
there was no warm feeling in the shoes.
No warmth or familiar smell in the clothing –
nothing.
And he left a gap in the word comfort able.

Hoot

From *Mama's Going to Buy You a Mockingbird*
JEAN LITTLE

*Jeremy's father is ill. For a long time he hasn't known how ill,
but at last the painful truth dawns. Sometimes, when something
huge is happening to us, a very small thing becomes important.
In this story it is Hoot, the little model owl. Sarah is Jeremy's
younger sister. Blue is the cat. And Tess is the unlikely friend
Jeremy has made because his father wanted him to help her.*

How long was Dad going to be away?

'How long...?' [Jeremy] started to ask, speaking softly so as not to
disturb Dad if he really had fallen asleep.

The man on the bed sighed a long sigh. He opened his eyes but he
didn't say anything. Jeremy backed away from him a little. Then his
father's voice reached out to him.

'I don't know how long, Jeremy. Nobody knows. Even the doctor
doesn't know.'

Silence swallowed the thin, tired voice again and Jeremy was
out the door, running for his own room. Once there, he stood still
panting as if he had come a long way and blinking hard as though
he were on the verge of crying, even though his eyes were dry.

'It's not fair,' he said in a low choked voice. 'It's not fair.'

He wished there was something he could do to help. He'd go with
Dad if they would let him. He could stay by him and bring him pills
and water. When he felt better, they could talk. He could say,
'Remember when we saw the owl?' And Dad would smile.

But they wouldn't let him. He knew that much. If they only would, he really would go... even if it were awful, even if his father just lay with his eyes shut and his hands limp and empty.

Then, all at once, Jeremy knew what he could do.

A minute later he was picking up one of his father's hands and putting Hoot into it.

'I want you to take him with you tomorrow,' he said, not turning to look at Mum as she came back into the room, concentrating his whole attention on this stranger who was his father. 'He's neat to hold, you know. He's small but heavy and smooth.'

'He's neat all right,' Dad agreed, looking not at Hoot but at Jeremy. Then he held the tiny owl up and smiled exactly the smile Jeremy had been missing.

'Yeah,' Jeremy said. His mother reached out and put her hand on the back of his head, the way she had often done ever since he was a little boy. It was a loving touch, an approving touch.

'Put him with my things, Melly,' Dad said.

Mum moved away from Jeremy and took Hoot. Turning, she put him into her purse. Dad laughed.

'Don't you take him, lady!' he warned. 'I can see you covet that owl. But he's Jeremy's. He's only loaned to me.'

'Don't worry,' Mum said lightly. Jeremy, looking at her, saw that her face was shadowed with sadness. 'You already told me, remember? "You can't have everything Melly," you said. "The bird is Jeremy's." I'll pack it with your other things in a minute.'

'Good,' Dad said. The tiredness was back.

The morning after the funeral, the three Talbots left Blue with Mrs Barr and went to the cottage. It was cold but sunny and the trees were ablaze with autumn colour. They read, went for hikes and picnics despite the nip in the wind. Mum spent a lot of time sitting looking out over the lake.

They all missed Dad but they had been there without him before. It felt more as if he were coming to join them soon than as if he would never be with them again.

One evening, Sarah, in a subdued voice, asked Mum what heaven was like. Their mother sat quietly for a moment. Neither Jeremy nor Sarah spoke. Then Melly Talbot said slowly, 'I don't know, Sarah. Nobody really knows.'

'But is Daddy an... an angel?'

Jeremy wished she would shut up. But while he was trying to come up with a way to squelch her, Mum went on.

'Think of some of the wonderful surprises there are in this world. Think of a caterpillar turning into a butterfly. Think of a brown seed growing into a flower. If God has arranged things like that for a caterpillar and a seed, I trust him to know what to do with us. But the picture we have of heaven as a place with golden streets and pearly gates, where angels play on harps and God sits on a big throne, comes from a book in the Bible called Revelations.'

She paused for a moment.

'I think the writer was trying to say that heaven must be more beautiful than anything we can imagine. I don't think he meant us to believe it was really the way he said it was. But there is one part in that book that I love. It was read at the funeral but you probably didn't take it in. Let me find it and read it to you.'

She fetched her Bible and found the place. Jeremy liked listening to her read the Bible. She used her own voice, not a special Bible-reading voice like the minister's. As she read the words, he did remember hearing them before.

Then I saw a new Heaven and a new Earth, for the first Heaven and the first Earth had disappeared and the sea was no more. I saw the holy city, the new Jerusalem, descending from God out of Heaven, prepared as a bride dressed in beauty for her husband. Then I heard a great voice from the throne crying, 'See! The home of God is with men and he will live among them. They shall be his people and God himself shall be with them, and will wipe away every tear from their eyes. Death shall be no more and never again shall there be sorrow or crying or pain. For all these former things are passed and gone.'

When she stopped reading, neither of them said anything. She closed the book and took it back into her bedroom. When she came out again, Jeremy could see she had been crying. But she said, 'Put on some music, Jeremy. I'm going to get marshmallows for us to toast when the fire dies down a little.'

The months pass, and Christmas comes. They know it will be different and lonely without Dad. But Mum and Jeremy work hard to make it good for

Sarah. If only it could be good for Jeremy too – that's what his Mum wants most of all. But Jeremy can feel no joy...

It was almost morning when he woke up. Four or five o'clock maybe. He wasn't sure how he knew. He just did. And it was Christmas.

He couldn't wake Sarah because she was in with Mum. Yet he knew he couldn't go back to sleep, either. He peered over the edge of his covers at Blue.

'Merry Christmas, cat,' he said.

If she heard him, she gave no sign. Not even a whisker moved. He poked her gently. She opened her blue eyes a slit, yawned, covered her face with one paw and refused to wake up.

'What I need is some food,' Jeremy said, as if his cat were listening. He tiptoed out to the kitchen, nobly not letting himself so much as glance into the living room where the presents waited. He got himself a banana. When he eased open the door of the refrigerator so that he could pour himself a glass of milk, he heard Blue thump to the floor and come running.

'You're disgusting,' he said to her softly. 'You won't even say "Merry Christmas" without a bribe.'

Blue polished off the last drop of milk, looked up to see if he had anything further to contribute, accepted the fact that he had not and, turning her back on him, stalked off into the living room. He knew what she was after. She took every chance to go and sit in front of the tree and play with the decorations on the low branches. What she had not broken, they had long since moved up out of her reach, but she still had high hopes.

'No, Blue!' he called after her in a stage whisper. 'Come on out of there.'

He glanced at the clock on the stove. It was twenty to six. He definitely was not supposed to go near the presents but he had to get Blue, didn't he? She might do some damage.

Blue, to his surprise, was not under the tree but curled up in the big armchair Mr Medford liked best. Maybe when the lights were not switched on, the tree lost its appeal for her. He left her where she was and turned to look at the row of stockings.

Sarah's was fat and knobbly and so were Aunt Margery's, Tess's and Mr Medford's. He kept his eyes averted from his own but he couldn't help putting his hand out to feel it. He snatched his fingers away as he recognized the shape of the special pen he had asked for that wrote in six different colours. He grinned. Then he saw that Mum's stocking, which was next to his, was half empty.

He lifted it to be sure he was right. There was a candy cane hooked over the top, but despite that cheerful note, it hung limply. He peered in and saw one mandarin orange and a Christmas cracker. Why hadn't she filled her own?

Jeremy sat down on the couch, pulled the afghan there around his shivering body, and thought. It was the kind of thinking he had not let himself do for a long time. But now there was no stopping it.

Clearly, as if it were happening right now instead of last year and all the years before that, he saw his parents laughing as they dug into their Christmas stockings. They had acted every bit as silly and excited as he and Sarah.

'They didn't know what was in theirs, either,' he said aloud. 'They never knew what they'd find next any more than we did.'

Last year his father had got a paperback murder mystery, some play money 'to help with the mortgage', a rubber spider, a chocolate cigar... and a little book saying how many calories were in everything. And Mum had had some pills with a poem about how sorry Santa was that she had to live with 'three pains in the neck'. There had been a small bottle of perfume and a little wooden animal with pink fuzzy hair...

Jeremy did not remember what else. He did not need to. He had just figured out something that had been obvious for years but that he had never before realized. Each of his parents had filled the other's stockings.

It must have been fun for them, he thought.

Pain closed in on him as he lived back in those other Christmasses and saw, really saw, what fun it had been. This time he did not push the pain away.

In the next hour, he was sure, over and over again, that he would waken them all and get caught. First he replaced the skimpy little sock she had hung up for herself with one of his own, one of the socks he wore over all the others when he went skating. Then he found a fifty-cent piece he had saved in a little box in his desk. He added an apple. That helped. Yet he knew there had to be more.

The scarf he had bought for her! He fetched it from his bottom dresser drawer. He had wrapped it just in tissue paper so it squashed up small enough to go in.

Now something funny.

He stood there, worried about the minutes ticking by, unable to think. He hadn't a single funny thing. Not one... Then he had an inspiration. George! George was a tiny plastic frog he had got out of a bubble gum machine. He couldn't find him right away but then he remembered. He dug his old cords out of the bottom of the dirty clothes hamper. George was in the left pocket.

There. He stood back and looked. He wished he could write a poem the way his father had but he was lousy at poems. Still her stocking did look beautifully lumpy now.

She hadn't even bothered to put her name on the one she had hung for herself, although she had made sure the rest had labels. He printed her name, 'Melly', on a sheet of paper from the telephone scratch pad and pinned it on. Now hers looked just like the others.

He had done it! Yet he went on standing there. It needed one more thing, something special, something...

Really he knew what it needed. He was trying not to say it to himself, trying not to give in to his own knowledge.

Hoot. That was what she would love.

But Hoot was his.

'She wouldn't want me to give it up,' Jeremy told himself.

He knew better. Didn't her hand go out to it every time she passed his desk? Maybe it was because the owl was so small and yet so unexpectedly heavy. Maybe it was simply because she remembered.

Jeremy went to his room and brought it back. Standing there, the smooth roundness of it still in his hand, still belonging to him, he remembered, too.

'You can't have everything, Melly,' Dad had said, smiling. 'Hoot is for Jeremy.'

It wasn't as if the owl was his only gift from Dad. He had other special things. The copy of *Kim*, for one. And Blue, of course!

And Tess, he thought with a grin.

He went to the telephone table again and got another sheet of paper. Then he saw it was really getting light outside and he hurried. He didn't wonder if Mum would remember, too. He knew she would.

'You can't have everything, Mum,' he wrote, 'but you can have Hoot. Merry Christmas. Love, Jeremy.'

He taped the piece of paper onto the little owl. He stroked it once more and slipped it in quickly. There. It was done.

He wrapped his arms around his body because the furnace had not come on yet and the air was cold. He felt different.

The joy he had so longed for the night before had come. And yet this was a more difficult joy than he had known other years. It was so real, so wonderful, that he felt almost afraid. He stood very still, looking back to the man he no longer wanted to forget, looking ahead to this Christmas which was now, at last, fully his.

What time was it? It didn't matter. He could not bear to wait another second. He wanted them, his whole family. Not even glancing at the clock, Jeremy flew to wake them.

Tony's Mum

From *I Carried You on Eagles' Wings*
SUE MAYFIELD

For as long as he can remember, Tony has had to help his Mum.
Once she could walk, but now she can't feed herself and it's hard
even to speak. Tony knows that she longs to be free, 'to soar on
wings like eagles'. But it is hard to say goodbye.

'Ovaltine, Mum?'

'Mmm, please.'

Tony's mum nodded stiffly and smiled. *Eastenders* was just
finishing as Tony switched off the TV, and walked through to the
kitchen. He liked watching telly with his mum in the evenings.
There were so few things they could do together and she found
talking difficult and tiring. It was nice just to sit together in the
living room by the gas fire.

He made her Ovaltine and a coffee for himself. Poking his head
round the door he asked, 'Biscuits?'

'Mmm. How was the trip?' It was the first opportunity she'd had
to ask him.

'It was good. There was a brilliant eagle – it must have been
twelve feet across!'

Tony spread his arms wide and scowled to look eagle-like. His
mum laughed.

He held the feeder cup up to her lips for her to sip the milky
liquid. Giving her a drink without spilling it or choking her was a

delicate operation. Tony grasped the top of her head with one hand to stop her shaking and placed the spout of the cup in her mouth. Then he tipped the drink slowly until she indicated with her eyes that her mouth was full and she was ready to swallow. He did it expertly, naturally, without any fuss. As long as he could remember he'd fed his mum or helped her to drink. He could remember as a very small child, climbing on to her knee to put Smarties in to her mouth. She'd been able to do more then. When he was a baby she could still walk. Tony had no memory of ever seeing her do it, but there were photos and people had told him. Now she could do almost nothing. Even her speech was slow, jerky, difficult to understand.

'Bed, then?' asked Tony. She nodded. 'They've got such small eyes, haven't they?' he continued, 'and massive, talony claws. It was quite fierce looking – just like you!'

His mum grinned as he slipped a blue canvas sling under her legs and round her shoulders. He clipped it on to the hoist that was fixed to a rail on the ceiling and pulled the blue cord – blue for up, white for down, red for left, green for right – he knew the drill without thinking about it. There was a whirring sound and his mum was lifted out of the armchair until she dangled in a sitting position in the hammock seat. She looked fragile and helpless like this, her legs flopping limply below her.

'Have a nice flight!' Tony teased. He pulled the red cord and slung her across so that she was suspended about a foot above the wheelchair that was beside her chair. Then he pulled the white cord and lowered her gently down.

When Tony had transferred his mum to her bed, he wiped her hands and face with a wet flannel and spread face cream from a pink pot on to her cheeks. She was still quite pretty, he thought. She had lovely pale skin and mysterious-looking eyes. Tony had a photograph of her in a scrap book in his bedroom. She could only have been about eighteen when it was taken and was leaning against a fence in a pair of jeans and a floppy sunhat. She looked lively, sparkly – sexy even – although it was weird to think of your mum being sexy, Tony thought. Now her face had a stiff look, as though she was wearing a mask that might crack. The muscles had grown weak and even smiling looked strange and forced.

Tony put the lid on the jar of cream and sat down on the edge of the bed.

'Would you like me to read to you?' he said. He had read to his mum for years – ever since he could read aloud. First his school reading books, and easy children's stories – now, snippets from the newspaper or part of a novel. His mum's eyesight was too poor to read herself but her mind was as sharp as ever and she liked to have plenty to think about. At the moment they were reading *Great Expectations* because Tony had to read it for school.

'I'm not sure I'm in the mood for Dickens,' she said.

Tony was quite relieved. 'He is a bit long-winded, isn't he?' he said. 'I get jaw ache reading it aloud!' Tony waggled his jaw and grimaced with pretend pain.

'I'll tell you what,' he continued, 'how about a special treat in memory of our beaky friend – since I saw him in the flesh today! I'll read you the eagle bit.'

Tony stretched his arms out and did his eagle face again.

He took his mum's Bible off her bedside table where she kept it beside her lamp and a little framed picture. The picture was a drawing of an eagle that Tony had given her last Christmas. He'd spent ages copying it from a nature book and had painstakingly coloured its plumage with pencil crayons. The eagle was flying across a lake edged with pine trees and in the corner Tony had written the words 'Isaiah 40 verse 30'.

His mum often asked him to read to her from the Bible or from paperback books about God and things. Sometimes she closed her eyes and a beautiful smile spread across her face, as if she was somewhere else, dreaming of a wonderful far-off place.

Tony opened the Bible at the book of Isaiah and started to read. The words were familiar to him and gave him a strange, stirring feeling, almost as if he wanted to cry.

'"Do you not know? Have you not heard? The Lord is the everlasting God, the creator of the ends of the earth. He will not grow tired or weary, and his understanding no one can fathom. He gives strength to the weary, and increases the power of the weak. Even youths grow tired and weary, and young men stumble and fall, but those who hope in the Lord will renew their strength..."'

Tony paused before the last bit and looked at the little framed drawing. He thought of the massive taloned bird in the glass case overhead, and of Clare, and he read slowly.

"'They will soar on wings like eagles, they will run and not grow weary, they will walk and not be faint.'"

He closed the book and they sat together in silence for a moment. Then Tony jumped up.

'I'd better do my maths homework now, okay?' he said. His mum nodded. He kissed the top of her head, switched off the light, and crept out.

His mum lay in the dark, looking up at the ceiling. As she stared into the gloom, tears ran down her cheeks and soaked her pillow, and she sobbed quietly.

Tony spends much of his spare time on an angry seagull called Bono. The bird doesn't give him much thanks, but at last its broken wing is mended. Bono is ready to fly again, but by this time Tony's own leg is in plaster – and his mum has grown very much worse. She is in hospital...

'You go on up, and we'll join you soon – I think she'd like to see you on your own.'

Tony's dad laid his hand on his shoulder. Tony smiled and nodded. He watched as his dad and his grandma walked along the polished white corridor and out into the hospital grounds.

His mum's room was full of flowers and sunlight was streaming in through the parted blinds. She lay, propped up on piles of white pillows, covered only in a thin sheet. A nurse was lifting her arms, wiping her skin with a wet sponge.

'I'll be only a few minutes,' she said to Tony, 'this is just to cool your mum down. Her temperature's very high.'

Tony sat on a chair beside the bed. His mum craned her head round very slowly and mouthed 'Hi'. Tony grinned and raised his hand in a Red Indian salute. 'How!' he said. He thought how thin she looked – her legs were like sticks, blue and brittle-looking. The nurse ran a wet cloth across his mum's face. Her skin looked flaky and yellowed, like old parchment.

'All right then, love,' the nurse said, tucking the sheet in round her, 'I'll leave you alone now. Do you want a cup of tea, Tony?'

The door clicked shut. Tony pulled his chair round so that his mum was facing him, and rested his cast on the edge of the bed.

'How's... your... leg?' she said slowly. She could hardly talk. Her voice was thick and hoarse, as though her throat was closing up. It was like lip reading.

'I think it's just about better.' Tony spoke quickly, filling the room with chatter. There was so much he wanted to say.

'I've to come to outpatients on Wednesday for them to take the plaster off... it feels like it's healed okay... I can't wait to get rid of it... hopefully I'll be back in the team for the last few games of the season – there are a couple of "Friendlies" in the holidays – if I haven't lost my touch... And I can start doing my paper round again, which is good because I'm skint!'

His mum listened. She tried to nod and smile, but every movement took an enormous effort. 'How's... Bono?' she mouthed.

Tony thought of Saturday morning. He remembered the thrill of watching through the garage window, his nose pressed against the glass, as Bono flexed his wings. And he remembered Clare squeezing his hand, sharing his excitement.

'He flew yesterday!' he said, triumphantly. Tony stretched out his arms and imitated Bono, gliding across the garage.

'Just a few yards, but he used the wing. The vet seemed to think it had mended perfectly. He's even more bad-tempered than usual though – now that the bandage is off! Somehow I don't think he'll miss me much once he's back in the wild!'

Tony laughed. He looked into his mum's face. Her eyes had a kind of faraway look, as though she was there, but not quite there – moving on another plane. She looked serious, lost in thought.

She turned her head and raised her hand a few inches off the bed, gesturing to the cabinet beside her bed.

'Do you want something?' Tony jumped up, scanning the cluttered shelf.

'A drink?' He reached out for the jug of water. She rolled her head slowly from side to side.

'Eagle,' she murmured.

The framed picture was standing between a box of tissues and some grapes. Tony reached out and took it. He tried to press it into her hands but she pushed it away and said, in a jerky whisper,

'I... want... you... to... have... it...'

Tony fingered the silver frame and looked at the golden bird, flying over the forest of pine trees. He remembered drawing it, sat hunched over an encyclopaedia in his bedroom, trying to get the plumage right, and the shape of the beak. He'd done a good job. He remembered his mum's face when he'd helped her tear the Christmas paper off it. She'd asked him to hold it close to her face so she could see it clearly, take it all in. Her eyes had been full of tears.

Tony slipped it into the pocket of his coat. He felt himself choking with tears. There were so many things he'd wanted to say to his mum and had never been able to. Now he felt urgent, as though time was slipping through his fingers like grains of sand. He took hold of her hand. It was cold. He thought of the marble saint in the cathedral and gripped tight. His eyes were stinging with tears, hot and prickling, welling up against his eyelids like a dam about to burst.

'I love you, Mum...' he blurted out. Then he buried his face in her sheet and sobbed. When he looked up her face was wet. He pulled a wodge of tissues from the box and mopped her cheeks and the dribbles that were coursing down her chin. She smiled weakly, painfully. Tony took another tissue and blew his nose very noisily.

'Fog on the river!' he said, as he trumpeted into the handkerchief. She tried to laugh.

The door opened. Dad and Grandma stood in the doorway with a tray of tea that the nurse had just pressed into their hands. Tony sniffed and stood up.

'I'll pass on the tea, thanks, Dad. Do you mind if I go for a walk? I'll meet you back at the car...'

There was a park across the road from the hospital with some flower beds and an empty paddling pool. Here and there, there were clumps of crocuses, plump and egg yellow. Tony sat on a swing. The afternoon sun was quite warm. He unbuttoned his coat.

He watched a little boy in red wellies splash through a muddy puddle and scramble, laughing, up the wooden steps of the slide.

'Look, Mummy! I'm high!' he said, standing on the top, stretching his tiny fingers up to the sky. He plopped to his bottom and slid down, arms flailing. His mother scooped him up as he reached the ground and threw him up in the air, with a toss of her head.

'Again!' he shouted with delight. 'Do again!'

Tony put his hands in his pockets. He felt the shape of the picture frame and ran his thumb around the edge of it. Taking it out, he held it on his knees, tracing his fingers across the glass, following the course of the outstretched bird. As he rocked gently backwards and forwards, scuffing his feet on the tarmac and listening to the creaking of the unoiled swing, he thought of the words he knew so well – the words his mum loved so much.

'He gives strength to the weary... They will soar on wings like eagles, they will run and not grow weary, they will walk and not be faint...'

'Uphill'

CHRISTINA ROSSETTI

Does the road wind uphill all the way?
Yes, to the very end.
Will the day's journey take the whole long day?
From morn to night, my friend.

But is there for the night a resting-place?
A roof for when the slow, dark hours begin.
May not the darkness hide it from my face?
You cannot miss that inn.

Shall I meet other wayfarers at night?
Those who have gone before.
Then must I knock, or call when just in sight?
They will not keep you standing at that door.

Shall I find comfort, travel-sore and weak?
Of labour you shall find the sum.
Will there be beds for me and all who seek?
Yea, beds for all who come.

Mary, Mary

From *The Manger is Empty*
WALTER WANGERIN

*Miz Odessa Williams, an old, black lady in the storyteller's
church has died. His daughter, Mary, just seven years old,
will not be comforted. She loved Miz Williams, and it's
Christmas time, and it's going to snow...*

On Tuesday, the twenty-second of December, Odessa Williams died.

It had been a long time coming, but was quick when it came. She
died in her sleep and went to God without her dentures.

Quick when it came, I say: Odessa left us little time to mourn for
her. Gaines Funeral Home had less than a day to prepare her body,
because the wake would take place on Wednesday evening. The
funeral itself had to be scheduled for Thursday morning. There was
no alternative. Friday was Christmas Day; Saturday and Sunday were
the weekend; Gaines would be closed for three days straight, and
Monday was too far away to make Odessa wait for burial. She would
be buried, then, on Christmas Eve Day.

And I, for my own part, was terribly distracted by a hectic week.
This was the very crush of the season, you see, with a children's
pageant and extra services to prepare. My pastoral duty was already
doubled; Odessa's funeral tripled it. So I rushed from labour to
labour, more pastor than father, more worker than wise.

Not brutally, but somewhat busily at lunch on Wednesday,
I mentioned to my children that Miz Williams had died. They

were eating soup. This was not an unusual piece of news in our household; the congregation had its share of elderly.

I scarcely noticed, then, that Mary stopped eating and stared at her bowl of soup.

I wiped my mouth and rose from the table.

'Dad?'

I was trying to remember what time the children should be at church to rehearse the Christmas programme. Timing was everything. I wanted to give them a last instruction before I left.

'Dad?'

One thirty! 'Listen – Mom will drive you to church at one fifteen. Can you all be ready then?'

'Dad?'

'Mary, what?' She was still staring at the soup, large eyes lost behind her hair.

'Is it going to snow tomorrow?' she said.

'What? I don't know. How would I know that?'

'It shouldn't snow,' she said.

'You always wanted snow at Christmas.'

In a tiny voice she whispered, 'I want to go to the funeral.'

Well, then that was it: she was considering what to wear against the weather. I said, 'Fine,' and left.

Thursday came grey and hard and cold and windless. It grudged the earth a little light and made no shadow. The sky was sullen, draining colour from the grass and the naked trees. I walked to church in the morning.

We have a custom in our congregation: always, before a funeral service begins, we set the casket immediately in front of the chancel and leave it open about an hour. People come for a final viewing of the body, friends who couldn't attend the wake, acquaintances on their way to work, strangers out of the past, memories, stories that will never be told. The dead one lies the same for all who gaze at her, infinitely patient. So people enter the church, and they creep up the aisle, and they look, and they think, and they leave again.

Soon some of the mourners remain. They keep their coats on, but they sit in the pews and wait. They remind me of winter birds on telephone wires, their plumage all puffed around them, their faces closed, contemplative.

And then, ten minutes before the service, I robe myself and stand in the back of the church to meet the greater flow of mourners. Last of all the family will arrive in limousines. I keep peeping out of the door to see whether the silent cars have slid to their places at the curb –

And so it was that on Christmas Eve at eleven in the morning I discovered Mary outside the door. In fact, she was standing on the sidewalk while her mother parked the car. She was staring at the sullen sky.

'Mary?' I said. 'Are you coming in?'

She glanced at me. Then she whispered, 'Dad?' as though the news were dreadful. 'It's going to snow.'

It looked very likely to snow. The air was still, the whole world bleak and waiting. I could have agreed with her.

'Dad?' she repeated more urgently, probing me with large eyes – but what was I supposed to do? 'It's going to snow!' she said.

'Come in, Mary. We don't have time to talk. Come in.'

She entered the church ahead of me and climbed the steps in the narthex, then she started up the aisle towards the casket. She was seven years old. She was determined. Though robed and ready to preach, and though people sat face-forward on either side, I followed her.

Mary hesitated as she neared the chancel – but then took a final step and stopped.

She looked down into the casket. 'Oh, no,' she murmured, and I looked to see what she was seeing.

Odessa's eyes seemed closed with glue, her lips too pale, her colour another shade than her own, a false, woody colour. Her skin seemed pressed into its patience. And the bridge of her nose suffered a set of glasses. Had Odessa worn glasses? Yes, sometimes. But these were perched on her face a little askew, so that one became aware of them for the first time. Someone else had put them there. What belonged to the lady any more, and what did not?

These were my speculations.

Mary had her own.

The child was reaching her hand towards the tips of Odessa's fingers, fingers like sticks of chalk; but she paused and didn't touch them. Suddenly she bent down and pressed her cheek to the fingers, then pulled back and stood erect.

'Dad!' she hissed. Mary turned and looked at me and did not blink but began to cry. 'Dad' she whispered, accusing, 'It's going to snow, and Miz Williams is so cold.' Immediately the tears were streaming down her face. 'Dad!' she wept. 'They can't put Miz Williams in the grave today. It's going to snow on her grave. It's going to snow on Miz Williams...'

All at once Mary stepped forward and buried her face in my robes. I felt the pressure of her forehead against my chest – and I was her father again, no pastor, and my own throat grew thick.

'Dad,' sobbed Mary. 'Dad, Dad, it's Christmas *Eve!*'

Later, at Oak Hill Cemetery, the people stood in greatcoats round the casket, shivering. My breath made ghosts in the air as I read of dust and ashes returning to dust and ashes. Mary said not a word nor held her mother's hand nor looked at me – except once.

When we turned from the grave she hissed, 'Dad!' Her blue eyes flashing, she pointed at the ground. Then she pointed at the sky. At the roots of the grasses was a fine, white powder; in heaven was a darker powder coming down. It was snowing...

On Christmas Eve at the church each year there is a children's pageant of the birth of Jesus. This year the pastor's daughter Mary is to be the *Mary. But she is so sad, her father is worried about her...*

We drove to church. The snow lay a loose inch on the ground. It swirled in snow-devils at the backs of the cars ahead of us. It held the grey light of the city near the earth, though this was now the night, and heaven was oblique in darkness. Surely, the snow covered Odessa's grave as well, a silent seamless sheet.

These, I suppose, were Mary's thoughts, that the snow was cold on a new-dug grave. But Mary's thoughts confused with mine.

The rooms of the church were filled with light and noise, transfigured utterly from the low, funereal whispers of the morning. Black folk laughed. Parents stood in knots of conversation. Children darted, making ready for their glad performance, each in a different stage of dress, some in blue jeans, some in the robes of the shepherds two millennia and twenty lands away. Children were breathless and punchy. But Mary and I moved like spirits through this company, unnoticed and unnoticing. I was filled with her sorrow, while she seemed simply empty.

In time the wildness subsided. The actors huddled in their proper places. I sat with the congregation, two-thirds back on the right hand side. The lights in the sanctuary dimmed to darkness. The chancel glowed a yellow illumination. The pageant began, and soon my daughter stood with pinched lips, central to it all.

'My soul,' said Mary, both Marys before a little Elizabeth – but she spoke so softly that few could hear, and my own soul suffered for her – 'My soul,' she murmured, 'magnifies the Lord, and my spirit rejoices in God my Saviour...'

And so: the child was surviving. But she was not rejoicing.

Some angels came and giggled and sang and left.

A decree went out.

Another song was sung.

And then three figures moved into the floodlit chancel; Joseph and Mary – and one other child, a sort of innkeeper-stage-manager who carried the manger, a wooden trough filled with old straw and a floppy doll in diapers.

The pageant proceeded, but I lost the greater part of it in watching my daughter.

For Mary stuck out her bottom lip and began to frown on the manger in front of her – to frown fiercely, not at all like the devout and beaming parent she was supposed to portray. At the *manger* she was staring, which stood precisely where Odessa's casket had sat that morning. She frowned so hard, blacking her eyes in such deep shadow, that I thought she would break into tears again, and my mind raced over things to do when she couldn't control herself any longer.

But Mary did not cry.

Instead, while shepherds watched over their flocks by night, my Mary played a part that no one had written into the script. Slowly she slipped her hand into the manger and touched the doll in diapers. She lifted its arm on the tip of her pointed finger, then let it drop. *What are you thinking, Mary?* All at once, as though she'd made a sudden decision, she yanked the doll out by its toes, and stood up, and clumped down the chancel steps, the doll like a dishrag at her side. People made mild, maternal sounds in their throats. The rhythm of a certain angel faltered. *Mary, where are you going? What are you doing?* I folded my hands at my chin and yearned to hold her, hide her, protect her from anything, from folly and from sorrow. But she carried the doll to the darkened sacristy on the right and disappeared through its door. *Mary? Mary!*

In a moment the child emerged carrying nothing at all. Briskly she returned to the manger, up three steps as light as air, and down she knelt, and she gazed upon the empty straw with her palms together like the first Mary after all, full of adoration. And her face – Mary, my Mary, your face was radiant then!

O Mary, how I love you!

Not suddenly, but with a rambling, stumbling charge, there was in the chancel a multitude of the proudest heavenly host, praising God and shouting, 'Glory to God in the highest!' But Mary knelt unmoved among them, and her seven-year face was smiling, and there was the flash of tears upon her cheeks, but they were not unhappy, and the manger, open, empty, seemed the receiver of them.

'Silent night, holy night – ' All of the children were singing. 'All is calm, all is bright – ' The deeper truck-rumble of older voices joined them. 'Round yon virgin mother and child – ' The whole congregation was singing. Candlelight was passing hand to hand. A living glow spread everywhere throughout the church. And then the shock of recognition, and the soft flight followed: Dee Dee Lawrence allowed her descant voice its high, celestial freedom, and she flew. 'Holy infant, so tender and mild – ' *Mary, what do you see? What do you know that your father could not tell you? Mary, mother of the infant Jesus, teach me too.*

'Sleep in heavenly peace – ' Having touched the crystal heaven Dee Dee descended. The congregation sighed. Everybody sang: 'Sleep in heavenly peace.'

Mary sat immediately beside me in the car as we drove home. A sifting snow made cones below the streetlights. It blew lightly across the windshield and closed us in a cotton privacy. I had been driving in silence.

Mary said, 'Dad?'

I said, 'What?'

She said, 'Dad, Jesus wasn't in the manger. That wasn't Jesus. That was a doll.' Ah, Mary, so you have the eyes of a realist now? And there is no pretending any more? It was a doll indeed. So death reveals realities –

'Dad?'

'What?'

She said, 'Jesus, he doesn't *have* to be in the manger, does he? He goes back and forth, doesn't he? I mean, he came from heaven, and he was borned right here, but then he went back to heaven again, and because he came and went he's coming and going *all* the time – right?'

'Right,' I whispered. Teach me, child. It is so good to hear you talk again.

'The manger is empty,' Mary said. And then she said more gravely, 'Dad, Miz Williams' box is empty too. I figured it out. We don't have to worry about the snow.' She stared out the windshield a moment, then whispered the next thing as softly as if she were peeping at presents: 'It's only a doll in her box. It's like a big doll, Dad, and we put it away today. I figured it out. If Jesus can cross, if Jesus can go across, then Miz Williams, she crossed the same way too, with Jesus – '

Jesus, he don't never let one of us go. Never. [Odessa Williams had said that.]

'Dad?' said Mary, who could ponder so much in her heart. 'Why are you crying?'

Babies, babies, we be in the hand of Jesus, old ones, young ones, us and you together. Jesus [I could hear Odessa say], he hold us in his hand, and ain' no one goin' to snatch us out. Jesus, he don't never let one of us go. Never. Not ever –

'Because I have nothing else to say,' I said to Mary.

Acknowledgments

Thanks go to all those who have given permission to include material in this book, as indicated in the list below. Every effort has been made to trace and contact copyright owners. We apologize for any inadvertent omissions or errors.

'Winston's Important Weekend' copyright © Rachel Anderson. 'A Half-Baked Bannock Cake' from *Princess Jazz and the Angels* by Rachel Anderson, published 1994 by William Heinemann Ltd. Reprinted by permission of Reed Consumer Books. 'Mum, Dad and Me' from *When I Dance: Poems by James Berry* (Hamish Hamilton Children's Books, 1988) copyright © 1988 by James Berry. Reprinted by permission of Penguin Books Ltd. 'My Hard Repair Job' from *When I Dance: Poems by James Berry* (Hamish Hamilton Children's Books, 1988) copyright © 1988, 1991 (US) by James Berry. Reprinted by permission of Penguin Books Ltd (UK) and Harcourt Brace & Company (US). Extract from *Malcolm and the Amazing Technicolor Waistcoat* by Hilary Brand, published by Lion Publishing plc. 'Calum's Swan' copyright © Elaine Brown. Extracts from *Ramona and her Mother* by Beverly Cleary, published Hamish Hamilton Children's Books, 1979. 'Davie's Rabbit' from *Shadrach* by Meindert DeJong, Lutterworth Press 1953. Text copyright © 1953 by Meindert DeJong. Used by permission of HarperCollins Publishers Inc. (US). 'Look' by Emily Douglas, copyright © Turning Heads. Excerpts from *The Hundred Dresses* by Eleanor Estes, copyright 1944 by Harcourt Brace & Company and renewed 1971 by Eleanor Estes and Louis Slobodkin, reprinted by permission of the publisher. 'Friends For Ever' from *Beyond the Rainbow* by Christine Marion Fraser, published by HarperCollins Publishers Ltd. 'Being Black' by Rachel Gillies, copyright © Turning Heads. 'Kizzy's Plan' from *The Diddakoi* by Rumer Godden, published by Macmillan Children's Books, copyright © Rumer Godden. 'The One and Only Delgado Cheese' by Bob Hartman, published by Lion Publishing plc. Extracts from *I am David* by Anne Holm, published by Methuen Children's Books. Reprinted by permission of Reed Consumer Books. 'Heaven' and 'I, Too' from *Selected Poems* by Langston Hughes. Copyright © 1926 by Alfred A. Knopf Inc. and renewed 1954 by Langston Hughes. Reprinted by permission of the publisher. 'Misfits' copyright © Nan Hunt. Text of *Mama, Do You Love Me?* by Barbara Joosse and Barbara Lavallec, copyright © 1991, published by Chronicle Books, San Francisco. 'Anna-Magdalena Makes a Friend' from *Anna-Magdalena: the little girl with the big name* by Kay Kinnear, published by Lion Publishing plc. 'The Night Ben Died' from *Red Sky in the Morning* by Elizabeth Laird, published by William Heinemann Ltd (UK). US title: *Loving Ben*. Copyright © 1989 by Elizabeth Laird. Reprinted by permission of Reed Consumer Books (UK) and Dell Books, a division of Bantam Doubleday Dell Publishing Group, Inc. (US). 'The Choosing' from *Indian Captive: The Story of Mary Jemison* by Lois Lenski. Used by permission of the Lois Lenski Covey Foundation, Inc. 'Aslan's Country' from *The Voyage of the Dawn Treader* by C.S. Lewis, published by HarperCollins Publishers Ltd. 'Farewell to Shadowlands' from *The Last Battle* by C.S. Lewis, published by HarperCollins Publishers Ltd. 'The Fight' from *The Twelfth Day of July* by Joan Lingard (Hamish Hamilton Children's Books, 1980), copyright © Joan Lingard. Reproduced by permission of Penguin Books Ltd. 'Hoot' from *Mama's Going to Buy You a Mockingbird*. Copyright © Jean Little, 1984. Reprinted by permission of Penguin Books Canada Ltd. 'Third Time Lucky' by Pawandeep Lochab, copyright © Turning Heads. 'The Christmas Mittens' from *Cowboy Jess* by Geraldine McCaughrean, published by Orion Books. 'I See Music' copyright © Linette Martin. 'Tony's Mum' from *I Carried You on Eagles' Wings* by Sue Mayfield, published 1990 by Andre Deutsch Children's Books. Used by permission of Scholastic Ltd. 'Faster than Thought' by Rebecca Mockford, copyright © Turning Heads. The extracts printed on

Also from Lion Publishing

STAR OF WONDER

A Special Collection compiled by Pat Alexander

Here is a book for the whole family to enjoy this Christmas and
for years to come. Beginning with the Christmas story – in the
familiar words of the Bible, then retold for younger readers –
this special collection brings together stories and poems from
a wide variety of sources to explore the joy, the fun and the
mystery at the heart of Christmas. Here are stories of angels,
shepherds and wise men, legends, folk tales and customs,
stories of Christmas past and of Christmas plays today.

Extracts from *A Christmas Carol, Little Women* and *The Lion,
the Witch and the Wardrobe* rub shoulders with texts from modern
picture storybooks. There are tales here from around the world
– from sources as far apart as Russia and Finland to America
and Australia. Stories from well-known authors sit alongside
those from less familiar names, all offering an enjoyable read.

An ideal gift, *Star of Wonder* is a book for the whole family to
enjoy reading together, and an unrivalled resource for schools
and churches. Charming illustrations complement the text and
make the collection a delight to return to again and again.

ISBN 0 7459 2264 3

SONG OF THE MORNING

A Special Collection compiled by Pat Alexander

This is a book for the whole family to enjoy this Easter and the whole year round. The Easter events form the climax to a story that began long before. So this book starts with the creation and spoiling of the world, God's rescue plan and the coming of Jesus. The Bible's stories of Palm Sunday, Good Friday and Easter Day are placed in context.

Stories and poems have been brought together from a wide variety of sources to explore the meaning, mystery and joy at the heart of Easter – and the great themes of love, generosity, forgiveness and hope.

Extracts from classic tales such as *The Lion, the Witch and the Wardrobe* and *Charlotte's Web* sit alongside the texts from modern picture storybooks and real-life stories. Each story and poem has been chosen to illuminate some aspect of the unforgettable Easter story.

An ideal gift, *Song of the Morning* is a book for the whole family to enjoy reading together, and is an unrivalled resource for schools and churches. Charming illustrations complement the text and make the collection a delight to return to again and again.

ISBN 0 7459 3209 6

TALES FROM THE ARK

Avril Rowlands

Mr Noah could not sleep. He lay in bed, listening to the wind howling round outside, and the snuffles and grunts of the animals inside, and he talked to God.

'Listen God,' he said. 'It's not too late. You need a lion-tamer for this job, or a big game hunter, or at least a zoo keeper. I'm very grateful, of course, that you want to save me and my family, but honestly, I'm not cut out for the job.

'And I'll tell you something, God,' Mr Noah went on. 'I'm scared of spiders and we've got two on board.'

Spiders aren't Mr Noah's only problem. The lion wants to be in charge, a sheep goes missing and the animals threaten to revolt because of the smell from the skunks. Worst of all, the ark begins to leak.

AVRIL ROWLANDS worked for the BBC for many years and has written screenplays for children's television as well as books. She now works as a freelance writer and runs training courses in television production. Her hobbies include swimming, walking, theatre and steam railways.

ISBN 0 7459 2375 5